Rethinking 'Mixed Race'

Edited by David Parker and Miri Song

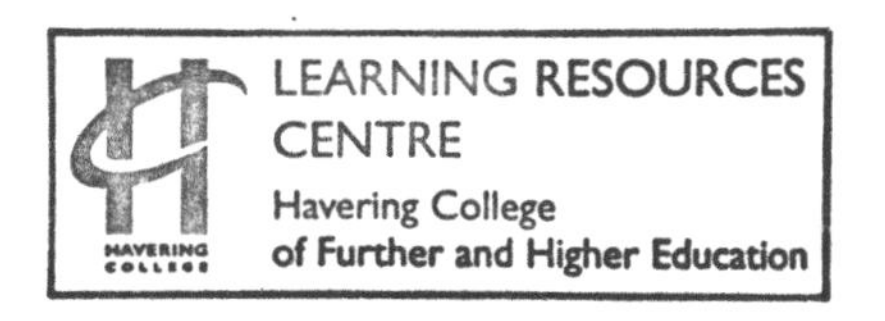

Pluto Press
LONDON • STERLING, VIRGINIA

First published 2001 by Pluto Press
345 Archway Road, London N6 5AA
and 22883 Quicksilver Drive, Sterling, VA 20166-2012, USA

www.plutobooks.com

British Library Cataloguing in Publication Data
A catalogue record for this book is available from the British Library

Library of Congress Cataloging-in-Publication Data

Rethinking mixed race/edited by David Parker and Miri Song.
p. cm.
ISBN 0-7453-1572-0 (hardback)
ISBN 0-7453-1567-4 (pbk.)
1. Racially mixed people. I. Parker, David. II. Song, Miri.
HT1523 .R38 2001
305.8'04–dc21
00-010447

ISBN 0 7453 1572 0 hardback
ISBN 0 7453 1567 4 paperback

10 09 08 07 06 05 04 03 02 01
10 9 8 7 6 5 4 3 2 1

Designed and produced for Pluto Press by
Chase Publishing Services, Fortescue, Sidmouth, EX10 9QG
Typeset from disk by Gawcott Typesetting Services
Printed in the European Union by TJ International, Padstow, England

Contents

Introduction: Rethinking 'Mixed Race'

David Parker and Miri Song

The topic of 'mixed race'[1] can bring out the worst in people. From the vicious harassment of couples in 'mixed' relationships to the hatred expressed on white supremacist websites, few subjects have the same capacity as racial mixture to reveal deep-seated fears and resentments. Conversely, proponents of interracial love can express a naïve celebration of 'mixed race' relationships and children as 'living proof' of the transcendence of racism and the ultimate expression of multicultural harmony. In this introduction we eschew such extreme positions. Our intention is not to hail 'mixed race' individuals and families as embodying the solutions to problems of racial antagonism or to essentialist thinking about 'race'. Neither do we wish to reinforce the centuries-old history by which racial mixture has been demonised and pathologised. Instead we wish to think critically about 'mixed race' in a variety of settings, through a variety of methodologies and perspectives.

This collection of chapters by scholars in Britain and the USA highlights the strategic importance of conceptions of racial mixture in the development of multicultural societies. The aim to place 'mixed race' firmly within mainstream debates about 'race' and ethnic identity lay behind the conference out of which this volume has emerged.[2] Far from being a marginal appendix to racial and ethnic studies, the experiences of the rapidly growing populations of mixed descent worldwide are central to the racialised dynamics of social and cultural change. Of course racial mixture is nothing new – it has been the history of the world. What stand out as novel are the forms of political contestation gathering around the topic of 'mixed race'. These include campaigns of racial harassment directed against 'mixed race' couples,[3] profound debates about the suitability of trans-racial adoption policies, and the development of 'mixed race' activism.

The growing importance of 'mixed race' in the USA and Britain reflects the increasing commonality of interracial cohabitation and relationships in both societies.[4] Although only 1.8 per cent of all marriages in the USA were interracial in 1990, this figure does not tell us about cohabiting couples or young couples who are dating – a number which is surely higher.[5] In the USA, Native Americans, Hispanics, and Asian Americans – particularly women in those groups – exhibit fairly high rates of exogamy.[6] A recent national survey of 5,196 ethnic minorities and 2,867 whites in Britain found that 50 per cent of African Caribbean men (and 30 per cent of African Caribbean women) born in Britain, and who are married or cohabiting, have a white partner.[7] The most recent data give Britain the highest rate of interracial relationships in the world, with a rate ten times that of the European average. According to this study, 90 per cent of black men aged 20 and in a relationship were with women who were not black.[8]

The first population censuses of the new century in Britain and North America will, in different ways, give administrative and political recognition to the growing multiplicity of ethnic genealogies. In Britain the April 2001 census question on ethnic origin, for the first time, offered respondents the category 'Mixed'.[9] The US census of 2000 enabled respondents to tick all the racial categories they feel apply to them.[10] Both of these new procedures, however clumsily and imperfectly, will redraw the map of ethnic boundaries and contribute to the emergence of a new vocabulary which goes well beyond the 'black/white' binary. As demographic patterns shift, there is an urgent need to reflect on the meaning of 'mixed race'.

In this volume we address the following questions:

- Can we conceive of 'mixed race' without reifying 'race'?
- How diverse are the experiences of 'mixed race' people, and do they share something in common by virtue of their 'mixed' status?
- What are the implications of 'mixed race' for social and cultural theory, and what political and institutional responses will engage with these developments?
- What new identities will emerge in the future?

Appreciating both the complexity of these questions and the provisional nature of the answers, we have not set out to resolve all the debates about terminology and the political implications of a 'mixed race' category. Rather, our aim is to utilise sober reflection to stimulate further discussion and research.

Until recently, 'mixed race' people had been the objects of scrutiny rather than the subjects of their own stories. We hope this book changes the terms of the debate and gives all those interested in racialised politics cause to rethink fixed positions.

From Pathologisation to Celebration

> The children themselves will and do wonder where they belong ... look deep into the eyes and expressions, you can almost feel their confusion.

> People with attitude towards us had better get used to us being around; the way the world is integrating, mixed race people will run the world. We are beautiful people with beautiful features and believe it or not beautiful experiences and a lot to offer Britain.

These quotations[11] neatly encapsulate the dramatically polarised responses to 'mixed race' people which this book tries to problematise and to understand. Few social groups have evoked such dichotomous reactions, while simultaneously lacking a clearly articulated and self-defined social identity.

The first quote echoes the many classical formulations of 'mixed race' pathology in modernity's metaphysics. The spectre of 'mixed race' has recurrently haunted modern thought. An antipathy to racial mixture was a constitutive element in the development of the human sciences.[12] For thinkers in the late nineteenth and early twentieth centuries, the emergence of 'mixed race' children was an ominous portent of the genetic deterioration of the nation, and indeed the human race itself.[13]

Accordingly, the existence of 'mixed race' populations posed serious questions for worldviews predicated on a clear separation of 'the races'. The interwar years saw investigations of 'mixed race' children in Britain's seaports. Their physical dimensions were carefully documented for evidence of abnormality.[14] However, these studies on the whole refuted the more alarmist pronouncements against mixing. Thereafter, the postwar reaction against Nazism fostered a low-key endorsement of pluralism. The 1950 UNESCO declaration summarised the anti-racist consensus that 'race' was a social myth, and that no scientific evidence could legitimate the presumption of 'mixed race' inferiority.[15] Yet the fear of racial mixture continued to resurface periodically in British discussions of immigration.[16] In the USA, legislation prohibiting intermarriage persisted in some States until as recently as

1967. The alleged threat to racial purity posed by 'mixed race' people and relationships continues to energise racist discourses circulating in the pamphlets and Internet sites of white supremacists.[17]

By contrast, in recent years both the popular and theoretical discussion of 'mixed race' has taken a more positive turn. Popular discussions in newspapers, radio, and television programmes laud 'mixed race' people as embodiments of the progressive and harmonious intermingling of cultures and peoples.[18] Among theorists, Donna Haraway has observed, 'Cross-overs, mixing and boundary transgressions are a favourite theme of late twentieth century commentators (...)'.[19] Inverting received wisdom; hybridity, mongrelisation and syncretism are no longer pathologies, but celebrated as exemplars of contemporary cultural creativity.[20] However, there is a lack of clarity over whether hybridity refers to the particular case where allegedly biologically separate 'races' intermingle; or more widely and metaphorically to all forms of cultural borrowing, recombination and fusion. Consequently the relationship between hybridity, 'mixed race' and 'race' has yet to be elaborated clearly.[21]

In the USA, some analysts have celebrated the very existence of 'mixed race' people as embodiments of social and cultural transgressions, whose lives make a mockery of distinct racial categories. Maria Root has even declared a 'bill of rights' for multiracial people, in which she exhorts 'mixed race' people to assert the identities which they have chosen for themselves, however uncomfortable or confused these may make others.[22]

In the context of ever-increasing cultural entanglements (as expressed by the notions of hybridity and cross-over cultures), the understanding of what 'mixture' means is a pressing concern. An important prerequisite is the clarification of current thinking about the modern category most associated with purity: 'race'.

Towards a Complex Ontology

The first dilemma underlying the analysis of 'mixed race' is whether the very term lends credence to the scientifically bogus and politically dubious category of 'race'. The emerging scientific orthodoxy credits modern genetics with undermining the ontological status of 'races' as discrete, immutable and intergenerationally stable biological entities.[23] There is as much genetic variation within as there is between so-called 'races'. Yet at the same time sociologists acknowledge the continuing significance of assumptions and practices predicated on a belief in the existence of 'races'. Accordingly most social scientists describe 'race' as a social construction with potentially pernicious effects, while recognising that racialised identities can be an important mobilising force for those struggling against discrimination and disadvantage.

This equivocation between recognising the scientific invalidity of 'race' and yet acknowledging the continuing power of racism and racialised identities is evident in the 'racial constructivism'[24] of the American philosopher Charles Mills. The constructivist dimension of his position highlights the role of historically specific processes of racialisation which give a social reality to categories such as black and white, 'which correspond to no natural kinds'.[25] However, he acknowledges the force of 'race' as a social fact that is deeply embodied, phenomenologically weighty and socially significant. Irrespective of the scientific invalidity of 'race', 'an objective ontological status is involved which arises out of intersubjectivity, and which, though it is not naturally based, is real for all that'.[26] Accordingly, racism can only be understood through an acknowledgement of the power of 'race' as a social category, not by an attempt to deny the existence of 'race'. Thus most North American discussions use the term 'race' without scare quotes on the grounds, firstly, that most people act as if stable, intergenerationally reproduced collectivities do exist; and secondly, that 'race' can be written of as a causal factor in its own right.[27]

In European sociological debates there is far less confidence in the validity of 'race' as a tool of analysis. Possibly due to the greater influence of Marxism and class analysis, many European sociologists tend either to enclose 'race' within scare quotes, or to argue for avoiding the term altogether. For Robert Miles, sociologists should not legitimate the reification of false abstractions such as 'race' which have no scientific basis.[28] Rather, their priority should be an analysis of the processes of racialisation and racism.[29] Michel Wieviorka's important work echoes this in demanding that 'we affirm, without ambiguity, the subjective, socially and historically constructed character of the recourse to that notion, which belongs to the discourse and consciousness of the social actors, and not, in any sense, to sociological analysis'.[30]

In our view, everyday social consciousness and sociological theory cannot be so rigidly separated. Rethinking 'mixed race' should serve as one means for exploring their complex interconnection rather than legislating their interplay out of existence prematurely. The status of 'race' cannot be determined by purely theoretical reflection. It must be analysed through specific instances, of which 'mixed race' is one of the most important and most neglected.

It is surprising that until recently, and in stark contrast to the formative decades of the discipline, the sociological analysis of racialisation has largely overlooked the phenomenon of 'mixed race'. In spite of its strategic importance for interrogating the presuppositions of racialised ontologies; discussions of 'race' and racism in both Britain and the USA have either not mentioned 'mixed race' at all, or only in passing.[31] However, in the last decade, a more concerted set of reflections has been initiated, largely by those who define themselves as 'mixed race' – especially in the USA.[32] This sets the terms for a renewed debate.

In the following pages we briefly review the social science literature on 'mixed race' and explore the implications of 'mixed race' for the understanding of 'race' and identity more generally. Broadly speaking, three kinds of arguments about 'mixed race' can be discerned:

1. Some analysts have developed diverse formulations that recognise 'mixed race' as a viable social category.
2. In the USA in particular, scholars and activists have elaborated the notion of 'multiracial' people and experiences.
3. There is a series of arguments at different levels of abstraction that call on social scientists to abandon the concept of 'race' as a step towards a 'post-racial' world.

'Mixed race' is a stable social category

The first strand of writing identifies 'mixed race' as a viable social category. In British social research this became evident in studies of 'mixed race' families and young people by Susan Benson and Anne Wilson in the 1980s and more recently the work of Barbara Tizard and Ann Phoenix.[33] These studies were limited by a regional focus in the South East of England, and their samples were confined to those with one black and one white parent, thus ignoring the many families with white, Asian, Chinese and other ancestries. However, as in the edited volumes on the diverse experiences of 'mixed race' people in the USA (such as by Maria Root and Naomi Zack), their sensitive renditions of personal testimony countered the pathologising and patronising representations of 'mixed race' that had dominated previous academic research. The term 'mixed race' is now widely recognised not only in relation to 'mixed race' families and individuals, but also in discussions of policy issues such as trans-racial adoption.[34]

This recognition of 'mixed race' people was evident in the press reception given to a major survey of ethnic relations in Britain in the late 1990s – the Fourth National Survey of Ethnic Minorities.[35] The research study itself contained very few reflections on 'mixed race'. Yet the growing population of 'mixed race' people was seized upon as a sign of peaceful integration and Britain's success as a multicultural society. The *Guardian* newspaper of 22 May 1997 also called attention to the theme of 'mixing' with an article titled 'Mixed marriages help close the race divide'. However, the tensions within the discourse on 'mixed race' can be read even within such a short piece. For, on the one hand, the closing of the race divide is welcomed and yet, on the other hand, a new 'mixed race' race is announced. The feature is illustrated by a racially diverse collage of 35 faces, captioned: 'Beige Britain: A new race is growing up. It's not black, it's not white and it's not yet officially recognised. Welcome to the mixed-race future.' Unfortunately, this reference to 'mixed race' in Britain has remained largely descriptive, without an elaboration of its conceptual presuppositions or the political implications of hailing the emergence of 'mixed' people.

Clearer statements on how the concept of 'mixed race' might disrupt conventional understandings of 'race' have appeared in the USA. Although, as in Britain, interest in 'mixed race' people and couples is predominantly focused on people with black and white parentage, the range of recognised 'mixes' is now broader (see Chapter 3, Mahtani and Moreno). Partly due to this, there is a far more evident 'mixed race' presence on university campuses, ethnic studies curricula, and on the Internet.[36]

Many recent writers on 'mixed race' have claimed that 'mixed' people have a unique experience. As research gathered in this book and elsewhere demonstrates, people of 'mixed race' often have distinctive experiences of their parents and family life, unique patterns of identity formation, and are subject to exceptional forms of discrimination that cannot be addressed within existing conceptions of 'race'. As discussed in Chapter 5 by Laurie Mengel, these particular experiences include: falling outside dominant racialised categories; facing distrust and suspicion from both 'sides' of their family; being profoundly and hurtfully misrecognised by others, enduring the 'What are you?' question; enjoying the potential for multiple allegiances and identities.

Yet the claim to a distinctive 'mixed race' experience has not gone unchallenged. According to some critics in the USA in particular, the white parents of 'mixed race' children and sometimes 'mixed race' people themselves, are charged with a covertly anti-black impulse. Especially in the case of people with black and white parentage, the assertion of a 'mixed race' identity is said to express a desire to dilute, or even disavow, their black heritage and seek the privileges of whiteness.[37] The philosopher Lewis Gordon believes that in a world deeply structured by a white/black antagonism, the claim for a 'mixed race' identity is an attempt to escape from being tainted by blackness.[38] He argues that analysts should accept the lived experience of racialised difference as a foundation for social identities: 'offsprings who are biracial mixtures with blacks are pretty much excluded from most racial categories except for black.'[39] Yet if lived experience is the criterion for judging the efficacy of a social identity, it seems disingenuous of Gordon to kick the ladder away from 'mixed race' people defining their own identities in a way which reflects both their mixed genealogies and their ongoing lives as 'mixed' individuals. Gordon's acknowledgement of the distinct social experiences of 'mixed race' people is brief, grudging and patronising. He leaves no room for complex combinations of black and 'mixed race' affiliations of the kind analysed by Jayne Ifekwunigwe and others.[40] Moreover, Gordon pays virtually no attention to those who are 'mixed race', but who have neither white nor black ancestry.

The emergence of a new multiracial discourse

The term 'multiracial' grates on a British ear. For here the word is associated with paternalistic governmental strategies of the 1970s and 1980s.[41] However, British dismissals of the prefix 'multi-' in 'multiracial' may be premature. They fail to recognise the distinct relationship between the multiracial and the multicultural in the USA. The 'multi-' prefix is used to index a more radical racial pluralism that goes beyond a simple black/white binary.

Recent work by those who initiated critical reflection on 'mixed race' or bi-racialism in the early 1990s now deploys the term 'multiracial'. Maria Root defines 'multiracials' as 'people who are of two or more racial heritages'.[42] Used in this way, the term 'multiracial' is intended to encompass a far more extensive diversity than 'mixed race'. As April Moreno argues in this book, the notion of 'mixed race' can imply the impurification of whiteness, and disavow more complex family histories.

Underlying the advocacy of 'mixed race' is the claim that 'mixed race' people experience most acutely how multiplicity is the modality of contemporary identity formation. Their complex genealogies of multiple ancestry draw on far more diverse 'sources of the self' compared to the modern quest for unity, authenticity and security set out in the work of thinkers such as Charles Taylor and Anthony Giddens.[43] Accordingly, the term 'mixed race' itself may not reflect the complexity of its own formation through historical entanglements and contemporary redefinitions. This may account for the gradual displacement of 'mixed race' by a notion of 'multiraciality' that points to multiplicity being the form of contemporary identity itself.

In the work of some writers, 'mixed race' people are the people of the future who embody most directly the transgressive theoretical motifs of hybridity, nomadism and border crossing. This new subjectivity of mixture and multiplicity is expressed most vividly in the writing of Gloria Anzaldúa.[44] Her notion of 'mestiza consciousness' is an explicit validation of living with multiple allegiances and the creative tensions that might arise. Jayne Ifekwunigwe's earlier work proposed the related term 'metissage' as a new means of understanding 'mixed race' subjectivities.[45] However, the derivation of some of these words from animalistic codes of breeding needs to be worked through and justified, clarifying the precise sense in which a term is being wrought free from negative associations to signify positively in the current conjuncture.[46]

Furthermore, the over-exuberant deployment of a notion like hybridity can connote an uncomfortable claiming of heterosis, the inherent biological superiority of 'mixed race'. As Anzaldúa declares: 'At the confluence of two or more genetic streams, with chromosomes constantly "crossing over", this mixture of races, rather than resulting in an inferior being, provides hybrid progeny, a mutable more malleable species with a rich gene pool.'[47] However well-intentioned, this eulogy for mixture is problematic. It implies the intermingling of separate streams of blood and genes whose mystical alchemy orchestrates a virtuous medley of mixed cultural practices. Yet such tropes of mixing and blending are predicated on heterosexualised reproduction, and an accentuated definition of ancestral loyalty which, though complex in origin, is still the genealogy of identity being traced. In addition these metaphors of intermixing only make sense if you hold a notion of purity constant for at least one of the generations prior to that being designated as 'mixed'.

There is the additional danger of assuming all mixes are on equal terms, the product of a harmonious balance between the mixing elements. The reasons for, and consequences of, the 'mixture' cannot be reduced to a universally positive designation. Thus the specific power relations and historical influences shaping this 'mixture' require careful specification. Furthermore, the existence of 'mixed race' populations does not in itself end racism. Instead, a different racial hierarchy can be set in place, where divisions and exclusions are far from dissolved. In this vein, Jon Michael Spencer offers a cautious account of the place of 'coloured' people in South Africa, and Steven Ropp highlights the persistence of racial discrimination in multiracial Belize.[48]

The term 'multiracial' thus harbours a number of inconsistencies. There is a tension between simply multiplying the number of 'races', and thereby multiplying the scientifically ungrounded allegiance to 'race', and deconstructing 'race' by unravelling its inherent, but all too often disavowed, multiplicity. To identify someone as 'multiracial' is to enumerate a genealogy that combines a number of distinct 'races' which that person now embodies. It merely displaces the monoracial designation to a higher branch of the family tree. This reinscribes the notion of multiraciality within the discourse of mono-racialisation. Furthermore, often associated with this use of 'multiracial' is the conservative impulse to preserve aspects of all of one's heritages. A seemingly forward-looking concept of 'multiraciality' can in fact depend on an exacting genealogy of ancestor correspondence where forebears are traced, matched and blended. The present-day self is then dissected into fractional components, each bearing a little of the weight of tradition that the term 'heritage' implies, but these individualised fragments might not coalesce into a social constituency with political effectivity. 'Multiraciality' therefore could simply be the latest episode in a specifically North American drama of ethnic rootedness, a privileging of relations of vertical kinship and descent rather than the horizontal affiliations of consent.[49]

A more rigorous and innovative deployment of 'multiraciality' requires a dialogue with attempts to theorise multiplicity in social and cultural theory.[50] Some of these efforts, far from validating notions of 'mixed race' or 'multiracial', argue that the time has come to go beyond 'race' altogether.

Beyond 'race'?

This third strand of argument sees 'mixed race' people as the leading edge of a much broader project to discredit the modern project of racial categorisation, and perhaps of categorisation itself. One sociologist claims: 'The next century ... will be a time in which the traditional methods of drawing sociological distinctions among human beings will crumble.'[51] Advocates of 'mixed race' hail the existence of 'mixed race' people for revealing the shifting and arbitrary nature of the boundaries between so-called 'races': 'The presence of racially mixed persons defies the social order predicated upon race [...] the existence of racially mixed persons challenges long-held notions about the biological, moral and social meaning of race.'[52]

But if the notion of 'mixed race' undercuts attempts to identify and perpetuate stable racially defined collectivities, then how can 'mixed race' itself be a sustainable category? Is it not simply reinscribing people within racialised boundaries, admittedly less fixed than before, but still there? The term 'mixed race' is itself contradictory; either it applies to everyone, or must assume at some time past there were pure 'races' which when mixed produce a new third 'race', a new category that only makes sense by combining existing racialised categories. David Goldberg defines the paradox: 'The challenge to the project of racial purity in the celebration of mixed-race identities is at best ambiguous, (re) fixing the premises of the racialising project in place as it challenges that project's very terms of articulation.'[53]

However, Goldberg's somewhat fraught reflections are not alive to the productive potential of antithetically juxtaposing mixture and 'race' in the same concept. Pointing out the 'mixedness' of 'race' in itself might begin to question the unreflective division of the population into discrete racial categories. It is not a criticism of 'mixed race' to cite its ambiguity, for that may be its distinctive contribution – troubling previously taken for granted distinctions.

Those who argue that 'mixed race' leads to the dissolution of 'race' have yet to develop a fully thought out position and tend to remain at the level of utopian speculation. In these accounts, a personal narrative often exemplifies a more general social change which the life story in question embodies – the transcendence of 'race': 'My journey has taken me past constructions of race, past constructions of mixed-race, and into an understanding of human difference that does not include race as a meaningful category.'[54] This move towards post-raciality requires a repudiation of the vocabulary of 'race'. To merely mix 'race' is to concede too much to those who would divide and judge human beings on the grounds of biologically inherited characteristics.

The most sophisticated aspirations to 'post-raciality' have affinities with authors who have not written explicitly on 'mixed race'. Thinkers such as Rosi Braidotti, Judith Butler and Elspeth Probyn express an impatience with the political and intellectual premises of modern thought, and a desire to unsettle previously foundational social categories such as gender, sexuality and 'race'.[55]

Paul Gilroy expresses the clearest translation of this perspective into a post-racial worldview in a review of Richard Dyer's study of whiteness. Here Gilroy makes clearer what his earlier work has occasionally implied. He chides Dyer for not following 'the line of constructionist thinking right through to the obvious destination. This would require saying, boldly and clearly, that "race" is an especially pernicious illusion which we need to purge from our thinking and our actions,'[56] and that the idea of 'race' is no longer secure as a way of understanding the world. In a subsequent journal article, Gilroy states that '"race" might best be approached as an after-image – a lingering symptom of looking too intently or too casually into the damaging glare emanating from colonial conflicts at home and abroad.'[57]

Unfortunately, Gilroy's declaration – 'Race ends here' – hesitates between daring and defensiveness. Even in his most extended development to date of the 'post-racial' case, he has yet to fully specify the political or moral destination after 'race' has been dispensed with.[58] He places too much emphasis on new visual imaging technologies in genetic science and medicine which operate beneath the surface of the skin as in themselves implying the transcendence of classification schemes based on visible racial difference. This focus on modes of scientific representation short-circuits questions of how institutional practice and politics should counter racism. These issues will require more than Gilroy's admittedly provisional formulation of a 'pragmatic, planetary humanism'.[59]

Critics of the 'post-racial' aspiration see it as naïve at best, at worst wilfully dismissive of how anti-racist initiatives depend on the pragmatic recognition and monitoring of social outcomes along racialised lines. Amidst racial discrimination, hatred and violence, is it not premature to already proclaim the end of anti-racism and the arrival of a 'post-racial' world?[60]

The problematic implications of 'post-raciality' can be discerned through an investigation of contributions to the bi-monthly Internet journal for 'mixed race' people, Interracial Voice. The editor of this site, Charles Byrd, states: 'Mixed race folk have not only a golden opportunity but an obligation to guide America beyond antiquated "racial" thinking.'[61] For all its self-professed wisdom, this position amounts to an uncompromisingly romantic reassertion of liberal individualism, as evidenced by Byrd's assent to the ideal that 'individuals should have the right to exercise sole dominion over their own lives'.[62] These libertarian 'post-racial' declarations overlook the impossibility of a generic pre-constituted and unmarked self, free from social determination. Furthermore, they disregard the possibility of a racism which can thrive without explicit reference to 'races'. This 'racism without races' has been described as postmodern racism or neo-racism.[63] It will require more than the semantic excision of 'race' from social science to defeat deep-seated racialised inequalities.

An Agenda for Rethinking 'Mixed Race'

We have now laid out three kinds of arguments in recent writings on 'race' and 'mixed race' which argue respectively in favour of the recognition of 'mixed race' people; the emergence of a 'multiracial' discourse; and advocacy of 'post-raciality'. However, the challenge of 'mixed race' can only be realised with a more precise analysis of the conceptual structure of 'mixed race' itself. This calls for a closer investigation of the processes which have defined 'mixture' and the practices of 'mixed race' identity formation.

Understandings of 'race' and ethnic identity in contemporary societies require an engagement with the legacies of colonialism and global migration; the processes through which cultures thereby brought into contact have mixed; and the complex formations of identity arising from the first two processes. As Chapter 1 by Frank Furedi documents, modern British and American social science has been implicated in 'race-management' projects throughout the world. Furedi's work in this book and elsewhere[64] illustrates how an intense focus on racial mixture through the prism of eugenics was a formative dimension in the emergence of sociology, particularly in the USA. The context of world war, population depletion and demographic anxiety fostered concern at the implications of migration, social mobility and cultural fluidity for the quality of the nation's future offspring.

It is also important to acknowledge the frequently far from benign sources of racial mixture. 'Mixed race' populations have often emerged through the deeply felt historical violations of imperial sexual conquest and enslavement.[65] 'Mixed race' bodies can bear the burden of these legacies, deep-seated traumas inscribed on people's skin, and this should not be evaded.

However, these histories are highly specific. No one nation's experiences should be taken as paradigmatic. Even within the English-African diaspora, Jayne Ifekwunigwe, in Chapter 2, shows how distinctive individual 'mixed race' subjectivities can be. Ifekwunigwe's testimonies of three women – Nigerian and English Ruby, Northumberland Yoruba Bisi, and Bajan (from Barbados) and Irish Akousa – demonstrate how subtle combinations of the local and transnational cut across monoracial national boundaries. Through these three narratives, Ifekwunigwe critiques the contested dialectics of Blackness and Whiteness as they delimit constructions of Englishness and the English-African diaspora.

Unfortunately, the sharpest criticisms of the emerging discourse on 'mixed race' often overlook such complexities. They can fail to mark their own conditions of production in the USA where a specific legacy of slavery and acquisitive white male sexuality structures the debate on 'mixed race'. The nation with the most exceptional racialised social formation dominates the global discourse on these questions, without acknowledging the historical and geographical particularity of the 'one drop' rule, where the existence of one known black ancestor sufficed for an individual to be designated black in law. The reduction of 'mixed race' to an anti-black identity by critics in the USA such as Lewis

Gordon and Lisa Jones[66] should not be applied indiscriminately.[67] Nor should such a narrow conceptualisation of 'mixed race' eclipse the experiences of other 'mixes'.

In Chapter 3, Minelle Mahtani and April Moreno pointedly stress the dangers of 'mixed race' discourse itself overlooking those with histories going beyond black and white mixture. As women of Canadian South-east Indian and Iranian descent (Mahtani) and Chinese and Mexican-American ancestry (Moreno), Mahtani and Moreno raise the fundamental question: Whose voice deserves to be and is heard in 'mixed race' discourse? In many academic and popular accounts, and in most policy formulations in both Britain and the USA, voices such as theirs have been notably neglected.

Paul Spickard's incisive review in Chapter 4 of the recent boom in biographies and autobiographies on and by 'mixed race' people shows the interweaving of large-scale racialised processes with intimate portraits about growing up 'mixed race' and 'mixed race' family life. As noted by Mahtani and Moreno, Spickard observes that most of these books are by or about people who are of Black and White ancestry, not other ethnic ancestries. However, as Spickard also documents, there is a notable flowering of autobiographically based fiction concerning Eurasian experiences in both the USA and Britain.[68]

Much of the writing on 'mixed race' has highlighted a distinctive form of 'mixed race' embodiment characterised by an intimate relationship between racialisation and facialisation.[69] Facialisation refers to the designation of a limited set of facial types, how these are taken as metonyms for the racialised body, and are associated with character traits. In the case of 'mixed race' people, their experiences tell of how the face gets figured as the repository of racial truths and suggestive of where you 'really' come from. As the title of Minelle Mahtani's chapter itself dramatises (Chapter 9, 'I'm a blond-haired, blue-eyed black girl'), falling in between these socially constructed norms leaves one open to statements which doubt corporeal integrity: 'You don't *look* Chinese ...' on a par with 'You don't look quite *right*.' Running through all these chapters is a vigorous contestation of the recurrent portrayal of 'mixed race' people as inauthentic dilutions of racial essences.

The particularities of Eurasian experience and the politics of authenticity and belonging – which are integrally shaped by how one's physical appearance is socially recognised – are outlined in Chapter 5 by Laurie Mengel. Mengel argues for a growing sense of commonality and shared experiences among multiracial people – regardless of their particular racial ancestries – which is fundamental for the creation of a panethnic identity based upon mixedness *per se*. The publishing trend by 'mixed race' authors, discussed by Paul Spickard, also suggests the reading public's awareness of a population of multiracial people.

Through a careful analysis of both media and government texts, Stephen Small demonstrates in Chapter 6 the interplay between racialised discourses and institutional practices. In comparison with Laurie Mengel's more optimistic view of an emerging panethnic multiracial identity and movement, Small's cautious appraisal of the 'mixed race movement' is a salutary reminder of the continuing force of racialised processes in determining social outcomes.

The policy and practice implications of how we understand 'mixed race' are now enormous. As Charlie Owen's paper (Chapter 7) on 'mixed race' in official statistics argues, the creation and recording of ethnic and racial categories does not occur in a vacuum. There is a politics of recognition and representation involved in these processes which has been given scant attention in the academic literature.[70] In the USA debates over the possible inclusion of a 'multiracial' or 'mixed race' category for the 2000 census were heated and vehement, yet resulted in the 'check all that apply' option, not the single category called for by some (though not all) within the 'mixed race movement'. By contrast, in the United Kingdom the inclusion of a 'mixed' category in the 2001 census question on ethnic origin has thus far gone largely uncontested. As the figures are counted over the next few years, researchers should ask: For whose benefit are these categories formulated? How do they alter past response patterns? Will a new constituency be consolidated by the very act of being counted?

As with ethnic monitoring in the census, Barbara Lal illustrates in Chapter 8 how definitions of 'mixed race' have shaped adoption policies in Britain and the USA. Lal argues that essentialist models of ethnic identity are erroneously employed by many child welfare professionals who oppose transracial adoption, and who see adoptees as irrevocably tied to the ethnicity of their birth parents. Lal shows how the administrative definition and regulation of 'mixed race' in adoption policies needs to be based upon an understanding of ethnic identity as learned culture, rather than as biologically determined.

One emerging paradigm for understanding the complexity of social relations and identities centres on the notion of intersectionality:[71] the idea that identity politics takes place at the site where multiple categories intersect. At first sight, 'mixed race' identity would appear a paradigm case of intersectionality. However, intersectionality can imply that social identities arise from social relations meeting at a single point, with a resolution at that site. This seems too static a rendition of the interactions between the multiple histories, images and transnational networks comprising any social identity, but most especially 'mixed race'. A more conceptual analysis demonstrates how 'mixed race' reveals the transectional nature of identity formation.

The idea of transection refers not simply to the spatial dimension of the intersection of social relations, but also to the temporal dimension of how distinct historical trajectories may be asynchronous, incommensurable and thus confound additive combinations through their interactive dissonance.[72] Particular experiences of migration, enslavement or displacement may permeate the present and influence the current time-horizons and senses of history in different social groups. Theorising transection requires sensitivity to such discrepancies, and a willingness to appreciate new iterative structures in intergenerational transmission. These refer to the growing complexity of origins, the ever-accelerating intensity of cultural practices as a means of handing things down, and consequently the reduced certainty of past entities being replicated over time. In this regard 'mixed race' may serve as an exemplary transectional identity. For the concept of 'race' depends on uninterrupted continuity, the persistence of genetically inherited characteristics, and thus the fragile injunctive temporality of 'same race' intergenerational reproduction. As Taguieff notes,[73] this temporality surfaces most notably when grandparents express concern at what their children's 'mixed race' offspring might look like – radically unlike them! It reflects an anxiety that 'mixed race' children will somehow dilute the family blood and lack the readily visible bodily signatures of ancestry. The injunction against interracial relationships is defined by loyalty to the lineage, the preservation of a physically apparent family line through time. The subversive potential of 'mixed race' consists in a conjoining that may disrupt this model of replication and resemblance in favour of a less predictable, non-linear outcome: no-one should be forced to deny their ancestry, no-one can be wholly defined by their heritage.

Minelle Mahtani's chapter, Chapter 9, works in this spirit. She uses the geographically inspired idea of 'paradoxical space' but takes its application to 'mixed race' identity well beyond a one-dimensional spatialism. Her ideas bear an affinity with Sara Ahmed's perceptive assessment of the temporal dimensions of 'passing' and 'mixed race' identity.[74] A transectional analysis does not assign 'mixed race' to a single 'third space' safely beyond the black/white binary. Nor does it reify 'the hybrid' as an inherently transgressive figure of intercultural bricolage. A transectional understanding of 'mixed race' highlights the transformation of categories and social relations when they do not merely intersect, but transect one another in antithetical combinations where the component parts may not be aligned in the same plane. Attention to diversity within 'mixed race' experiences brings home how racialisation is transected by other formative social relations: class, gender and sexuality. The results of these transections cannot be resolved neatly into pre-assigned fractions, and require analysis grounded in particular performative contexts.[75]

It is important in future research, therefore, to foreground 'mixed race' not just in itself, but rather as offering more general insights into dense, multifaceted 'textured identities'.[76] The rethinking of 'race' through 'mixed race' disrupts the certainty of a social category central to the organisation of modern societies. For the notion of 'mixed race' thwarts the ideal of pristine, pure 'races' with the undeniable historical truth of mixture, while simultaneously highlighting the inescapable contemporary fact of racialisation.

In the longer term, only a combination of greater conceptual rigour, sober historical analysis and sensitive gathering of testimonies will further the debates we initiate here. Many of the arguments we have identified about 'mixed race' may be in dispute for many decades to come. Just as with the ethnicity boxes on population census forms we shouldn't be forced to choose one perspective as all-encompassing. For now, the term 'mixed race' refers to distinctive experiences which cannot be accommodated within existing frames of reference. These experiences may be too diverse to share a name for too long, too dynamic and dispersed to hold still for sustained political action, but they are undoubtedly too important to dismiss.

Notes

1. In this introduction we have decided to utilise quotation marks around 'mixed race' and 'race' to signal our unease at invoking the notion. However, we have left each contributor's chosen formulation intact. The issues of terminology and the ontological status of 'race' and 'mixed race' are yet to be determined conclusively. Similarly we have followed each contributor's chosen style for Black/black and White/white.
2. The conference 'Rethinking "Mixed Race"' was held in December 1997 at the National Institute for Social Work, London. We thank all those who attended and participated, in particular Margaret Boushel, Chris Smaje, Erika Tan, Jill Olumide, John Dixie.
3. The recent case of a Black British athlete whose white boyfriend was initially alleged to have been the victim of a racist attack called forth a number of articles from those in 'mixed-race' couples. For example 'Race hate in Britain is rife – just ask my wife' written by Richard Ellis, about his experiences married to a Black British woman, *Observer*, 26 March 2000.

The most dramatic example of the everyday harassment faced by many is the case of Mal Hussain and Linda Livingston, an Asian–white couple. Their house in Lancaster has been the subject of over 2,000 attacks since 1991. See the *Guardian*, 13 April 2000.

4. Y. Alibhai-Brown and A. Montague, *The Colour of Love* (London: Virago: 1992); M. Root (ed.), *Racially Mixed People in America* (Newbury Park: Sage, 1992); R. Frankenberg, *White Women, Race Matters: the Social Construction of Whiteness* (Minneapolis: University of Minnesota, 1993).
5. M. Thornton, 'Hidden Agendas, Identity Theories, and Multiracial People', in M. Root (ed.), *The Multiracial Experience* (Newbury Park: Sage, 1996).
6. C.M. Snipp, 'Some observations about racial boundaries and the experiences of American Indians', *Ethnic and Racial Studies*, 20, 4 (1997), p.672.
7. T. Modood and R. Berthoud, *Ethnic Minorities in Britain: The Fourth National Survey of Ethnic Minorities* (London: Policy Studies Institute, 1997).
8. 'Britain leads in mixed-race romance', *Sunday Times*, 9 April 2000, p.7. The statistics are taken from a study by Richard Berthoud, Institute for Social and Economic Research, University of Essex.
9. The Stationery Office, 2001 census (London: The Stationery Office, 1999). The precise question to be used can be found in Chapter 7, p.147.
10. The United States census 2000 Web site offers an explanation of its new system of categorisation: 'Each respondent decides his or her racial identity. For the first time ever, people with mixed heritage may select more than racial category. The groups shown in the census race question can be collapsed into the minimum race categories needed by the federal government: "White", "Black or African American", "American Indian and Alaska Native", "Asian" and "Native Hawaiian and Other Pacific Islander".' See http://www.census.gov/dmd/www/genfaq.htm#ethnic
11. These were comments in the visitor's book for 'Deep', the exhibition of photographs of 'mixed race' people, by Clement Cooper. This was held at the Drum Arts Centre, Birmingham, England, Summer 1998.
12. For example in a paragraph titled 'the purification of the races' Nietzsche writes: 'There are probably no pure races but only races that have become pure, even these being extremely rare. What is normal is crossed races, in which together with a disharmony of physical features, there must also go a disharmony of habits and value-concepts'. F. Nietzsche, *Daybreak* (Cambridge: Cambridge University Press, 1997 [1881]), p.149.

    For further examples of how pervasive fear of racial mixture has been in the canon of Western thought see E. Eze, *Race and the Enlightenment* (Oxford: Blackwell, 1997); and P. Taguieff, *Les Fins de l'anti-racisme* (Paris: Éditions Michalons, 1995) esp. Ch.4. This theme of the interplay between corporeal disharmony and psychological instability is of course dramatised in the fictional construct of the tragic mulatto, so evident in American literature. See J. Williamson, *New People: Miscegenation and Mulattoes in the United States* (New York: New York University Press, 1980).
13. M. Grant, *The Passing of the Great Race* (New York: Charles Scribner, 1918).

14. See E. Barkan, *The Retreat of Scientific Racism* (Cambridge: Cambridge University Press, 1992); M.E. Fletcher, 'Report of an investigation into the colour problem in Liverpool and other ports' (Liverpool: Liverpool Association for the Welfare of Half-Caste Children, 1930).
15. A. Montagu, *Statement on Race* (London: Oxford University Press, 1972).
16. See J. Solomos and L. Back, *Race, Politics and Social Change* (London: Routledge, 1995).
17. This is evident in the study by Abby Ferber: A. Ferber, *White Man Falling* (Maryland: Rowman and Littlefield, 1998).
18. Y. Alibhai-Brown, 'Every mixed race marriage is building a better Britain', *Independent*, 4 March 1999; Y. Alibhai-Brown, *Beyond Black and White*, BBC Radio 4 documentary, 5 March 1999.
19. D. Haraway, *Modest_Witness@Second_Millenium. Female Man _Meets_OncoMouse* (New York and London: Routledge, 1997), p.52.
20. See S. Rushdie, *Imaginary Homelands* (London: Granta, 1991); S. Hall, 'The Question of Cultural Identity', in S. Hall, A. McGrew and D. Held (eds), *Modernity and Its Futures* (Cambridge: Polity Press, 1992); H. Bhabha, *The Location of Culture* (London: Routledge, 1994).
21. Critical discussions of hybridity can be found in Robert J.C. Young, *Colonial Desire: Hybridity in Theory, Culture and Race* (London; New York: Routledge, 1995); P. Werbner and T. Modood (eds), *Debating Cultural Hybridity* (London: Zed Books, 1997); N. Papastergiadis, *The Turbulence of Migration* (Cambridge: Polity Press, 2000).
22. M. Root, 'A bill of rights for racially mixed people', in M. Root (ed.), *The Multiracial Experience* (Newbury Park: Sage, 1996).
23. R. Lewontin, S. Rose and L. Kamin, *Not in Our Genes* (New York: Pantheon Books, 1984); R. Lewontin, *Human Diversity* (New York: Scientific American Library, 1995).
24. C. Mills, *Blackness Visible* (Ithaca: Cornell University Press, 1998), p.47.
25. *Ibid*, p 48.
26. *Ibid.*
27. See for example the popular sociology textbook J. Macionis, *Sociology* (Englewood: Prentice Hall, 1995); and the collection R. Torres, L. Miron and J. Inda (eds), *Race, Identity and Citizenship* (New Malden: Blackwell, 1999).
28. Miles's views are stated clearly in R. Miles, *Racism* (London: Routledge, 1989); R. Miles, *Racism after 'Race Relations'* (London: Routledge, 1993).
29. Stephen Small's work in this collection and elsewhere has pursued this analysis with important modifications. See S. Small, *Racialised Barriers* (London: Routledge, 1994).
30. M. Wieviorka, *The Arena of Racism* (London: Sage 1995), p.34.
31. For example, see J. Solomos, *Race and Racism in Contemporary Britain* (London: Macmillan 1993); M. Omi and H. Winant, *Racial Formation in the United States* (New York and London: Routledge, 1994), p.59

32. Ground-breaking studies included M. Root (ed.), *Racially Mixed People in America* (Newbury Park: Sage, 1992); M. Root (ed.), *The Multiracial Experience* (Newbury Park: Sage, 1996); N. Zack, *Race and Mixed Race* (Philadelphia: Temple University Press, 1993).
33. S. Benson, *Ambiguous Ethnicity* (Cambridge: Cambridge University Press, 1981); A. Wilson, *Mixed Race Children* (London: Allen and Unwin, 1987); B. Tizard and A. Phoenix, *Black, White or Mixed Race* (London: Routledge, 1993).
34. See *Sunday Times*, 18 July 1999. The story concerned 'a mixed race couple' whose application to adopt a child was refused.
35. T. Modood and R. Berthoud, *Ethnic Minorities in Britain* (London: Policy Studies Institute, 1997).
36. A small selection of relevant Internet sites:
    - Interracial Voice (Bi-monthly journal and forum) http://www.webcom.com/intvoice
    - Project RACE (Reclassify All Children Eqaully) http://www.projectrace.com/
    - Hapa issues forum (Bay Area, California) http://www.hapaissuesforum.org
    - MAVIN (On-line journal) http://www.mavin.net
    - The Multiracial Activist (on-line journal) http://www.multiracial.com/
    - The longest established British group is 'People in Harmony' http://www.pih.org.uk/
    - Anglo-Indian Home page http://www.alphalink.com.au~agilbert/index.html
37. 'Mixed race' celebrities have become the objects of almost fetishistic attention, especially in the United States; for example, Mariah Carey, Tiger Woods, Dean Cain.
38. See L. Gordon, *Her Majesty's Other Children* (Lanham: Rowman and Littlefield, 1997) esp. Ch.3.
39. *Ibid.* p.56.
40. See in particular J. Ifekwunigwe, *Scattered Belongings* (London: Routledge, 1999).
41. These were defined by a liberal pluralist philosophy which sought to manage and pacify minority communities whose cultures where homogenised and at best tolerated by the majority. B. Parekh, 'National Culture and Multiculturalism', in K. Thompson (ed.), *Media and Cultural Regulation* (London: Sage, 1997).
42. M. Root, *The Multiracial Experience* (Newbury Park: Sage, 1996), p 11.
43. The contours of modern identity are traced in C. Taylor, *Sources of the Self* (Cambridge: Harvard University Press, 1989) and A. Giddens, *Modernity and Self Identity* (Cambridge: Polity Press, 1991).
44. G. Anzaldúa, *Borderlands/LaFrontera: The New Mestiza* (San Francisco: Aunt Lute Books, 1987); G. Anzaldúa (ed.), *Making Face, Making Soul* (San Francisco: Aunt Lute Books, 1990).

45. See J. Ifekwungiwe, *Scattered Belongings* (London: Routledge, 1999).
46. A useful and concise argument detailing the contradictions of Latin American discourses on 'racial mixture' can be found in A. Bonnett, *Anti-Racism* (London: Routledge, 2000).
47. G. Anzaldúa, *Making Face, Making Soul* (San Francisco: Aunt Lute Books, 1990), p.377
48. J. Spencer, *The New Colored People* (New York: New York University Press, 1997); S. Ropp. 'Do Multiracial Subjects Really Challenge Race?', *Amerasia Journal*, vol.23, no.1 (1997), pp.1–16.
49. The distinction between descent and consent as sources of identity is defined with great acuity in W. Sollors, *Beyond Ethnicity* (New York: Oxford University Press, 1986).
50. See A. Brah, *Cartographies of Diaspora* (London: Routledge, 1996).
51. J. Stanfield, 'Preface', in A. Montagu, *Man's Most Dangerous Myth: The Fallacy of Race* (Walnut Creek: Alta Mira Press, 1997), 6th edn, p.25.
52. M. Root (ed.), *Racially Mixed People in America* (Newbury Park: Sage, 1992), p.3.
53. D. Goldberg, *Racial Subjects* (New York and London: Routledge, 1997), p.61.
54. R. Spencer. 'Race and Mixed Race: A Personal Tour', in W. Penn. (ed.), *As We Are Now: Mixblood Essays on Race and Identity* (Berkeley: University of California Press, 1997), p.137.
55. See in particular R. Braidotti, *Nomadic Subjects* (New York and London: Routledge, 1994); J. Butler, *Gender Trouble* (New York and London: Routledge, 1990); J. Butler, *Bodies that Matter* (New York and London: Routledge, 1993); E. Probyn, *Outside Belongings* (New York and London: Routledge, 1996).
56. P. Gilroy, 'White man's bonus', *Times Literary Supplement*, 29 August 1997, p.10, reviewing R. Dyer, *White* (London: Routledge, 1997).
57. P. Gilroy, 'Race ends here', *Ethnic and Racial Studies*, vol.21, no.5 (1998), pp.838–47.
58. Paul Gilroy's latest book was published in the final stages of this collection's preparation. It is a bold challenge to all forms of racialised thought and is likely to reshape many current debates. We cannot do it justice here. However, it is notable that the topic of 'mixed race' is not directly engaged in the text. See P. Gilroy, *Against Race: Imagining Political Culture Beyond the Color Line* (Cambridge: Belknap Press, 2000), published in Britain as *Between Camps* (London: Allen Lane, 2000).
59. P. Gilroy, *Against Race*, p.17.
60. L. Gordon, *Her Majesty's Other Children* (Lanham: Rowman and Littlefield, 1997).
61. http://www.webcom.com.intvoice/editor22.html.
62. http: //www. webcom.com/intvoice/editor13.html. Other 'multiracial' Internet sites express various forms of post-racial libertarianism. These are marked by an opposition to the census question on ethnicity itself and

thereby to affirmative action programmes; and unqualified support for transracial adoption. See in particular 'The Multiracial Activist' site at http://www.multiracial.com/about.htm which states its outright opposition to all forms of racial classification. The enterprise of racial categorisation and identification is critiqued at greater length in the work of Yehudi Webster: *The Racialization of America* (New York: St Martin's, 1992).

63. See E.Balibar, 'Is there a neo-racism?', in E. Balibar and I. Wallerstein, *Race, Nation, Class* (London: Verso, 1991) and L. Gordon, *Her Majesty's Other Children* (Lanham: Rowman and Littlefield, 1997), p.67.
64. F. Furedi, *The Silent Race War* (London: Pluto Press, 1998).
65. See N. Gist and A. Dworkin, *The Blending of Races* (New York: Wiley-Interscience, 1972).
66. L. Gordon, *Her Majesty's Other Children* (Lanham: Rowman and Littlefield, 1997); L. Jones, *Bulletproof Diva* (New York: Doubleday, 1994).
67. Scholarly attention should turn to more multifaceted racialised settings: South Asia, East Asia, South America and the Caribbean, where the matrix of racialisation cannot be encompassed by a binaristic black/white framework. See J. Forbes, *Black Africans and Native Americans* (Oxford: Basil Blackwell, 1988); A. Stoler, *Race and the Education of Desire* (Durham and London: Duke University Press, 1995); A. Marx, *Making Race and Nation* (Cambridge: Cambridge University Press, 1998).
68. See Chang-Rae Lee, *Native Speaker* (London: Granta Books, 1995), Peter Ho Davies, *Equal Love* (London: Granta Books, 2000), and Mira Stout, *One Thousand Chestnut Trees* (New York: Putnam, 1998).
69. L. Alcoff, 'Towards a Phenomenology of Racial Embodiment', *Radical Philosophy*, no.95 (1999), pp.15–26.
70. David Goldberg's charting of the extraordinary shifts in the categories used to record 'race' in the USA is a notable exception. See D. Goldberg 'Taking Stock: Counting By Race', in D. Goldberg, *Racial Subjects* (New York and London: Routledge, 1997).
71. A. Brah, *Cartographies of Diaspora* (London: Routledge, 1996).
72. P. Harper, A. McClintock, J. Munoz and T. Rosen, 'Queer Transexions of Race, Nation and Gender', *Social Text*, vol.15, nos.3&4 (1997), pp.1–4.
73. P. Taguieff, *Les Fins de l'anti-racisme* (Paris: Éditions Michalons, 1995), p.77.
74. S. Ahmed, 'She'll Wake Up One of These Days and Find She's turned into a Nigger: Passing Through Hybridity', *Theory, Culture and Society*, vol.16, no.2 (1999), pp.87–106.
75. S. Gregory, *Black Corona* (Princeton: Princeton University Press, 1998); D. Kondo, *About Face* (New York and London: Routledge, 1997).
76. T. Campt, 'Afro-German Cultural Identity and the Politics of Positionality: Contests and Contexts in the Formation of a German Ethnic Identity', *New German Critique*, no.58 (1993), pp.109–26.

1
How Sociology Imagined 'Mixed Race'

Frank Furedi

The discipline of race relations emerged as a response to widespread Western anxieties concerning impending conflict on an international scale. 'Race', which was a positive ideal in the self-image of the West, had become a source of concern by the end of the First World War. By the 1920s, the Anglo-American foreign policy élites regarded racial thinking as having the potential to disrupt the world system; and by the end of the Second World War racial ideology was so discredited that Western diplomats were forced to devote considerable resources to eliminating it from international affairs altogether.[1] This chapter focuses on academic and policy concerns about 'mixed race', which was one of the key debates shaping the race relations industry in the first half of the twentieth century. Although American, British and South African analysts shared some common beliefs and concerns about the implications of race mixing, specific influences in these countries differentially shaped the intellectual discourses concerning 'race' and 'mixed race'.

These political concerns about race mixing stimulated collaboration and research between institutions in Britain, South Africa and the USA. Western missionaries associated with the International Missionary Council (IMC) were in the forefront of co-ordinating and promoting research on the subject. It was their influence that led to the establishment of the Institute of Pacific Relations in the USA, the International Africa Institute in Britain and the Institute of Race Relations in South Africa. Research on race relations during the interwar period was informally co-ordinated by a small group of individuals affiliated to the Carnegie Corporation, the Phelps-Stokes Fund, the Rockefeller Foundation, the IMC and specialists from the British Colonial Office.

The research agenda of the emerging race relations industry was dominated by the imperative of damage limitation. One of the key questions identified by the new group of experts was whether stability could be maintained if the Colour Bar was eliminated and if disparate races lived and interacted at a closer proximity with one another. Private deliberations indicated a particular preoccupation with racial and cultural mixing. Leading scholars, such as the British anthropologist Bronislaw Malinowski, sought funding for projects on the subject. In a memo written to the Rockefeller Foundation in 1926, he drew attention to the importance of studying 'the mixing of races' in the colonial world.[2] Such concerns found resonance among American Foundations. Frederick Keppel, the President of Carnegie, was intensely committed to the maintenance of the prevailing racial boundaries. The first major race relations project commissioned by Carnegie, *The Poor White Problem in South Africa*, was inspired by the fear of what would happen if poor whites in South Africa began to 'go native'. In Britain, the earliest investigations into the condition of people of colour in seaport towns were actually about the position of 'half-caste children'.[3] This preoccupation with the problems posed by people of mixed heritage was widely reflected in American sociological journals such as the *American Journal of Sociology* and *Social Forces*.

So why did the issue of race and cultural mixing assume such significance for the policy makers and academic experts associated with the newly established race relations industry? This question is particularly interesting because the problematisation of mixing coincided with the gradual acknowledgement of the principle of race equality. Historical records suggest that the gradual reorganisation of the prevailing racial etiquette around the principle of formal equality raised important questions about how to retain a boundary between white people and people of colour. For Western policy makers, the stigmatisation of race mixing served to retain social distance between people, and to assuage white racial fears.

During the 1930s, the liberal head of the South African Institute of Race Relations, Alfred Hoernle, justified segregation on the grounds that it would reassure those who might otherwise, because of a concern with race mixing, oppose economic reforms for Africans. He argued that:

> In the conditions at present prevailing in South Africa, the barrier against race mixture is worth maintaining, so that we need not be deterred from a liberal native policy by the fear that race mixture throughout the community will be the inevitable result.[4]

This was a South African version of the case put by American southern liberals for the maintenance of vertical segregation. Anson Phelps-

Stokes, head of the Phelps-Stokes Fund, echoed this argument in the American context, when he stated that the call for eliminating segregation in the USA should be postponed to avoid creating 'Southern antagonism'.[5]

In fact, as Saul Dubow pointed out, many of the intellectual authors of apartheid such as Maurice Evans and Charles Templeman Loram were strongly influenced by the experience of the American South. Evans's call for the 'separation of the races to an extent hitherto never attempted' so as to preserve their 'home life and race integrity' was viewed by British missionaries as a humane way of coping with the consequences of change.[6] Elsewhere in Africa, imperial publicists, missionaries and officials tended to view some form of segregation as essential for 'protecting' the African. As the historian Andrew Roberts noted:

> Mixing cultures made trouble; it was better to keep them apart. The crudities of a legalised colour bar might indeed be abhorrent, but more subtle forms of discrimination were not necessarily to be opposed.[7]

Such paternalism was presented as a reasonable compromise necessary for the healthy evolution of the African.

In Britain and the USA the case for segregation was justified on the grounds that it was a matter of individual preference. It was claimed that in any case, people did not like to mix. An editorial in the *Spectator*, which concluded a series of articles on the Colour Bar, explicitly distinguished between the economic and personal aspects of the issue. According to the editor, it was everyone's duty to 'unceasingly' help 'the coloured races', both 'politically and economically'. But 'socially each man and woman must judge for him or herself,' observed the editor.[8] In 1940, Eleanor Roosevelt, during lunch with Ralph Bunche, an up-and-coming black American official, put matters concisely. According to her, race problems were most 'effectively attacked on the economic front'. She added that 'social equality ought to be crossed out of the equation because that is strictly a personal and individual matter.'[9] By designating 'social equality' as off-limits, Eleanor Roosevelt outlined the constraints to the accommodation of demands for equality. Social equality served as a euphemism for personal relationships between different races. For race relations reformers, this was deemed off-limits. The deliberate construction of a special sphere of 'social equality', where individual preferences could legitimately prevail, provided the foundation for the redrawing of racial boundaries. In this way the reform of race relations within wider society did not need to intrude into any sphere deemed personal. Race mixing was the clear target of this newly emerging etiquette.

White Racial Fears

The issue of race mixing was driven by white racial fears about the threat it posed to the integrity of the white race. It was widely believed that contact would encourage mixing and that this would both undermine what was referred to as 'white prestige' and lead to the deterioration of the white race. 'As it is impossible to prevent miscegenation between races when intermingled by work or residence the safer policy is to restrict the mass association of the different races,' argued a columnist for the British *Spectator* in 1931.[10] In particular, there was widespread concern that the lower classes would not abide by the existing racial boundaries and that they would contribute towards the 'lowering' of the white race to the level of the so-called inferior races. Characteristically, white people who mixed were described in pathological terms as immoral and weak. In Britain, concerns about race mixing constituted an important part of what Phil Cohen calls a 'code of breeding', in which selective notions of breeding were invoked to protect against racial and class degeneration.[11]

Interwar British studies of miscegenation described English mothers partnered with black men as 'immoral'. Their children invariably grew up in an 'atmosphere overcharged with sex'.[12] A 1944 report titled the 'Condition of the Coloured Population in A Stepney Area', but which was actually about the effects of race mixing in this district of east London, manifested a strong sense of repulsion against the poor white. Concern about the moral fitness of the white poor was explicit. It complained that Negroes 'have no opportunity of meeting English people with good moral standards'. White women who took up with black migrants were described as 'prostitutes' or 'daughters of prostitutes'. The author of the report, Phyllis Young, stated that most of these women were 'below normal intelligence and, according to officials who have dealt with them, over-sexed'. Young observed that 'these women have very little moral sense'. Her description of 'this tragic corner of Stepney' reflected deep anxieties about the erosion of the race line.[13]

The Carnegie Commission's *The Poor White Problem in South Africa* reflected this body's own preoccupation with America's own poor white population. South Africa provided a laboratory where racial anxieties could be studied more openly than in the USA. This report was thankful that 'the great majority of poor whites are still imbued with the conviction of their superiority over the non-European' and that this 'feeling has played an important part in preventing miscegenation'. However, the report warned that growing contact and association between the two groups would lead to greater miscegenation.[14] In South Africa itself, proposals to ban mixed marriages in 1938 were driven by the concern that poverty would help erode the racial boundary between white and black. 'In conditions under which children were growing up in city slums it was impossible to guarantee that they would retain their prejudice against mixing their blood with that of the coloured races,' argued J. G. Strydom, a leading figure in the United Party.[15]

British and American social scientists accepted that racial contact and mixing were disruptive. Having accepted the problematisation of mixing, specialists in race relations turned their attention to the study of the offsprings of such unions. Intuitively, academics were convinced that people of mixed origins were likely to be 'problem people'. The question was how to conceptualise the problem. Studies of the in-between person became a leading theme of the new discipline of race relations.

The Marginal Man

Race relations theory drew extensively on theories of maladjustment, which influenced the Anglo-American sociological tradition of the interwar period. This perspective regarded colonial and racial conflict in terms of the maladjustment of individuals and groups to the conditions of change and modernity. From this standpoint the problem was not so much the impact of imperialism or of racism but the failure of colonial people subject to Westernisation to adjust to new circumstances. It was proposed that those who could not adjust became racially conscious, anti-white or unstable. Neither rooted in their own society nor accepted by the West, the maladjusted individual lived in between two worlds. The uprooted colonial intellectual or the racially conscious mulatto became symbols of the problem of instability. Maladjustment also underlined a mental state that was problematic. The experience of being uprooted from one's traditional culture and a lack of acceptance into the dominant culture were seen to expose intense insecurities.

According to this simplistic paradigm, Westernisation and in particular Western education in the colonies produced individuals with unrealistic aspirations for a better life. Educated blacks in America would also suffer from the same pretensions. One of the most sensitive commentators on American race relations wrote in the twenties that the 'rising consciousness of the negro race is slowly surpassing the capacity of present racial adjustments'.[16] When one sociologist addressing the American Sociological Society in 1919 informed his audience that the condition of maladjustment led to a 'hyper self-consciousness', which when 'carried far enough' could 'result in a definite neurotic condition, as is often seen among the Jews', no one voiced dissent.[17]

Since such aspirations would inevitably be rebuffed by European society, anti-white bitterness and hatred would be the likely outcome. Rejection by the European was bad enough. However, the aspirant maladjusted individual could no longer go back to his people. Such maladjusted individuals were doomed to a life of perpetual instability. Unable to live on either side of the cultural divide, they became a recruiting ground for troublemakers. The model of maladjustment suggested that they, rather than ordinary colonial subjects, represented a danger to the maintenance of the existing racial lines.

The British policy of indirect rule through local intermediaries sought to minimise disruption and maladjustment through the conservation of tradition. Indirect rule was motivated by the imperative of confining people within their cultural and racial boundaries. Lord Lugard, the author of this policy in Africa, was concerned to curb the expectations generated by modernisation and in particular regarded the 'educated native' as an important threat to colonial order. The educated colonial subject in Africa who aspired to Western standards in an environment which depended on the maintenance of racial and social distinctions, personified the problem. Such thwarted individuals were represented as impudent charlatans who sought to be something they were not.[18]

The American sociologist Everett Stonequist, author of the influential text *The Marginal Man: A Study in Personality and Culture Conflict*, was a key theorist of the 'marginal man'. The label 'marginal man' was applied indiscriminately to anyone who was not firmly rooted in a specific culture. In the first instance, the term referred to cultural hybridity, but it was also used to describe the biological hybrid's existence. Insecurity was said to drive the marginal man to intensify 'his concern about status'. Stonequist argued that it was this preoccupation which explained such people's political involvement:

> His anxiety to solve his personal problems forces him to take an interest in the racial problem as a whole. Consequently he has an

> important part in defining and eventually changing the general pattern of race relations.[19]

This model interpreted anti-racist agitation as an instrument through which the maladjusted individual coped with life. Shorn of any principles or idealism, anti-racism was represented as a form of mendacious special pleading by self-centred individuals. The 'marginal man' thesis suggested that the reaction to racism or colonial domination was best understood as the reaction of the psychologically frustrated. The need to compensate for a sense of inferiority led to a 'new feeling of self-appreciation and even self-exaltation'. For Stonequist, it was this feeling that 'heralds the birth of a nativistic or nationalistic movement'.[20]

Much of the Anglo-American literature continually emphasised the theme of envy and the absurd and futile attempt of the educated colonial to imitate the European. Such motives were at once proof of inferiority but also suggestive of desperation. The thesis of maladjustment was based on the premise that the uprooted individual was by definition an agent of subversion. The very attempt to cross the lines between races, to seek to be what they were not, indicated that these individuals were capable of doing anything – thus the counterposition between the traditional 'honest' native and the scheming 'detribalised' individual. According to the American academic Raymond Buell, in his influential survey, 'The Native Problem in Africa', 'The African "intellectual" is probably the most sensitive in the world.'[21] Buell's quotation marks around the word intellectual signified scepticism regarding the moral and educational claims of such individuals. Academics concerned with colonial matters and social scientists interested in the problem of change were increasingly drawn towards the study of the 'Europeanised' or 'detribalised native'. Such people, by existing outside the conventions of tradition, but not yet being assimilated into modernity, personified the problem of cultural change. These marginal men became an important focus for sociological discussion during the interwar period. The concept of marginality reflected the interwar shift from a biological to socio-cultural focus on race. Early investigations into the hereditary effects of race mixture gave way to a preoccupation with its psychological and social consequences. Nevertheless, Kenneth Little, one of the foremost British race relations experts, was still engaged in studying the biological features of 'Anglo-Negro' children in the mid-1940s.[22] Although concern with the biological classification of mixed race people did not disappear, it became subordinated to the discourse of marginality.

A review of the literature on the theme of maladjustment indicates that it soon turned into a sociological condemnation of race mixing. The tendency to psychologise dissent by labelling it as maladjustment dominated the literature.

Anglo-American Cross-Fertilisation of Ideas

The interaction between colonial officialdom and British anthropology in the twentieth century is well known. However, the influence of imperial views on the subject of maladjustment went beyond that of a single discipline. Correspondence and collaboration between colonial officials and social scientists on both sides of the Atlantic was widespread.[23] In this interaction it is often difficult to detect the actual origins of the ideas. An inspection of reading lists distributed to colonial administrators and university students in the interwar period suggests that there was significant cross-fertilisation of ideas.[24]

For example, Stonequist was a student of R.E. Park, the leading representative of the Chicago School of Sociology. Park was strongly influenced by the German sociologist George Simmel's ideas about the stranger, the early prototype for the marginal man.[25] There were other influences on Stonequist. In the preface to *The Marginal Man*, Stonequist acknowledged the influence of the Oxford academic and leading imperial publicist Sir Alfred Zimmern, on his writing. But more pertinent for this discussion was Stonequist's debt to Lord Lugard. Stonequist wrote in his preface, that his interest in his subject matter 'began with a lecture given by Lord Lugard at the Geneva School of International Studies in 1925 describing the effect of European ideas and practices upon native life in Africa'. He noted in passing that he was particularly interested in Lugard's comments 'upon the detribalised'. Such an acknowledgement is not surprising since *The Marginal Man* can be read as a systematic sociological defence of boundary maintenance.[26] Like Lugard, Stonequist considered the detribalised as a race apart from everyone else. The marginal man suffered from 'personal maladjustment' and possessed a victim mentality.

The pathology of the marginal man also made an appearance in the writings of many British thinkers. The influential British sociologist Morris Ginsberg strongly praised Lugard's *Dual Mandate*. Ginsberg's *The Psychology of Society*, published in 1921, condemned the semi-educated intellectual. 'They are often capricious and despotic, and exhibit all the characteristics of the parvenu,' wrote Ginsberg.[27] This pathology of the marginal man – be it in the form of the detribalised native, the half-caste or the colonial intellectual – became an integral element of Anglo-American arguments on the subject.

It is worth noting that, despite its conservative implications, many liberal social scientists felt at home with Lord Lugard's espousal of indirect colonial rule, which involved rule through intermediaries in order to conserve existing traditional institutions. American cultural anthropology and the growth of relativism in the 1930s converged on some crucial points with the policy of indirect rule. The preservation of tradition was consistent with the positive promotion of cultural differences. So, for example, in a collection of essays about the encounter of cultures written by liberal social scientists in the 1930s and early 1940s, every contribution sided with indirect rule as against assimilation.[28] British social anthropology was even more wholehearted in its promotion of indirect rule. This consensus on fundamentals may help explain the absence of a literature critical of the maladjustment thesis at the time.

The varied concerns and influences that shaped American and British thinkers meant that the ideas regarding the in-between person were expressed through different intellectual forms. In the USA it was the experience of racial tension in the urban North which gave focus to discussions led by American sociologists. The impact of collaboration with colonial officialdom and the maladjustment thesis on British social anthropology was straightforward. Malinowski warned the readers of the *American Journal of Sociology* that the 'anthropologist recognises more and more fully how dangerous it is to tamper with any part or aspect of culture, lest unforeseeable consequences occur'.[29] Malinowski promoted the policy of reshaping economic development so as to minimise the consequences of maladjustment. He was no less concerned with the 'African in transition':

> [who] finds himself in a no-man's-land, where his old tribal stability, his security as to economic resources, which was safeguarded under the old regime by the solidarity of kinship, have disappeared.[30]

Malinowski feared that Europeanised Africans would rebel against the limits imposed on their ambitions by colonial society. Consequently he had profound misgivings about European education and the African intellectual. 'The European, instead of regarding all education or any education as an asset, might consider here that what the African takes from the European culture may be a handicap and a malediction, a blight or an injury, if it opens horizons, develops ambitions, raises him up to a standard of living which cannot be achieved,' warned

Malinowski.[31] Ironically, others would hold up Jomo Kenyatta, future leader of Kenyan nationalism and one of Malinowski's ex-students, as the personification of the marginal man. And later, the Kenyan nationalist movement, the Mau Mau, would be interpreted as proof of the dangers inherent in the state of maladjustment.

The systematic development of the theme of maladjustment took place in the USA where sociologists were directly confronted with the problems of immigration and race relations. The subject of assimilating immigrants from different cultures and of integrating the black population into the mainstream of American society stimulated a focus on the in-between individual. Many sociologists focused on the mulatto, the American biological hybrid equivalent of the African detribalised – a cultural hybrid. Edward Byron Reuter's 1918 study, *The Mulatto in the USA*, provided an interpretative framework, which influenced academic discussion on the subject. Reuter regarded the 'mulatto' as a personality given to outbursts of frustration. His book sought to raise concern with the tendency of this group towards agitation. His diagnosis of the educated mulatto 'agitator' was expressed in the following terms:

> The agitators voice the bitterness of the superior mulattos of the deracialised men of education, culture and refinement who resent and rebel against the intolerant social edict that excludes them from white society and classes them with the despised race.[32]

Reuter's use of the term 'deracialised men of education' indicated that it was the aspiration to be freed from the conventional racial categories that defined the problem of the mulatto.

In the 1920s, Reuter's emphasis on a discourse cast in biological racial terms gave way to a more sociological one. The Chicago sociologist Robert Park played a major role in reorienting this discussion from its early biological emphasis on racial mixing to a more sociological focus. Park's theory of the marginal man was the American equivalent of the detribalised native of the British anthropological tradition. Although Park was unusually sympathetic to his subject matter, he evoked the tragic dimension of the marginal way of life. There is a kind of ambivalence, which sees the 'mulatto' as a leader of the black population as well as an individual that could never be at ease with him- or herself.[33] Park noted that:

> One of the consequences of migration is to create a situation in which the same individual – who may or may not be a mixed blood – finds himself striving to live in two diverse cultural groups. The

> effect is to produce an unstable character – a personality type with characteristic forms of behaviour. This is the 'marginal man'. It is in the mind of the marginal man that the conflicting cultures meet and fuse.[34]

Park's disposition towards psychologising led him to formulate a personality type. Such a personality type was not the product of any particular experience but of all forms of culture contact.

Consequently, for Park, the concept of the marginal man transcended the American situation. It was a generic concept that could be deployed to examine the dynamic of mixing in other contexts. Indeed Park was concerned to emphasise that marginality was not reducible to racial mixing but encompassed a wider cultural and indeed moral dimension.

> Ordinarily the marginal man is a mixed blood, like the mulatto in the USA or the Eurasian in Asia, but that is apparently because the man of mixed blood is one who lives in two worlds, in both of which he is more or less a stranger. The Christian convert in Asia or in Africa exhibits many if not most of the characteristics of the marginal man – the same spiritual instability, intensified self-consciousness, restlessness and malaise. It is in the mind of the marginal man that the moral turmoil which new cultural contacts occasion manifests itself in the most obvious forms.[35]

Park's sociology of race relations provided a synthesis of the hitherto fragmented accounts of culture contact, race mixing, theories of maladjustment, and the moral disintegration of the uprooted. Park himself was careful not to condemn the marginal man. The 'moral turmoil' of this mind is posed in relatively neutral terms. However, the symptoms that he identified, such as 'spiritual instability', 'intensified self-consciousness' and 'restlessness' were seen by others as a form of moral condemnation.

In previous discussions on the uprooted colonial there was a stress on cultural type rather than on personality. However, Park helped to orient the subsequent research towards a more systematic consideration of a personality type. Increasingly, marginality became associated with a state of mind. This perspective readily lent itself to an apologetic interpretation, where the maladjusted mind, rather than the problem of colonial domination or racial oppression, became the problem. The condition of hybridity was understood to inspire irresolvable personality problems. These character traits were central to the discourse of the interwar sociology of the marginal man.

Articles which appeared on the subject of culture contact in the *American Journal of Sociology* were preoccupied with the problem of the hybrid. So one account of the 'Eurasian in Shanghai', in the *American Journal of Sociology*, observed how this 'racial hybrid' tends 'toward exaggerated self-pity' and defensiveness. A discussion of Asian nationalism in the same periodical explained the problem of maladjustment in terms of a character flaw. 'An intellectual training had been provided which enabled them to understand Western ideas, but not the character formation which enabled them to function adequately in a dynamic competitive society,' was the conclusion of the author.[36] Elsewhere, the Anglo-Indian was targeted and condemned for his 'shabby and pathetic Britishness'.[37] The American sociological periodical *Social Forces* was no less concerned with the issue. Articles on miscegenation and marginality paralleled the attitudes expressed in the *American Journal of Sociology*. The Anglo-Indians 'reappear' as demoralised individuals prone to 'excessive drinking and gambling'. 'This demoralisation is reflected in the fact that in the large cities numerous Anglo-Indian women are to be found engaged in professional or semi-professional prostitution,' the reader was informed.[38]

Either explicitly, as above, or implicitly in the case of more detached observers, the character of the in-between person was called into account. Considerations of maladjustment tended to shift back and forth between the moral and the psychological spheres. It was the psychological dilemma of having to negotiate living in between two different worlds that shaped the behaviour of the marginal man. In this way the behaviour of the educated colonial or the American mulatto or the Eurasian could be interpreted as an expression of a weak personality.

The Marginal Man became one of the most influential works on the subject during the 1930s and 1940s. The concept of marginality was not only part of the prevailing sociological tradition, but it also influenced the non-academic discussion on the subject. Stonequist himself was involved with the Institute of Pacific Relations and was Director of Research of the Office of War Information, 1944–5. The importance of Stonequist's contribution was that while he recognised some of the extreme manifestations of Western domination, his arguments called into question the legitimacy of anti-imperialist or anti-racist movements. Such movements were interpreted as the irrational actions of psychologically frustrated individuals. The marginal man never acts but *overreacts*. To give some examples:

> The hypersensitiveness of the marginal man has been repeatedly noted. [This] may result in a tendency to find malice and discrimi-

> nation where none was intended ... The marginal situation produces excessive self-consciousness and race consciousness.[39]

By elevating the psychological state of marginality, there was a crucial redefinition of the issue at stake. It was not so much racism but the over-reaction to it that constituted the problem. It was not idealism, conviction or political passion but a psychological obsession which drove the anti-imperialism of the marginal man. From the vantage point of Stonequist, anti-racist politics became the means through which the maladjusted marginal man acquired self-esteem. Of course, this stress on adjustment left the reality of discrimination as unproblematic.

In *Orientalism*, Edward Said's well-known description of Western representation of the Orient focused on the recurrent theme whereby the:

> oriental is imagined to feel his world threatened by a superior civilisation; yet his motives are impelled, not by some positive desire for freedom, political independence, or cultural achievement *on their own terms* but instead by rancour or jealous malice.[40]

The durability of this theme shows the vitality of the thesis of maladjustment leading to moral disintegration.[41] The focus on the psychology of anti-Western sentiment invariably distracts from the wider social and historical structures of Western domination.

By representing the reaction to colonialism and racism as the pathology of the marginal man, sociological theories of race consciousness helped to intellectually discredit anti-colonial and anti-racist sentiments. The widespread influence of this outlook in the 1930s and 1940s helps place in perspective the intellectual climate on race. Precisely at a time when scientific racism was under attack and when ideas of race equality were gaining currency, a rearguard action was mounted to morally condemn race mixing and thereby retain the colour line.

Holding the Line

The discourse on the in-between person was a discussion of the maintenance of existing social, cultural and racial boundaries. By his very existence the marginal man was seen to question the durability of these boundaries. And by challenging these boundaries, the marginal man or the detribalised native threatened to encroach on the status of the European. That is why there was such a clearly articulated tendency to create a moral distance between the marginal man and the European. The insistence on moral difference represented an attempt to uphold a line and repulse those who claimed an equal status. Whatever they were, the marginal man and the detribalised native were not European. They might be 'in between' but they were not conceptualised as a bridge between the races. Mencke was surely right when he observed that in the USA, the discussion of the marginal man was interpreted by some as an argument to 'force mulattos back into the black race, at least morally'.[42]

A condemnation of miscegenation was almost always implicit in the literature on the maladjusted marginal man. According to the academic specialists in race mixing, the 'hybrid' that was produced was not just a racial but also a cultural hybrid. However, most studies of this subject either implicitly or explicitly assumed it was the effect of racial mixing that was the most far reaching. As Wirth and Goldhamer noted, 'the mixed blood is sometimes assumed to exhibit the characteristic personality traits of the marginal man more clearly than the purely cultural hybrid.'[43] According to this model, the most developed form of the condition of marginality was that of racial hybridity. The assumption – that with race mixing there was no way back – was rarely spelled out.

Academic writers qualified their condemnation of race mixing with the caveat that the problem was not so much with the hybrid as with the circumstances that isolated such people from both the dominant and subordinate classes. So Malinowski contended that the 'most dramatic, not to say tragic, configuration of racial relationships occurs' when 'whatever mixture takes place is socially degraded, and where in consequence, a rigid caste system comes into being.'[44] But while Malinowski was sensitive to the way that society could stigmatise the hybrid, he himself had serious doubts about the wisdom of miscegenation. 'It is a questionable blessing when a lower race ousts or absorbs a higher, or when a distinctly inferior mixed race is formed,' he concluded. Why? Because a 'mixed race does not rise to the level of the higher parent-stock.' Malinowski was pessimistic about the ability of a mixed race society to progress. He wrote:

> At best, we can hope, then, that the partly mixed, partly Europeanised population, such as the Negroes of the West Indies, will be able to hold their own and to establish a new polity and a new culture in their new home. The recent American invasion of Haiti is however, an ominous indication of the dangers which beset this type of solution.[45]

From this perspective, the avoidance of mixing and the strict maintenance of a racial line made the most sense.

In non-academic accounts the moral distancing of writers from the marginal man was often strident and deliberately insulting. Hybridity was invariably portrayed in unflattering terms and conveyed the warning that racial hybrids should 'not presume to be like the white man'. Articles on the subject dealt at length on the alleged tendency of hybrids to imitate the European. Such pretensions were invariably repulsed and the reader was reminded that the products of race mixing bore the stamp of moral inferiority. The American writer Gertrude Marvin Williams observed that 'the most pathetic of India's minority groups are the mixed bloods.' As symptoms of their pathetic state, she remarked that they 'always wear European clothes'. She added:

> They fawn upon the English and make pitiful advances to them. They always speak of England as 'home' though they may never have been there, and they are forever vainly trying to include themselves with the British.[46]

It was the idea that those of mixed race and the English could share the same 'home', that Williams found particularly preposterous. Such an aspiration was wholly unacceptable to the interwar racial imagination.

During the interwar period there was little criticism of the moral repulsion of the marginal man. White fears regarding race mixing were treated as natural and not worthy of critical reflections. This sentiment continued well into the 1940s. Anson Phelps-Stokes reminded his collaborators in 1946 that reports on the subject of race relations should avoid giving the impression that 'we favor inter-marriage.'[47] None of his associates in the American race relations industry took exception to this reminder. This was a subject which was seen to be above debate. Even postwar liberal academics such as Kenneth Little accepted this consensus.

One of the rare attempts made to analytically examine the moral condemnation of the hybrid was by the American writer Lewis C. Copeland. Copeland characterised 'moral distinctions' in race relations as the 'final rationalization of racial contrasts'. Copeland's analysis stressed the importance of moral distancing and moral repulsion against mixing in American racial thinking. He took the view that racial beliefs helped create 'two social orders and moral universes'. This outlook, according to Copeland, was rooted in white racial fears. 'There is a widespread fear of the invasion of the white social order by the black man,' observed Copeland. This fear of social invasion was illustrated by the tendency of white people to react most to those black people who stood closest to them. Copeland believed that it was this reaction which motivated the 'defamation of the mulatto'. For the person of mixed parentage was a 'moral anomaly' in the racial imagination.[48] Copeland's discussion of the 'defamation of the mulatto' clearly reveals the manner in which apparently neutral descriptions of the marginal man's state of mind helped to mask real moral condemnation.

Copeland's insights into fears concerning the invasion of the white social order helps place in perspective the race relations discourse in the interwar period. Such fears also expressed self-doubt and anxieties about the possible exposure of white pretensions. It was almost as if there was an expectation that nothing would be the same, if other races came too close and saw the European at 'home'. The fundamental assumption was that the racial line had to be maintained; otherwise white prestige would suffer. The racial line existed in both a metaphorical and physical sense. Even the existing world order was seen to depend on keeping everything in its place.

In Britain, Copeland's sentiments were echoed by the fierce anti-racist scientist, Lancet Hogben. His introduction to Cedric Dover's *Half-Caste* (1937), stands out as a rare critique of the contemporary pathologisation of race mixing. Hogben attacked 'eugenists, anthropologists, psychologists, sociologists and politicians' for their stigmatisation of mixed race people. In a typically robust vein he noted that they 'have contributed a vast mass of pseudo-science to the more delicate technics of bastard baiting and bluffing, and to the creation of a consciousness of genetic guilt in the *sang melé*.'[49]

Both Copeland and Hogben were considerably ahead of the academic profession in their thinking. They not only refused to accept the stigmatisation of mixed race people but also asked interesting questions about why academic experts appeared to be negative about this subject. Their research suggested that the emerging field of race relations remained wedded to élite prejudices of the period. It was only in the late 1940s that contributors to the subject began to adopt a more neutral 'value-free' language.[50] But more substantial critiques of the moral condemnation of hybridity would have to wait until the intellectual upheavals of the 1960s. Even now, there is no clear consensus about how we should define and conceptualise 'mixed race' relationships and individuals. Furthermore, attributions of marginality and pathology toward 'mixed race' individuals still seem to be common in the popular imagination.

Notes

1. See F.Furedi, *The Silent War: Imperialism and the Changing Perception of Race* (London: Pluto Press, 1998).
2. B. Malinowski, 'Memo For the Rockefeller Foundation Written for Mr Embree in March 1926', in *J.H. Oldham Papers, Box 2 File 2,* Rhodes House Library (RHL), Oxford.
3. See the discussion of a report issued by the Liverpool Association for the Welfare of Half-Caste Children in *The Nation & Athenaeum*, 9 August 1930.
4. R.F.A. Hoernle, 'Race-Mixture and Native Policy in South Africa', in I. Schapera (ed.), *Western Civilization and the Natives of South Africa* (London: George Routledge and Sons Ltd, 1934), pp.235–54.
5. Phelps-Stokes Fund Archives (PSF) *Box 27:4,* 'A. Phelps-Stokes to G.B. Johnson'. 15 August 1944.
6. See S. Dubow *Racial Segregation and the Origins of Apartheid in South Africa, 1913–1936* (Basingstoke: Macmillan, 1989), p.26.
7. A.D.Roberts, 'The Imperial Mind', in A. Roberts (ed.), *The Cambridge History of Africa, Vol.7, 1905-1940* (Cambridge: Cambridge University Press, 1986), p.50.
8. *Spectator*, 12 September 1931.
9. Cited in W. A. Jackson, *Gunnar Myrdal and America's Conscience* (Durham: University of North Carolina Press, 1990), p.126.
10. *Spectator*, 18 July 1931.
11. P. Cohen, 'The perversions of inheritance', in P. Cohen and H. Bains (eds), *Multi-racist Britain* (Basingstoke: Macmillan, 1988).
12. *The Nation & Athenaeum*, 9 August 1930.
13. IMC archives, School of Oriental and African Studies, (IMC/CBMS); *Africa Committee, Race Relations, Box 261*, 'Report On Investigation Into Condition of the Coloured Population In a Stepney Area by Phyllis Young, March 1944'.
14. Carnegie Corporation, *The Poor White Problem in South Africa*. Report of the Carnegie Commission (Stellenbosch: Pro Ecclesia – Drukkery, 1932), vol.1, p.xix, vol.5, pp.38–40.
15. *Cape Times*, 9 November 1938.
16. G.B. Johnson 'A Sociological Interpretation. of the New Ku Klux Movement', *The Journal of Social Forces*, vol.1, no.4 (May 1923), p.444.
17. See H.A. Miller 'Discussion', in J. Dowd 'Race Segregation in a World of democracy', *American Sociological Society*, vol.14 (1919), p.204.
18. An American sociologist who was an expert on South Africa, W.O. Brown, directly borrowed from the Lugardian perspective. See 'Race Consciousness Among South African Natives', *American Journal of Sociology*, vol.40, no.5 (March 1935).p.574.
19. E.V. Stonequist, *The Marginal Man: A study in Personality and Culture* (New York: Russell and Russell, 1961), 2nd edn, p.50.
20. *Ibid.* p.59.

21. R.Buell, *The Native Problem in Africa* (London: Frank Cass, 1965), 2nd edn, vol.2, p.80.
22. See K. Little, 'Some Anthropological Characteristics of Anglo-Negro Children; An Aspect of Racial Mixture in Britain', *The Journal of the Royal Anthropological Society of Great Britain and Ireland*, vol. 73 (1943–4), pp.57–73.
23. See for example the interwar correspondence deposited in the Archives of the International Africa Institute, London School of Economics.
24. These comments are based on an inspection of social science reading lists of Cambridge University and the London School of Economics.
25. See Donald Levine, Introduction to G. Simmel, *Georg Simmel on Individuality and Social Forms* (Chicago: University of Chicago Press, 1971).
26. E.V. Stonequist, *The Marginal Man: A study in Personality and Culture* (New York: Russell and Russell, 1961), 2nd edn, p.vii.
27. See M. Ginsberg, 'The Problem of Colour in Relation to the Idea of Equality', in *Journal of Philosophical Studies*, 1, 2 (April 1926), p.222; M. Ginsberg, *The Psychology of Society* (London: Macmillan, 1964), 2nd edn, p.139.
28. A. Locke and B. Stern (eds), *When People Meet: A Study in Race and Culture Contacts* (New York: Progressive Education Association, 1942).
29. B. Malinowski, 'The Pan-African Problem of Culture Contact', *American Journal of Sociology*, vol.48 (1942–3), p.651.
30. *Ibid.*
31. Cited in F. Furedi, *The Silent War* (London: Pluto Press, 1998), p.141.
32. E.B. Reuter, *The Mulatto in the United States* (Boston: Scribner, 1918), p.364.
33. An interesting account of Park's ambivalence toward the marginal man is well explored in R.F. Wacker, *Ethnicity, Pluralism, and Race: Race Relations Theory in America Before Myrdal* (Westport: Greenwood Press, 1983).
34. R.E. Park, 'Human Migration and the Marginal Man', *American Journal of Sociology*, vol.33 (1928), p.881.
35. *Ibid.* p.893.
36. H.D. Lamson, 'The Eurasian in Shanghai', *American Journal of Sociology*, vol.41 (1935–6), p.647; and N.J. Spykman, 'The Social Background of Asiatic Nationalism', *American Journal of Sociology*, vol.32 (1926–7), p.406.
37. L. Hedin, 'The Anglo-Indian Community', *American Journal of Sociology*, vol.40, no.2 (September 1934).
38. P.F. Cressey, 'The Anglo-Indians: A Disorganized Marginal Group', *Social Forces*, vol.14, no.2 (December 1935). p.266.
39. E.V. Stonequist, *The Marginal Man*, pp.148, 150, 151.
40. E. Said, *Orientalism* (London: Penguin Books, 1985), p.249.
41. For an elaboration of the argument, see F. Furedi, *The New Ideology of Imperialism: Renewing the Moral Imperative* (London: Pluto Press, 1994).
42. J.G. Mencke, *Mulattoes and Race Mixture: American Attitudes and Images, 1865–1918* (Boston: UMI Research Press, 1976). p.ix.

43. L. Wirth and H. Goldhamer, 'The Hybrid and the Problem of Miscegenation', in O. Klineberg (ed.), *Characteristics of the American Negro* (New York: Harper, 1944), p.336.
44. B. Malinowski, 'Race and Labour', *Listener*, 16 July 1930, Supplement No. 8, p.vii.
45. *Ibid.*
46. Cited in L. Wirth and H. Goldhamer, *The Hybrid*, p.337.
47. PSF: *Box 27, folder 2*. 'A. Phelps-Stokes to Professor Liston Pope', 10 January 1946.
48. L.C. Copeland 'The Negro as a Contrast Conception', in E. Thompson, *Race Relations and the Race Problem* (Durham: Duke University Press, 1939), pp.158, 160, 169, 172.
49. Lancet Hogben, 'Preface On Prejudices', in Cedric Dover, *Half-Caste* (London: Martin Secker & Warburg, 1937), pp.16–17.
50. One of the first examples of this approach is provided in Robert Merton's 1941 essay 'Intermarriage and the Social Structure'. This is reprinted in Robert Merton, *Sociological Ambivalence and Other Essays* (New York: The Free Press, 1976), pp.217–50.

2

Re-Membering 'Race': On Gender, 'Mixed Race' and Family in the English-African Diaspora[1]

Jayne O. Ifekwunigwe

> Herein lie buried many things which if read with patience may show the strange meaning of being black here at the dawning of the Twentieth Century ... for the problem of the Twentieth Century is the problem of the color line.[2]

Beginnings: The Problematics of 'Race'

We have now reached the twenty-first century, and yet, as 'racial' ideologies and social practices, colour consciousness still persists. In this chapter, I will highlight the ways in which the public and political paradoxes of what I refer to as the popular folk concept of 'race' – as it pertains to social constructions of Blackness and Whiteness – inform the private and personal realities of 'mixed race'. More specifically, I will present and interpret extracts from the oral testimonies of three female project participants, Nigerian and English Ruby, Nigerian and English Bisi, and Bajan (from Barbados) and Irish Akousa. Each woman's narrative illustrates the different ways in which 'mixed race' subjectivities are both self-constructed as situational, negotiable and fluid as well as externally constrained by static, essentialist and binary notions of Blackness and Whiteness.

I will also critique the contested dialectics of Blackness and Whiteness as they delimit constructions of Englishness and the English-African diaspora. I suggest that the discourses of both territorialised Englishness and the de-territorialised English-African diaspora are themselves prescribed by the popular folk concept of 'race'. This mode of signification forms a potent dynamic social and cultural imaginary, the naturalisation of which attaches symbolic meanings to real or manufactured physical differences. These create, explain, justify and maintain social inequalities and injustices; and perpetuate differential access to privilege, prestige and power. My term dovetails with philosopher and critical 'race' scholar Lewis Gordon's compound definition of 'race' and racism: 'Both race and racism, for instance, emerge when the physical or the biological is invoked. Groups are therefore racialised at the point at which the values attributed to them are treated as material attributes of who or "what" they are.'[3] These daily practices of racialisation comprise what Dutch sociologist Philomena Essed would define as 'everyday racism'.[4]

These routine conceptions of 'race' and racism are predicated on false notions of purity and alleged 'racial' superiority.[5] Contemporary popular folk thinking about 'race' and its bedfellow 'hybridity' emerged from earlier eighteenth and nineteenth century pseudoscientific debates about 'race' mixing as a mode of 'racial' degeneration and contamination.

'Hybridity' and the Paradoxes of 'Race'

As Robert Young eloquently argues in *Colonial Desire*, it is the nineteenth-century marriage of discourses on biology and culture that lends so much weight to the contemporary persistence of the idea of 'hybridity' as the sexual transgression of so-called pure 'racial' boundaries: '... "hybrid" forms (creole, pidgin and miscegenated children) were seen to embody threatening forms of perversion and degeneration and became the basis for endless metaphoric extension in the racial discourse of social commentary.'[6] These false conceptions of 'racial' purity and pollution defy the established scientific fact that there are no discrete genetically homogeneous 'races', which means there are no pure 'races'.[7] Nevertheless, one of the many personal, political and categorical terms that emerges from this false belief in 'racial' homogeneity is 'mixed race'.[8]

At this juncture, my discursive reversion to the contested but decidedly popular folk term 'mixed race' demands explanation. In previous publications, I have invoked the doubly appropriated conceptual term *métis(se)* as a shorthand analytical stand-in response to what I believed were the inadequacies of the myriad and at times ambiguous terms deployed to name individuals with differently racialised parents – 'mixed race', 'mixed heritage', 'mixed parentage', 'biracial', 'multiracial', etc ...[9] The term *métis(se)* is a 'French-African' in particular Senegalese, reappropriation of the continental French *métis(se)*. In translated continental French, *métis(se)* is synonymous with the derogatory English 'half-caste' and 'half-breed'. However, in French-African contexts, linguistic informants, Senegalese comparative literature professor Samba Diop and Senegalese/Congolese ethnomusicologist Henri-Pierre Koubaka suggest that alternative translations of *métis(se)* both include and transcend Black/White discourses and in so doing encompass diasporic convergences across ethnicities, cultures, religions and nationalities.[10] For example, one is considered *métis(se)* if one has a Wolof parent and a Mandinka parent – two distinct Senegambian cultural groups, two different languages.

By redeploying this term in English milieux, my intention was to de-centre 'race' as a primary identity marker and to clear space for the interplay of other hierarchically positioned signifiers such as ethnicity, locality, generation, gender and social class. Hence, though both middle class, the fact that Bisi's mother hails from Northumberland in the North of England and her father is Yoruba from Western Nigeria should be as significant as the fact that her father is considered Black and her mother White. In terms of generational concerns, Ruby was socialised as culturally English in predominantly White English settings. Thus it is not surprising that she would choose a White English partner. Yet, it is the primacy of the popular folk concept of 'race' and its social application that cancels out any lived similarities between Ruby and her husband John. The public racialised recognition of her husband and children as White and of her as Black also denies them the collective right to claim 'ordinary' family status. In a different fashion, Akousa's mother is working class Irish and not English and her father is working class Bajan. Given the shifting historical, political and ultimately racialised status of the Irish in England, it is quite possible that initially Akousa's working-class parents saw their plights as more similar than different.[11]

However, though the de-privileging of 'race' remains both an important critical theoretical and research objective, I now believe that the term *métis(se)* does not sufficiently do this important job. My research has taught me that parents, carers, practitioners, educators, policy makers, academics and 'mixed race' individuals themselves are all hungry for a uniform but not essentialist term which carves out a space for the naming of their specific experiences without necessarily reinscribing and reifying 'race'. Utilising a French-African term in an English context, even if simply for discursive analyses, could be perceived as potentially exoticising and further marginalising 'mixed race' subjectivities.

Another self-critique is that the double linguistic othering of *métis(se)* downplays the fact that scattered and ambiguous belongings also characterise the lived realities of other members of designated minority ethnic and diasporic groups such as English-born children of continental African or African Caribbean immigrant parents in general, and those who have been transracially adopted and/or fostered in particular.[12] Furthermore, one could argue that partially deflecting attention away from the popular folk concept of 'race' to other forms of identification and stratification diminishes the significant and potent function institutionalised racism plays in the maintenance of privilege and power for some and disadvantage and discrimination for others.[13] Finally, in attempting to construct a new lexicon, I am perpetuating a fictional history which ignores the ways in which the social processes of 'racial' mixing are themselves old.[14] Rather, it is the localised and temporal reinterpretations of the designated status of the children of such 'interminglings' that keep shifting. In other words, in the case of African American communities, or for our purposes, African Caribbean communities in England, the legacy of slavery as both a mode of economic exploitation as well as a strategy for the diversification of African and European descent groups means that to be 'mixed race' is constitutive of the genealogies of most just Black or just White families.[15]

Therefore, although the previously outlined conceptual motivation underpinning my temporary deployment of *métis(se)* – that of rupturing allegedly stable racialised faultlines – has not changed, I now problematise the utility and potential application of this or any other mediating term. Our unanswered conundrum is twofold. First, how do we create textual and conceptual space for the contestation and construction of complex and multi-layered identities without either reproducing a South African apartheid typology or promoting what Donovan Chamberlayne critically refers to as 'I amism': 'I am not Black or White, I am just me'?[16] Second, how do we create political alliances forged from shared marginal status while also acknowledging the varied and inherently hierarchical power dynamics within, between and among such disparate and differently racialised groups? For example, in a Whiteness-centred society such as Britain, those who can pass for White face a different set of psychosocial challenges than those individuals whose non-Whiteness is visibly marked.[17] In what follows I cannot resolve the existential challenge of reinscribing racialised terminology. I also cannot do justice to the other permutations and combinations of now multi-generational diasporic 'mixed race' such as South Asian/English, Chinese/English, South Asian/continental African, South Asian/African Caribbean. To construct such an inclusive grand narrative would downplay the significance of different lived racialised historical, social and cultural complexities within and without diasporic interwoven communities. In so restricting myself, I am mindful of the ways in which I am perpetuating a pervasive and exclusive critical 'mixed race' discourse which does not transcend the current dominant Black/White 'mixed race' paradigm.

So why 'mixed race'? Although as problematic as *métis(se)*, my revival of the term 'mixed race' is a necessary, deliberate and discursive political intervention. Unlike *métis(se)*, 'mixed race' is a term that is part and parcel of the English vernacular. Unlike 'mixed race', 'mixed parentage' and 'mixed heritage' retreat from a racialised discourse; thus someone with White Scottish and White Welsh parents could claim to be both 'mixed parentage'and 'mixed heritage'. To be 'mixed race' presumes differently racialised parentage. Therefore, for purposes of critical discussion, here I use the term 'mixed race' to describe individuals who according to popular folk concepts of 'race' and by known birth parentage embody two or more world views or in genealogical terms, descent groups. These individuals may have physical characteristics that reflect some sort of 'intermediate' status *vis-à-vis* their birth parents. More than likely, at some stage, they will have to reconcile multiple cultural influences. The degree of agency afforded a 'mixed race' individual is contingent in part upon local folk 'readings of their phenotype' in relation to systems of categorisation and classification that may reinforce eighteenth- and nineteeth-century 'race' science fiction.[18] By phenotype, I mean the visible physical markers of genetically inherited traits such as skin colour, hair texture and colour, eye shape and colour, general facial features, and body structure.

In addition to the social meanings of phenotype, social class, gender, generation and locality are also important variables. Moreover, as the chosen extracts will reveal, it is contradictory racialised perceptions of physical differences that frequently determine and undermine the lived experiences of those who, as active agents, identify as, and/or are socially designated as, 'mixed race'. These social applications of the term 'mixed race' highlight the paradoxes of kin and colour and pinpoint the problems of reinscribing a term predicated on the bases of scientifically dubious criteria.

Englishness and Normalised Whiteness

As I continue to set the stage, I would like to invoke the words of a recently departed English politician and scholar who was branded a visionary by some and a racist by others:

> ... sometimes people point to the increasing proportion of immigrant offspring born in this country as if the fact contained within

> itself the ultimate solution. The truth is the opposite. The West Indian or Asian does not, by being born in England, become an Englishman. In law he becomes a United Kingdom citizen by birth; in fact he is a West Indian or an Asian still. Unless he be one of the small minority – for number, I repeat again and again, is of the essence – he will by the very nature of things have lost one country without gaining another, lost one nationality without acquiring a new one. Time is running against us and them. With the lapse of a generation or so we shall at last have succeeded – to the benefit of nobody – in reproducing 'in England's green and pleasant land' the haunting tragedy of the USA.[19]

As the excerpt from Powell's now infamous 1968 'Rivers of Blood' speech suggests, the notion of Englishness was and still is based on the mythologies of indigeneity and 'racial' purity. Belonging in England is determined as much by social exclusion as by inclusion. For example, Catherine Hall defines Englishness as:

> not a fixed identity, but a series of contested identities, a terrain of struggle ... Englishness is defined through the creation of an imagined community: who is 'one of us' ... is quite as important in that definition as who is excluded. For the imagined community is built on a series of assumptions about 'others' which define the nature of Englishness itself.[20]

Although Hall describes Englishness as an ethnic designation, she also acknowledges that one of the primary criteria for determining English membership is in fact 'racial'. In other words, to be English is to be White.[21] Whiteness is the given, normative, naturalised, privileged and therefore the template category by which all other racialised 'deviations' are measured.[22] To be what Richard Dyer refers to as 'utterly White' is to be non-Black.[23] For as Gordon asserts: 'Blackness functions as the primary racial signifier. It is the element that enters the room and frightens Reason out.'[24]

However, though the maintenance of privilege and power may be the universal logic underpinning 'racial' ideologies, local meanings of Blackness and Whiteness do not travel easily. For example, in Britain, the social and political category Black has been used to incorporate South Asian, Chinese and in certain instances Irish communities.[25] Nevertheless, in Britain, there is by no means a consensus regarding the inclusivity of the designation Black. In fact, certain sectors of the religiously and ethnically diverse South Asian communities have rejected

Black affiliation in favour of an Asian identification.[26] On the other hand, in the USA, Black refers primarily to individuals of African descent.[27] In the specific context of Britain (and the USA), I define 'biracialisation' as a process which dictates the specific structural, symbolic and oppositional relationships forged between people deemed White and those socially designated as Black. As a substructure of the concept of racialisation,[28] biracialisation highlights the dominance of Black/White discourses on 'race' and 'mixed race' – one is either Black or White and never the twain shall meet. This binarism of 'mixed race' poses significant political and personal challenges for individuals who identify as 'mixed race' but do not have Black/White parentage.

The English-African Diaspora and Essentialised Blackness

> I searched but could not find myself, not on the screen, billboards, books, magazines, and first and last not in the mirror ... I longed for an image, a story, to speak me, describe me, birth me whole. Living in my skin, I was, but which one?[29]

Of Nigerian and English parentage, this quotation from Evaristo laments what another Nigerian and English writer Adewale Maja-Pearce refers to as 'the half-life of the outsider'.[30] Evaristo and Maja-Pearce, as well as the twenty-five individuals with whom I spoke, descend from lineages which cut across so-called differently configured and gendered Black/White 'races' and by extension ethnicities, cultures and classes. Yet, unlike the citizen children of immigrant parents to whom Powell denied English membership, by virtue of parentage, 'mixed race' citizens can claim both indigenous and diasporic roots or what Avtar Brah would refer to as 'diaspora space': 'the entanglement of genealogies of dispersion with those of "staying put"'.[31] In simple terms, they are White English *and* Black English-African diasporic.

However, two dominant and competing public discourses on nationalisms impede joint insider/outsider private identifications. Both link sociocultural constructions of 'race' to an ongoing political project demarcating the boundaries of belonging. I have already mentioned the first which is the notion that Englishness is synonymous with mythically pure Whiteness and an ancestral claim to territory. The second is based on the ways in which as both alleged deviation and resistance strategy the designation Black is associated with social and geographical misplacement as well as resilience.

I refer to this biracialised political space as the English-African diaspora. The English-African diaspora conventionally comprises

African (post)colonial constituents from the Caribbean, North and Latin America, and continental Africa and their descendants who find themselves in England for labour, schooling, political asylum, and frequently by birth. This contemporary formulation is derived from a re-assessment of the African diaspora, in its conventional, historical, static and monolithic formation, as the first and only major dispersal of continental Africans during the transatlantic slave trade.[32]

In the plural, contemporary African diaspora(s) constitute complex patterns of cultural practices, whose understanding demands new theoretical frameworks. Across continua of time and space, I redefine contemporary African diaspora(s) as dynamic, interlocking and interdependent networks of culturally specific geopolitical spheres. Each of these constituencies is sensitive to and historically impacted by the particular nation-states of which they are a part: the Brazilian-African diaspora; the Canadian-African diaspora; or in this case the English-African diaspora. Each of the African diaspora communities has common cultural roots emanating from the African continent. However, these geographical and cultural groupings represent diverse outcomes to a common heritage of slavery, colonialism and racism. These differences must be located in appropriate historical, social, cultural and political contexts that do not erupt simply in either/or, margin to centre, push/pull dichotomies.

Paul Gilroy 'heuristically' configures 'the black Atlantic' as a 'transcultural, international formation' which links the lived experiences, political projects and cultural products of 'Black Britons' and Black Americans.[33] My reconceptualisation of the African diaspora(s) in general, and the English-African diaspora in particular, also conveys a broader collective Pan-African diasporic consciousness. This is forged from different lived outcomes to similar post-slavery and post-colonial social, historical and economic legacies such as underdevelopment, globalisation, institutionalised racism, sexism and class discrimination.[34]

Scattered Belongings and the 'Half-Life' of the 'Mixed Race' Subject

The private and local family histories of most (post)colonial subjects are crafted from the public and global remains of slavery and imperialism as they are manifest in 'inter-racial', gender, sexual and economic relations.[35] Accordingly, in a genealogical sense, there are very few constituents of the African diaspora(s) who could not claim 'mixed race' ancestry.[36] However, here I am concerned with first generation 'mixed race' individuals,who according to the popular folk concept of 'race', have immediate birth parentage which is recognised as Black and White. Hence, neither the exclusionary discourse of White Englishness nor the inclusive discourse of the Black English-African diaspora completely represents their everyday lived realities. Black/White parentage and English/English-African-diasporic upbringings position them at complex and specific multiethnic, multicultural, multiracial and transnational intersections.

My ongoing biographical and autobiographical ethnographic research on 'mixed race' identity, family and memory focuses on this particular paradox of belonging.[37] The original Bristol, England-based project involved twenty-five participants: sixteen women and nine men.[38] Participation in this two-year-long project consisted of respondents providing me with a series of tape-recorded testimonies about their childhood, gender politics, racial and ethnic identity, class background, nationalism, family, sexuality, creativity, parenting and experiences of racism, among a variety of organic topics. I bonded with all twenty-five project participants to such an extent that as an outside-insider my daily challenge was maintaining those elusive objective boundaries.

After completing the interviews and while writing various versions of the ethnography, I oscillated between two positions and sat comfortably in neither. On the one hand, as the conduit for these stories, I was forced to make both general editorial decisions about which of the twenty-five testimonies would be included as well as specific selections of raw materials from these reconstructed lives. On the other hand, I could not justify presenting the narratives as mere anthropological 'data' wherein extracts of life experiences are cut and pasted for the primary purpose of authenticating the authority of the researcher. With the latter traditional approach, we learn more about the particular biases of the anthropologist and less about the lived realities of the respondents.[39] Over a two-year period, the testimonies I heard challenged my alleged sovereignty as social scientific mediator. I now wanted to produce a coherent final product that neither fragmented nor trivialised the lived experiences of the individuals with whom I had worked.

In the end, it was the centrality of kin in the retelling of all of their life stories which led me to focus in detail on the different pathways to womanhood forged by just six women – two sets of women growing up in the same family – as well as two women who create family within the contexts of children's homes.[40] Collectively, the six narratives illustrate the ways in which at different life stages and across age, class, gender, ethnicity and locality, 'mixed race' subjects construct integrated senses of self, family, and community which both encompass and transcend conventional, exclusive and hierarchical Black/White, English/English-African-diasporic subject positions. In the words of mestiza feminist Gloria Anzaldúa:

> I, a mestiza, continually walk out of one culture and into another, because I am in all cultures at the same time.[41]

I will now present and interpret extracts from just three of the six longer narratives featured in *Scattered Belongings*.[42] Each of these 'testimonies of redemption', as Behar describes them, sheds light on the paradoxes of identity, kin and ultimately 'race':

> Telling her story, turning her rage into a story, is part of her quest for redemption, the redemption of her past and the redemption of the present she is actively seeking to understand and forge.[43]

Ruby[44]

Marie Garson, an African Caribbean social worker, had introduced me to Ruby who is also a social worker. Her mother is English and her father is Nigerian. She grew up in a children's home outside London. She is married to a White Englishman and is the mother of two daughters and a son. Ruby is the only one of the original twenty-five participants whom I spoke with exclusively in my home. This deprived me of a fully contextualised sense of who she was. Nonetheless, profound sadness laced with occasional happiness are the words that best capture my sense of her. Like many 'mixed race' people, she is a survivor – a warrior on the frontlines by virtue of her bloodlines.

Her recollections of an incident in Morocco, en route to visit her father in Nigeria, highlight the profound and unsettling ways in which perceptions of 'race' and false assumptions about lineage converge. She is presumed to be the family's maid. Because Ruby's children 'look White', the family friend who is travelling with them is thought to be the wife of her husband John and the mother of their children:

> Then we went back to Africa. Took the kids, year after I left university. That was very good in terms of reinforcing the African connection as it were. It was nice to take the kids. That was also interesting, and had its aspects of upset. We took a White friend with us. She knew that we were going and wondered could she come for part of it. So, we said, 'Okay, join in.' So, we went. But what

> happened, particularly when we got to North Africa – Morocco, Algeria – that we would be travelling as a family and people would automatically think I was the maid – that my husband and my White friend were the man and wife, and that the kids were theirs. That was distressing.
>
> There was one particular occasion in Morocco where through a set of circumstances, the family was invited to supper by this chap. We all went along, and he had seats for everybody except for me. He didn't look at me, he didn't talk to me, he just looked straight through me. None of my family appeared to do anything about it. They hadn't picked up. They did eventually, but there were a couple of minutes when they did not actually pick up what was happening. So, I remember that very clearly, and how distressed I was about that.
>
> Because that also implicated my family, who hadn't picked up what this bloke was doing. Why he was doing what he did. The so-called White friend, far from seeing it as a distressing situation for me to be in, seemed to get some pleasure out of it – it wasn't overt – but there was something about, 'Oh, isn't it funny that people see me as John's wife?' Oh, yes, how odd, how strange, what a giggle! The kids did get quite upset about it. 'We know that you're our mum, and we don't like people saying that you're not.'

Ruby's experiences while travelling with her family demonstrate the ways in which public racial politics impact upon private family realities. In contrast to her own circumstance as someone with a White mother, but who is regarded as Black, Ruby, who is married to a White Englishman, has given birth to three children who look White. Based on the same biracialised folly that forces her White mother to figuratively and literally forfeit the right to claim Ruby, Ruby must now disown her own children. According to the popular folk concept of 'race' and not genealogical fact, they are White and she is Black.

As normatively White, English, middle class and male, Ruby's husband's paternal rights are never challenged nor contested. On the other hand, the imposition of different essentialist Black and White designations for mother and children respectively disrupts conventional notions of kinship and problematises the normal institution of the family. While their physical appearances enable Ruby's children to occupy the privileged space of Whiteness, for Ruby, being or becoming White is never presented as a public option. Accordingly, in a public domain Ruby must disinherit the very children to whom she has given birth and whom in the domestic sphere she nurtures, supports and parents. This forced paradox defies the reality that multigenerational 'mixed race' families such as Ruby's represent indigenous English and African-diasporic ethnic and cultural inheritances, which are themselves neither homogeneous nor static. One could say that such families are exemplary metaphors for the (post)modern condition. As heightened representations of a generic diasporic angst, Black English-African diasporic/White English households continuously undertake the complex and dynamic work of (post)modern identity politics within cauldrons characterising embodied multiple and fractured 'racial', ethnic, and gendered subjectivities. These double narratives of motherhood – public: Black non-mother of White children versus private: 'mixed race' mother of 'mixed race' children – reflect the hierarchical gender, generational, ethnic and biracialised tensions within English/English-African-diasporic society. They are also located outside it in imagined but not imaginary subverted 'mixed race' familial spaces.

Bisi

I first met Bisi in 1990 through an American woman in self-imposed exile in Bristol who by virtue of our similar backgrounds and involvement in the Arts thought we would enjoy meeting each other. However, Bristol being a very small city, Bisi had already heard about me through mutual friends. With one exception, of the twenty-five project participants, I have known Bisi the longest. Bisi refers to herself as a Northumberland Yoruba. Her father is Nigerian and her mother is English and she grew up with them and her two sisters in middle-class Ibadan, Nigeria. At the age of eighteen, she moved to England to study Art. In addition to being an accomplished visual artist, she is married to an Englishman and is the mother of three daughters and a son. Her reflections on 'race', family and what DuBois refers to as 'double consciousness'[45] reinforce the ways in which for 'mixed race' individuals, couples and families daily life comprises a series of complicated negotiations of public and private spaces wherein particular liberties are denied and reclaimed:

> After you have lived here for a bit, you get aware that, in fact there's a whole load of stuff that gets involved in mixed relationships, which maybe one would choose not to take on board ... these assumptions of what's strange and what's not. All that is a lot more theoretical once you've got children. Then perhaps the real stuff is gonna make the other stuff not matter so much ... the question of what race are my children? What do they think? How do they feel? It's difficult as well.

> I think Elizabeth said, 'I'm one-quarter Nigerian (very specific, very precise), but I'm three-quarters English, Mummy.' Which is true. I ask my son sometimes, 'Do you think you are White?' I don't know whether he says it to please me or not but he says,'Well, no, not really.' And they use this dreadful term – 'half-caste', ''alf-caste' [Bristolian pronunciation]. They say, 'You are, aren't you Mum?' I say, 'What kind of a word is that? Half of what? How can one call oneself half of something?' I don't think that's made any impression on them basically. Because it's the basic term they use at school, and everyone knows what it means. 'I'm qua'a caste [Bristolian pronunciation again], aren't I Mum?' 'What do you mean caste? Do you know what it means?'
>
> Of course, Julia looks completely English. What are they to feel? Julia's probably the child who'd have the least problems adjusting to a new country. She hasn't got this terrible sense of 'normal' Elizabeth has. She's outgoing. Actually, they are all quite shy funnily enough, apart from Emma. Julia is more sociable than Elizabeth. That's why she would have less problems. You can't actually feed thoughts into your children. They are aware that they are not completely British. Let's put it like that. I don't know how far that goes. The words I put it in then are negative. They are aware that they are not completely English. Is that being aware of something positive or not? It's only through talking and discussing that I know what they think.
>
> Being aware that one's system of ideas isn't absolute. It isn't the absolute, the one above all others. There are many and they are all sort of parallel and contradictory. If you are mixed race, you belong in two (or more) cultural traditions, which may be mutually contradictory, you just have to find that middle space.

Like Ruby's, Bisi's reflections illustrate the complexities of identity formation for 'mixed race' mothers and their near-White children. For example, in an English context, wherein Whiteness is normalised, naturalised and associated with Englishness, it is not surprising that Bisi's daughter Elizabeth would emphasise that in fractional terms she is only 'one quarter Nigerian'. Bisi does not deny her daughter this privileging of White Englishness. At the same time, Bisi does lament the fact that her four children are learning to reproduce the very colonial nomenclature – 'half-caste' and 'quarter-caste' – that has marginalised 'mixed race' subjects for centuries.[46] In addition, Bisi's observation that her daughter Julia, who looks 'completely English', and who is the one child who would have the least difficulty adjusting to another cultural context, is consistent with Ruby's ruminations about her own children. What both Ruby's and Bisi's extracts pinpoint are the specific and contradictory lived challenges confronting second generation 'mixed race' children. They do not look Black enough to be considered Black. Rather, isolated from their 'mixed race' mothers, Ruby's and Bisi's children are seen as White. It is only the recognition of their maternal parentage that calls into question the authenticity (and purity) of a White designation. For example, Bisi's children deduce that they must be 'quarter-caste' because their classmates have discerned that their mother is 'half-caste'.

The active contestation and shifting construction of multi-dimensional identities by second generation 'mixed race'/White children is an underexplored and fertile research area. Their evolving narratives could help us understand further the ways in which dominant 'racial' ideologies are internalised and reproduced in micro-familial contexts. Exploring the strategic ways in which these children's racialised identities shift across time and space – White at school, 'mixed race' at home – could also fortify the critical theoretical assertion that racialised identities in general and conceptions of Whiteness and Blackness or non-Whiteness in particular are neither fixed nor stable.

Akousa

When I first met Akousa, I remember thinking how much she sparkled – her eyes, her smile and her presence. My responding to her sparkling smile is humorous in light of the fact that until recently, Akousa has always hated her smile. She grew up working class in Liverpool with her Irish mother and without her Bajan (from Barbados) father. She is a Rastafarian[47] and yet is not seen as a typical Rasta woman. She sees herself as a Black woman and yet not everyone sees her as a Black woman. The lack of fit between the multilayered and textured complexities of Akousa's oral testimony and their flattened reduction to text reinforce for me the extent to which all of our lived experiences cannot be completely contained by the four sides of the page.

However, with the following extract, I have tried as much as possible to capture and preserve the lyricism of her Scouse (Liverpudlian) accent. In so doing, I am also emphasising the ethnomethodological tension between the written and the spoken word.[48] Akousa's recollections of biracialised bullying in school demonstrate the ways in which 'mixed race' children are forced to negotiate public and private spheres which negate and acknowledge their White English or in Akousa's case White Irish parentage respectively. By choosing to align herself with her Black friend who is the victim of a racist taunt, rather than to 'opt out' as a 'mixed race' person, Akousa also both submits to the indelible imposition of compulsory Blackness and legitimates Black as a powerful political affiliation:[49]

> School: school was an experience. Primary school wasn't too bad. There were a lot of Chinese kids and Black kids, and everyone skitted each other off, called each other 'Four Eyes' or 'Fatty'. It wasn't so heavy, there were certain racist undertones, but because you had other Black kids there, you had a bit of alliances with other people and things like that. But 'round the school, some of the streets we couldn't walk up. 'Cos the kids would come up, just particular streets, and call us 'nigger' or 'black bastard'. So we never walked up that street, we'd have to go two more streets down.
>
> It was mainly when I went to secondary school, which was like a horror story for me. I wouldn't go to that school again, I wouldn't do my school career over again. People reminisce a lot over their school days [kisses teeth]. My mum thought she was doin' a good thing, she was sendin' me to an all-girls' school – secondary modern school. Half of it was boys, half girls. We didn't mix, but we shared the hall, which was in the middle. I was the only Black girl there. The whole area is a White area. They called you 'nigger' and 'coon' and 'You need to get back where you came from.' All those things were goin' on in school. I remember the first couple of weeks of school and I missed the bus stop. It was only a simple thing – just one bus stop. I started cryin' me eyes out. I was totally terrified to walk up any of the streets to get to school rather than the way that I normally walked. I was frightened some White people might come out and pick on me.
>
> ... I was standing next to this White guy and he started to call this Black girl a 'nigger' and I said, 'Who are you callin "nigger"?' 'Oh, you're alright Akousa, there's nothin' wrong with you. You're fine.' I said, 'Listen love, if you're callin' her a "nigger", you're callin' me a "nigger".' And I walked away. School was heavy. Another heavy experience was during the first couple of weeks of school. There were skinheads in the area as well. There was a skinhead, and he was sittin' on the street. I'd just come from the shop up the road. He had his big boots on, and he said, 'Hey nigger come polish my boots for me.' Here I am eleven and a half, and being confronted with this guy. All I could do was run.

For 'mixed race' individuals then, such as Akousa, being Black, as both public mandate and personal survival strategy, is not always a straightforward process. In one situation, her classmate marks her as 'mixed race' and thus spares her the 'racial' abuse which he directs at her Black friend. In another context, the skinhead does not recognise her 'mixed race' parentage. He brands her a 'nigger' and confronts her with racialised aggression. Here Akousa is compulsorily Black. I reappropriate Adrienne Rich's theorising on the political institution of 'compulsory heterosexuality'[46] to describe what I call compulsory Blackness. Compulsory Blackness is a political institution wherein it is presumed that identification with Blackness is the implicit or explicit exclusive personal preference of most 'mixed race' women and men with one Black continental African or Black African Caribbean parent and one White British or White continental European parent. The ongoing challenge then remains coming to terms with one's Blackness as both affirmative and as a source for social discrimination in a manner that does not require partial genealogical or cultural annihilation.

For example, in her longer testimony, Akousa positions herself as a 'light-skinned Black woman'. At the same time she acknowledges and applauds the resilience of her White working-class Irish mother, who raised her and her three siblings on her own. In fact, she punctuates one of her discussions on Black identities politics with the statement: 'At the end of the day I have a White mother.' Akousa also had additional Black continental African, African Caribbean and African-American safety nets into which she could fall when identifying exclusively with her White Irish (and English) maternal culture was insufficient. As cultural surrogates, these women introduced Akousa to Black literature, taught her how to cook African Caribbean dishes, and showed her basic Black grooming skills – creaming the skin and oiling the scalp. Akousa fondly recollects the pivotal role played by these fictive kin in the form of continental African and African American surrogate sisters and African Caribbean 'other mothers'. Fictive kin are not biologically related to individuals. However, they perform the same functions as these family relations.

Both the schoolroom incident and the skinhead encounter example illustrate Akousa's consciousness of the contradictory way in which she is 'racially' positioned as both 'mixed race' and Black. Akousa also acknowledges the significant role her White Irish mother, Black African Caribbean 'other-mothers', continental African and African American surrogate sisters all played in her journey from girlhood to womanhood. I define Akousa's reconciliation of these biracialised public forces and private influences as Additive Blackness. Additive Blackness is a cumulative process of 'racial' reconciliation, wherein a 'mixed race' individual starts with her or his familiar social foundation and builds forward without having to sever ties with her or his often White English or in this case Irish roots. This particular psychosocial process of becoming Black as an individual and collective response to racialised oppression does not compromise the specific allegiances and attachments 'mixed race' individuals may have to White identities, cultures and family.

Parting Thoughts

> I have grown gradually more and more weary of having to deal with the effects of striving to analyse culture within neat homogeneous national units reflecting the 'lived relations' involved; with the invisibility of 'race' ... and, most importantly with the forms of nationalism endorsed by a discipline which in spite of itself, tends towards a morbid celebration of England and Englishness from which blacks are systematically denied.[50]

Gilroy's voicing of these 'strategic silences' was published almost thirteen years ago. As we enter the twenty-first century, we still witness the ideological and political policing of English boundaries which keeps Whites enclosed and Blacks at sea.[51] Independent of rapidly changing demographics indicating a rise in both the number of 'mixed race' marriages and the birth of 'mixed race' children,[52] there is still a deep-seated and now unspoken White English anxiety concerning 'racial' infiltration by Black and Asian 'alien-settlers'. 'Mixed race' children, couples and families occupy a critical location in this context:

> It is clear that mixed 'race' relationships (and children) are increasing and are 'here to stay'. The biggest difficulty facing such relationships, and therefore the children, is not one of inherent pathology or 'maladjustment' of children. The difficulty is one of *social stigma* [emphasis as in original text] which exerts outside pressures on relationships through discrimination and the ways in which people look at people of mixed 'race' and mixed 'race' families.[53]

Consequently, as a critical 'mixed race' researcher, I intend to continue addressing and critically assessing the extent to which public discriminatory social structures and practices affect the formation and maintenance of private 'mixed race' family units, whether comprised of children living with both birth parents, a lone birth parent, or foster or adoptive parents.

For example, in this chapter, Ruby's recounting of a humiliating experience in Morocco wherein she was forced to forfeit the right to claim her three children as her own because they look White illustrates the ways in which conventional notions of kinship are disrupted and the ordinary institution of the family is stigmatised. This particular incident took place in North Africa. However, in her longer testimony, Ruby recalls similar experiences in England wherein her maternal rights are also socially contested. In fact, she describes her position in her family as 'the only Black member in a totally White household'.

Similarly, Bisi describes the 'real stuff' of parenting four children who are struggling to make sense of their location within a crude 'racial' taxonomy that does not match their genealogies. Bisi's narrative illustrates the ways in which the popular folk concept of 'race' cannot easily accommodate phenotypic ambiguities which manifest themselves in individuals as a result of so-called 'inter-racial' mating across generations. In her response to an earlier version of this chapter, Katya Azoulay suggests that the privileging of the Whiteness of second generation 'mixed race' individuals may signal 'the emergence of a racial ambiguity which reinforces Whiteness as normativity'.[54] The unique demographics mentioned earlier provide an ideal opportunity for UK researchers to investigate Azoulay's important speculation among other pressing policy concerns. These include the separate census category debate (see Chapter 7), the politics of transracial fosterage and adoption (see Chapter 8), biographical explorations of the lived experiences of 'mixed race' men raised by White English, Irish, Scottish and Welsh mothers, and the over-representation of 'mixed race' adults in general and 'mixed race' men in particular in 'institutions of violence' such as prisons and psychiatric facilities.[55]

At the same time, to avoid further pathologisation and victimisation of historically marginalised 'mixed race' individuals and groups, we must emphasise and centralise situational and negotiated forms of political agency such as Akousa's strategic Black identification when recollecting her encounters with both the skinhead and the racist classmate. Thus, more than just presenting and interpreting three poignant narratives of 'mixed race' women's lives in the gendered contexts of families and communities, this chapter demonstrates the ways in which racialised boundaries are constructed, policed, maintained and ultimately transgressed.

Acknowledgements

I extend boundless gratitude to the sixteen women and nine men in Bristol without whose courage and honesty this ongoing organic project could not take textual flight. Many thanks also to David Parker and Miri Song who provided astute editorial assistance and created necessary discursive space for further critical exploration of this pervasive paradox. A final thank you to Katya Azoulay who provided important insights and feedback on an earlier version of this chapter.

Notes

1. A multimedia version of this paper was presented in June 1999 as part of a panel I co-organised titled, 'Kinscripts and Ancestors: "Mixed Race", Lineage and Representation in Historical and Biographical Narratives', at the 68th Anglo-American Conference of Historians, Institute of Historical Research, University of London, 30 June–2 July 1999.
2. W.E.B. DuBois, *The Souls of Black Folk* (New York: Signet, 1969 [1903]), p.xi.
3. Lewis Gordon, 'Race, BiRaciality, and Mixed Race', in *Her Majesty's Other Children: Sketches of Racism from a Neocolonial Age* (Lanham, Maryland: Rowman and Littlefield, 1997), p.54. See also Naomi Zack, *Race and Mixed Race* (Philadelphia: Temple University Press, 1995); Stephen Small, *Racialised Barriers* (London: Routledge, 1994); David Theo Goldberg, *Racist Culture* (Oxford: Blackwell, 1993); Floya Anthias and Nira Yuval-Davis, *Racialised Boundaries* (London: Routledge, 1992); Anthony Appiah, *In My Father's House: Africa in the Philosophy of Culture* (New York, Oxford University Press, 1992); Robert Miles, *Racism* (London: Routledge, 1989); Michael Omi and Howard Winant, *Racial Formation in the USA* (New York: Routledge, 1986).
4. Philomena Essed, *Understanding Everyday Racism: An Interdisciplinary Theory* (London: Sage, 1991), p.2.
5. See Kenan Malik, *The Meaning of Race* (London: MacMillan, 1996); Charles Mills, *The Racial Contract* (London: Cornell University Press, 1997); Ani Marimba, *Yurugu: An African-Centred Critique of European Cultural Thought and Behavior* (Trenton, New Jersey: Africa World Press, 1994); Frances Cress Welsing, *The Isis Papers* (Chicago: Third World Press, 1991).
6. Robert Young, *Colonial Desire: Hybridity in Theory, Culture and Race* (London; New York: Routledge, 1995), p.5.
7. See George Stocking, *Race, Culture and Evolution* (Chicago: University of Chicago Press, 1982); Marek Kohn, *The Race Gallery: The Return of Race Science* (London: Vintage, 1996); Noel Gist and Anthony Dworkin (eds), *The Blending of the Races: Marginality and Identity in World Perspective* (New York: John Wiley and Sons, 1972).
8. For a cogent discussion of the 'mixed race' terminology debate as it pertains to the census, see Peter Aspinall, 'The Conceptual Basis of Ethnic Group Terminology and Classifications', *Social Science and Medicine*, vol.45, no.5 (1997), pp.689–98.
9. For a more detailed unravelling of the 'tangle of terminology', see Jayne O. Ifekwunigwe, 'Cracking the Coconut: Resisting Popular Folk Discourses on "Race", "Mixed Race" and Social Hierarchies', in *Scattered Belongings:*

Cultural Paradoxes of 'Race', Nation and Gender (London: Routledge, 1999), pp.1–28.

10. Samba Diop, personal communication, 1993/1998; Henri-Pierre Koubaka, personal communication, 1993.
11. See Breda Gray, 'Unmasking Irishness: Irish Women, the Irish Nation, and the Irish Diaspora', in J. MacLaughlin (ed.), *Location and Dislocation in Contemporary Irish Society* (Cork: Cork University Press, 1997), pp.209–35.
12. See Ivor Gaber and Jane Aldridge (eds), *In the Best Interests of the Child: Culture, Identity and Transracial Adoption* (London: Free Association Books, 1994).
13. See Stephen Small, *Racialised Barriers* (London: Routledge, 1994); Floya Anthias and Nira Yuval-Davis, *Racialised Boundaries* (London: Routledge, 1992).
14. See Noel Gist and Anthony Dworkin (eds), *The Blending of the Races: Marginality and Identity in World Perspective* (New York: John Wiley and Sons, 1972).
15. See Jayne O. Ifekwunigwe, *Scattered Belongings* (London: Routledge, 1999).
16. Donovan Chamberlayne, personal communication, 1996.
17. See Debbie Storrs, 'Whiteness as Stigma: Essentialist Identity Work by Mixed Race Women', *Symbolic Interaction*, vol.22, no.3 (1999), pp.187–213.
18. See Stocking, *Race, Culture and Evolution* (Chicago: University of Chicago Press, 1982); Cheik Anta Diop, *Civilisation or Barbarism: An Authentic Anthropology* (New York: Lawrence Hill, 1991).
19. J. Enoch Powell, *Freedom and Reality* (Kingswood, Surrey: Elliot Right Way Books, 1969), p.313.
20. Catherine Hall, *White, Male and Middle Class* (Cambridge: Polity Press, 1992), p.26; see also Phil Cohen (ed.), *New Ethnicities, Old Racisms?* (London: Zed, 1999); Kwesi Owusu (ed.), *Black British Culture and Society* (London: Routledge, 1999); Paul Gilroy, *There Ain't No Black in the Union Jack* (London: Hutchinson, 1987); Les Back, *New Ethnicities and Urban Youth Cultures* (London: UCL Press, 1996).
21. See Vron Ware, *Beyond the Pale: White Women, Racism and History* (London: Verso, 1992); Robert Young, *White Mythologies: Writing History and the West* (London: Routledge, 1990).
22. The study of Whiteness is not a new research area, although recently there has been a 'revival', which is more apparent in the USA than in the UK. For examples, see David Roediger (ed.), *Black on White: Black Writers on What it Means to Be White* (New York: Schocken Books, 1998); Karen Brodkin, *How Jews Became White Folks* (New Brunswick, New Jersey: Rutgers University Press, 1998); Jane Lazarre, *Beyond the Whiteness of Whiteness* (Durham: Duke University Press, 1996); Michelle Fine, Lois Weiss *et.al.*(eds), *Off White*, (London: Routledge, 1997); Ruth Frankenberg (ed.), *Displacing Whiteness* (London: Duke University Press, 1997).
23. Richard Dyer, *White: Essays on Race and Culture* (London: Routledge, 1997), p.25.

24. Lewis Gordon, *Her Majesty's Other Children* (Lanham, Maryland: Rowman and Littlefield, 1997), p.53.
25. See Tariq Modood, 'Black Racial Equality and Asian Identity', *New Community*, vol.14, no.3 (1988), pp.397–404; Paul Gilroy, *There Ain't No Black in the Union Jack* (London: Hutchinson, 1987); Heidi Mirza (ed.), *Black British Feminism* (London: Routledge, 1997); Claire Alexander, *The Art of Being Black* (Oxford: Oxford University Press, 1996); Kobena Mercer, *Welcome to the Jungle: New Positions in Black Cultural Studies* (London: Routledge, 1994).
26. See Tariq Modood, 'Black Racial Equality and Asian Identity', *New Community*, vol.14, no.3 (1988), pp.397–404.
27. See James F. Davis, *Who is Black?: One Nation's Definition* (University Park: Pennsylvania State University, 1991); bell hooks, *Black Looks* (Boston: South End Press, 1992); Gina Dent (ed.), *Black Popular Culture* (Seattle: Bay Press, 1992); Lisa Jones, *Bulletproof Diva: Tales of Race, Sex and Hair* (New York: Doubleday, 1994).
28. For in-depth analyses of the concept of 'racialisation', see See Stephen Small, *Racialised Barriers* (London: Routledge, 1994); Floya Anthias and Nira Yuval-Davis, *Racialised Boundaries* (London: Routledge, 1992); Robert Miles, *Racism* (London: Routledge, 1989); Michael Omi and Howard Winant, *Racial Formation in the USA* (New York: Routledge, 1986).
29. Bernadine Evaristo, *Lara* (Tunbridge Wells, Kent: Angela Royal, 1997), p.69.
30. Adewale Maja-Pearce, *How Many Miles to Babylon?* (London: Heinemann, 1990), pp.12–13.
31. Avtar Brah, *Cartographies of Diaspora* (London: Routledge, 1996), p.181.
32. See Melville Herskovits, *The Myth of the Negro Past* (Boston: Beacon Press, 1958); Ivan Van Sertima, *They Came Before Columbus* (New York: Random House, 1976); Robin Cohen, *Global Diasporas* (London: UCL Press, 1997); Ronald Segal, *The Black Diaspora* (London: Faber and Faber, 1995); James Clifford, *Routes: Travel and Translation in the Late Twentieth Century* (London: Harvard University Press, 1997); Smadar Lavie and Ted Svedenburg (eds), *Displacement, Diaspora and Geographies of Identity* (London: Duke University Press, 1997).
33. See Paul Gilroy, *The Black Atlantic* (London: Verso, 1993).
34. See Jackie Brown, 'Black Liverpool, Black America, and the Gendering of Diasporic Space', *Cultural Anthropologist*, vol.13, no.3 (1998), pp.291–325; Barnor Hesse, 'Diasporicity: Black Britain's Post-Colonial Formations', in B. Hesse (ed.), *Un/Settled Multiculturalisms: Diasporas, Entanglements, Disruptions* (London: Zed, 2000), pp.96–120.
35. See Ronald Hyam, *Empire and Sexuality: The British Experience* (Manchester: Manchester University Press, 1990); Robert J.C. Young, *Colonial Desire: Hybridity in Theory, Culture and Race* (London; New York: Routledge, 1995); Calvin Hernton, *Sex and Racism in America* (New York: Grove Press, 1965); Beth Day, *Sexual Life Between Blacks and Whites* (New York: William and Morrow, 1974).

36. See J.A. Rogers, *Sex and Race*, vol.III (St Petersburg: Florida, 1944); J.A. Rogers, *Nature Knows No Color Line* (St Petersburg: Florida, 1958).
37. This project culminated in the publication of *Scattered Belongings* (London: Routledge, 1999) which weaves the narratives of six 'mixed race' women , two sets of biological sisters and two women who grew up in care in the UK in either Liverpool, Cardiff, suburban London or in Ibadan, Nigeria, with a critical assessment of historical and contemporary understandings of 'hybridities', social hierarchies and identities politics.
38. With the exception of three of the storytellers, everyone with whom I spoke was born and came of age elsewhere. However, for a two-year-long postmodern pregnant moment we were all living in Bristol, the setting for many reconstructions of childhood as well as collaborative exchanges and debates on the existential meanings of Whiteness, Blackness, Englishness and African diasporic identities.
39. See Renato Rosaldo, *Culture and Truth: The Remaking of Social Analysis* (Boston: Beacon Press, 1989); John Van Maanen (ed.), *Representation in Ethnography* (London: Sage, 1995); Margery Wolf, *A Thrice Told Tale: Feminism, Postmodernism and Ethnographic Responsibility* (Stanford: Stanford University Press, 1992).
40. For an in-depth rationale for the whittling down process in particular and the research methodology in general see Jayne O. Ifekwunigwe, 'Setting the Stage', in *Scattered Belongings* (London: Routledge, 1999), pp.50–61.
41. Gloria Anzaldúa, *Borderlands/La Frontera: The New Mestiza* (San Francisco: Aunt Lute Press, 1987), p.76.
42. With restrictions on word length, I have had to omit excerpts from the poignant narratives of the three other women. They include: Similola, whose mother is German and her father is Tanzanian and who grew up in a children's home outside Cardiff, Wales, as well as the stories of Yemi, Bisi's older sister and of Sarah, Akousa's younger sister.
43. Ruth Behar, 'Rage and Redemption: Reading the Life Story of a Mexican Market Woman', *Feminist Studies*, vol.16, no.2 (1990), p.233–58.
44. To protect the anonymity of those involved, all names and places have been fictionalised.
45. See W.E.B. DuBois, *The Souls of Black Folk* (New York: Signet, 1969); Paul Gilroy, *The Black Atlantic* (London: Verso, 1993).
46. See Robert J.C. Young, *Colonial Desire: Hybridity in Theory, Culture and Race* (London; New York: Routledge, 1995).
47. A Rastafarian – a member of a religious group (others refer to it as a 'cult') which originated in Jamaica and who reject Western ideas and values ('Babylon') and regard Haile Selassie, the former emperor of Ethiopia, as divine.
48. See Richard Price, *First Time: The Historical Vision of an Afro-American People* (Baltimore: Johns Hopkins University Press, 1983); Ruth Finnegan, *Oral Traditions of the Verbal Arts* (London: Routledge, 1992); Tunde Jegede, *African Classical Music and the Griot Tradition* (London: Diabaté Arts, 1994).

49. Each of the six women with whom I spoke has an acute awareness of the Black Power Movement in the USA and its global impact on people of colour in general and Black people in particular. However, most interesting are the different ways in which each woman reaches a critical Black consciousness.
50. Paul Gilroy, *There Ain't No Black in the Union Jack* (London: Hutchinson, 1987) p.12.
51. Paul Gilroy, *The Black Atlantic* (London: Verso, 1993).
52. For precise statistics, see Tariq Modood and Richard Berthoud, *Ethnic Minorities in Britain: The Fourth National Survey of Ethnic Minorities* (London: Policy Studies Institute, 1997).
53. Nick Banks, 'Mixed "Race" Children and Families', Rethinking Mixed Families and Mixed Parentage: Emerging Issues for the Millennium', papers from an Institute for Public Policy Research Seminar, (London: IPPR, 1998), p.8
54. Katya Azoulay, 'Personal and Collective Identities and the Politics of Mixed Race Narrative', commentary for 'Kinscripts and Ancestors: Mixed Race, Lineage and Representations in Historical and Biographical Narratives', 68th Anglo-American Conference of Historians, Institute of Historical Research, University of London, 30 June–2 July 1999.
55. The term 'institutions of violence' stems directly from the work of the founding father of the anti-psychiatry movement in Italy, Franco Basaglia, as well as from the writings of sociologist Erving Goffman and medical anthropologist Nancy Scheper-Hughes. The thrust of the idea is that social relationships within all institutions of violence are based on the dynamics of power: 'the common thread in all these situations is the violence exercised by those who hold the weapons against those who are hopelessly dominated'. Nancy Scheper-Hughes and Anne Lovell (eds), *Psychiatry Inside Out: Selected Writings of Franco Basaglia* (New York: Colombia University Press, 1987), p.60.

3
Same Difference: Towards a More Unified Discourse in 'Mixed Race' Theory

Minelle Mahtani and April Moreno[1]

April: I'm attending my first conference on 'mixed race' in London, England. I've been looking forward to this conference for ages, and I arrive enthusiastic and excited. I found out about the conference several months ago while I was still at home in California through the Internet. After a couple of hours, it begins to dawn on me that 'mixed race' issues take on a very different focus here compared to my past conference experiences in the US. At this conference, issues concerning 'mixed race' primarily address people of white and non-white heritage. I feel that none of the papers and presentations discussed at this conference addressed someone like me – a woman of Chinese and Mexican-American ancestry – a 'mix' that does not involve any white ancestry or experience.

When questions and comments circulate at the end of the conference, I feel that I have to say something; to make note of this absence. I clear my throat and say anxiously, 'Does anyone else here not claim white descent and yet still consider themselves 'mixed race'?' I see a woman in the back of the room glance up at me, but she says nothing.

Minelle: It's nearing the end of the conference, and I stifle a yawn. It's been a long day, and although I've been taking frantic notes, I can still hear a little nagging voice in the back of my head. I'm painfully aware that my own racialised experiences have yet to be discussed. As a Canadian woman of South Asian and Iranian descent, I'm often left wondering about my own place in the existing discourse of 'mixed race'. Can I identify as 'mixed race' even though I'm not part white? This is a difficult question for me to consider. I find that I'm sometimes seen as black or white depending upon where I am. For example, in Britain, where I lived for several years, I was identified as 'black' because this wide rubric often encompasses people of colour. In

America, my racialisation dramatically alters to the contrary – I am seen as 'white' in spite of my olive complexion. In Canada, I am often mistaken for Portuguese, French-Canadian, Italian, and Spanish, among a wide range of markings. For me, a politics of identity is intrinsically tied to a politics of location, where the question, 'Where are you from?' is largely relational, depending on where I am. The ways I am identified depend upon where I am located, at a particular time – and what I'm wearing, what my hair looks like ... and who I'm with, too. I'm beginning to nod off in the final plenary of the conference until I hear a confident voice ring out, 'Does anyone else here not claim white descent and yet still consider themselves 'mixed race'?' Her thoughts strongly resonate with my own, and I make a mental note to approach her after the conference.

April: After meeting at the conference in London, this paper emerged over the course of several meetings, in which Minelle and I shared our thoughts about future theorising on 'mixed race'. Our paper is like a map.[2] We would like to travel along some new routes in this ever-changing map we are sketching. We hope to contemplate new ways of thinking through 'mixed race' theory stemming from some of these questions: Who is considered 'mixed race'? Whose voice deserves to be heard in 'mixed race' discourse? We would like to open up the term 'mixed race', so that we move beyond the dominant understanding of 'mixed race' as predominantly a black and white issue. In this chapter, we explore the struggle for integration in existing 'mixed race' circles. We would like to address the fracturing and divisions emerging in the discourse on 'mixed race'. It has come to the point where I personally feel the need to witness change in the existing 'mixed race' discourse, or else abandon it completely. We want to dispel popular and limiting conceptions of what 'mixed race' constitutes. We hope to negotiate a new space for fresh theorising on 'mixed race' identities to emerge. We want to make space for the forging of new alliances in 'mixed race' discourse.

Minelle: Before we embark on this, however, we want to stress that we certainly don't want to dismiss the importance of the work on black/white interracial identity to date. Obviously, the work of researchers like Jayne Ifekwunigwe, Maria Root, Naomi Zack and France Winddance Twine has played a crucial role in bringing to life the voices of other 'mixed race' individuals.[3] Their contributions have revitalised the terrain of 'mixed race' studies, successfully integrating many voices which may have otherwise been submerged and demonstrating the importance of the black/white colour line in North America and Britain. However, we think that the ideas articulated by these authors may require further thought and disentangling. After all, there may be many other marginalised voices which are lost in the existing discourse on 'mixed race', like those of April and myself. In the recent explosion of writings about multiraciality, we have seen a plethora of discussion about white/black crossings, and white/Asian crossings (and we want to remind you that we are using these terms very suspiciously). But we worry that we have not yet seen a great deal of discussion about people who are of dual minority mixes, or who are not part white.

This concerns us because researchers have indicated that the numbers of people who identify as being of multiple racial origin are growing quickly. In both the UK and the USA the census data from the early 1990s revealed the growing inability of the racial categories employed to reflect the complex ancestry of the population. The assumption that 'mixed race' equals 'part white' cannot be sustained. As Charlie Owen demonstrates in Chapter 7 of this volume, the 'other mixed' grouping in the 1991 UK census exceeded both the black-white and Asian-white groups. Much of this can be attributed to the arbitrary coding of respondents who are partially white, but not all. Likewise in the USA a large number of respondents (9.8 million) did not fit the five main racial categories in the 1990 census and fell into the 'other' category. Nearly a quarter of a million wrote in some form of multiracial self-description.[4] Although impossible to document precisely, there is a growing constituency who are 'mixed race', and who do not have white parentage. We want to map the voices of those who tend to be excluded in the binary conceptualisation of our racialised societies.

April: It has become disturbingly clear at this point that there are majority and minority camps within those researching and writing about 'mixed race'. Minelle and I are real-life examples of the fact that 'mixed race' is a concept which transcends black and white, or white and non-white identities and experiences. What do we mean by that? We would like to discuss our own personal experiences to explain why we wish to open up the category of 'mixed race'.

Minelle: I initially found myself wholly identifying with the 'mixed race' movement because my parents' ethnic, cultural and class backgrounds were so radically different. I am of South Asian and Iranian descent. My father was raised in Bombay, India. My Dad's Hindu, working-class family owned a restaurant, and my last name loosely translated means 'purveyor of sweets'. My mother grew up in Tehran, Iran in a relatively wealthy, Muslim household. My parents met in London, and after they married, they decided to move to Canada, in large part because of the enormous racism they faced in Britain. I was born in Toronto in 1971, the same year that official multicultural policy was inaugurated in Canada.

Having two parents of different backgrounds significantly shaped my experience of growing up. I felt that my mother's Iranian side of the family never accepted me as a 'real' Iranian – I was always seen as an outsider at family gatherings. When my mother and I flew across the Atlantic to visit my Dad's family in Bombay one summer, I felt a coldness from my aunts and uncles towards us, as if we were not welcome there without my father. The dynamics surrounding the marginalisation and racism from family members on both sides of my family were complex. At times, I felt isolated from both groups.

Although I feel that there are some similarities between my experiences and those of people who are part white, I believe that there are different situations and challenges facing people of dual minority heritage, and I can see this through the dynamics within my family. Both sides of my family have tended to compartmentalise who I am, by seeing one half of my ethnicity as odd, strange and foreign. My Indian family seems to be perplexed by my Iranian side, and are especially concerned about my family's relationship to Islam. Similarly, some members of my Iranian family seem to shower disdain on my Indian family, imagining Indian and Hindu culture as 'uncouth' or even 'dirty'. It has also been insinuated to me that I would be more valued if I was part white, instead of being of two minority groups, primarily because of the high value placed upon whiteness and fair skin. For some people in my family, I would have been 'alright' if I had only been part white, instead of being completely 'different'. I feel that my relationship to whiteness is fraught with a different kind of tension than those who claim partial white heritage.

I've also noticed that people tend to privilege one of my ethnicities over the other. Often, my ethnicities are ranked by individuals as if it is a matter for debate, as if my parents' cultural backgrounds are fighting a battle for ownership over my identity. Perhaps this isn't hugely different from those whose who claim some white heritage. However, I find it startling how my ethnicities are privileged differently in different places. My Iranian heritage has been praised by friends and strangers as more 'exotic' than my Indian side at times, but I cannot help but wonder if my Iranianness is only preferred because it is seen as more 'white' than my Indian background. Yet, at other times, such as when I'm travelling abroad, my Iranianness marks me as a criminal or a terrorist. I have been denied access to flights, and have had my bags ransacked simply because of my Arabic name and Iranian heritage. I've also noticed how this privileging alters as I become older.

The racism I experienced growing up was largely directed at my Indian identity. Children pelted me with hateful racial slurs based on my skin colour, awful names that I didn't understand until my mother explained them to me when I got home from school. Now it seems that my Iranianness has been drawn out for spectacle, where I face greater prejudice based on unfair stereotypes of Iran and Islam respectively. The fact that both my parents are considered ethnic minorities means that I experience a different sort of ethnic and racial prejudice because I am of dual minority heritage.

These experiences led me to wonder what further differences could exist between the experiences of those of dual minority backgrounds and those with part-white backgrounds. In contemplating that question, I turned to Dr Andrew Gotowiec, a research psychologist in Toronto who has just finished the largest study on 'mixed race' identity in Canada and its links to mental health. His work has demonstrated that people of dual minority heritage may experience lower self-esteem and may be less socially confident than 'mixed' people with some white heritage.[5]

My own experiences have led me to question my own place in the 'mixed race' movement. Can I identify as 'mixed race' even though my parents are only occasionally identified as being from two different racial groups? I have been told coolly at conferences that I should not be allowed to identify as 'mixed race' because I am not 'multiracial' at all; rather, 'multiethnic'. It has even been oddly suggested to me that I am not even really 'multiethnic' because India and Iran supposedly share such similar cultures – after all, aren't they very close to one another geographically?! Although we are all well aware by now that racial categories are but social inventions, who gets to decide whether or not I can be considered 'mixed race'? Who are the gatekeepers of such a category? Some believe that my parents are from two different ethnic groups – others feel that the differences are racial ones. How can we open up spaces for alliances between those who identify as 'mixed race' and those who identify as 'multiethnic'?

April: I believe that being a third-generation Mexican-Chinese American is an unusual experience. My mother is a Chinese American, born in Las Vegas, Nevada and my father is a Mexican American who was born in El Paso, Texas. They met during high school in Los Angeles. Partly for this reason, I was only taught to speak English in my family, and I could only speak a few sentences of Chinese to my maternal grandmother, even though I attended elementary school in the Los Angeles Chinatown. I found my third-generational status to be relatively unusual, as my friends were either first- or second-generation

Americans who still had close cultural and linguistic ties to their Chinese or Latin American ancestry.

In Chinatown, I was prey to prejudicial comments about my dark skin colour and my mixed non-white heritage by students and teachers alike. I believe that if I were of a mixed white background, I would not have experienced many of these comments, since white physical features were often praised at school.

When I am outside of Los Angeles, people very frequently assume that I am newly arrived in the USA, despite the fact that the US is where not only I, but also my parents, were born and raised. I believe that my appearance as a non-white 'mixed race' person contributes to this continual attribution of foreignness. In addition, when people ask me about my 'background', they often respond with comments about how interesting it must be to be mixed, yet very often follow with their comments on their 'favorite' mixes, which usually involve 'mixes' with white heritage. I often feel insulted by this, as people (indirectly) seem to be telling me that 'being mixed is beautiful and exotic, but you would be even more attractive if you were part white.'

My sister, who is also Mexican-Chinese American, appears more Mexican while I appear more Chinese, and Spanish-speakers will approach her in Spanish, while they will often choose not to speak to me. This is ironic, as I actually speak more Spanish than my sister does. In addition, when we visit the Mexican side of the family, I am treated as if I am less related to my grandmother than my cousins, who are Latina. When I am with my cousins, we are often referred to as 'the Chinese cousins'. Although we are just as related to each other as any other cousins, I feel that the validity of our kinship ties is questioned, not only by my family members, but also by outsiders. I believe I would be treated very differently if I were half white instead, as Mexicans are often already of mixed white heritage. For example, my paternal grandmother is light-skinned with green eyes. I think that I would feel more included as part of my Mexican family if I were of partly white heritage.

With the Chinese side of my family, I have felt more included, although there is also a slight sense of distancing when my Mexican father is mentioned. My Chinese grandmother always chided my mother as being 'crazy' for deciding to marry a Mexican, but accepted him nonetheless. In contrast, my uncle's decision to marry a white woman was never joked about, but was considered to be acceptable. Furthermore, my Chinese-white cousins live a more privileged life here in the USA, in comparison with my family. However, this is not simply due to their being part white. My uncle's university education lifted the family into the middle class. My cousins have white college-educated partners. Perhaps due to this social mobility they have chosen to opt out of maintaining close ties with the working-class Chinese side of the family, choosing to visit the white side of the family more often. Based upon the differences in interethnic experiences within my family, I have concluded that there are differences in the experiences of non-white 'mixed race' individuals compared to those who are part white. However, not all of these differences are due to racialisation. Disparities in class and education are also significant in shaping family relationships.

Minelle: We cannot help but observe that non-white 'mixed race' voices are marginalised in current debates, and are not given equal and valuable consideration. We have found that discussions in 'mixed race' circles, as well as public conceptions of 'mixed race', have tended to disregard the experiences of non-white 'mixed race' people. As mentioned before, this is reflected in the common societal perception that the term 'mixed race' is synonymous with a black and white 'mix'. Part of our concern stems from the theoretical assumptions inherent in many writings on 'mixed race.' It is apparent that a privileging of particular voices is taking place. The current discussions in 'mixed race' theory perpetuate a kind of crude asymmetry that has tainted many critical analyses of race theory, where race is a code word for non-white. The binary logic of race, in which the world is perceived in terms of oppositions (white versus non-white) encodes a hierarchy, with the first term of these oppositions superior to the second.

April: It is important, as Judith Butler reminds us, to trouble these categories.[6] As in the changing historical status of Italian and Jewish immigrants to the USA in the early twentieth century (who gradually came to be regarded as 'white'), who qualifies as white or raced changes over time and space. The categorisation of who is permitted to be white and who is marked as non-white fluctuates, and is a highly politicised and contested matter. 'Mixed race' people themselves participate in these dynamics. Yet, in spite of the instability surrounding racial and ethnic categorisation, popular conceptions of 'mixed race' remain predominantly characterised in terms of a white–non-white dichotomy.

Another example of this binary construction and the exclusion it produces can be seen in Amy Iwasaki Mass's study on Japanese-Americans in Southern California. The title of her study is 'Interracial Japanese Americans: The Best of Both Worlds or the End of the Japanese Community?'[7] It is interesting that although she uses the term 'interracial', she does not deconstruct her use of the label. She seems to imply that 'interracial' only refers to people of Japanese and white descent. From personal experience, I have met several Southern Californians who identify as interracial Japanese Americans who do not fit into the category that Iwasaki Mass employs in her article – for example, Japanese-Mexican-Americans. Her use of the term 'interracial' solely to represent Japanese-white-Americans glosses over the differences and demographic diversity characteristic of Southern California.

Minelle: We have no easy answers to these thorny issues, but we hope that by raising them, it will lead to extensive debate. How should 'mixed race' be conceptualised? As discussed in the introduction to this volume, how can we talk about 'mixed race' without reifying the notion that someone who is 'mixed' is descended from two distinct and 'pure' lineages, whatever 'pure' means? Given the common polarisation of white and black heritages (and the accompanying mythologisation of whiteness and white purity in particular), it is vital that we move away from a sole focus on white/black 'mixture'.

We find ourselves at an ironic impasse, because we do not want to dissolve the category of 'mixed race' altogether. We want to acknowledge the wide range of voices, some of which are marginalised within the current 'mixed race' discourse. If we do not begin to assert and give consideration to alternative perspectives on 'mixed race', we fall prey to binary traps of categorisation, where a majority 'mixed race' group (with some white heritage) exists and other minority 'mixes' find themselves silenced or ignored. Other groups should not be negated or overshadowed in the generalised discourse on 'mixed race'.

We believe that there is a lack of interconnectedness among the various groups who study and write about 'mixed race'. At times, discussions at conferences about 'mixed race' seem to disintegrate quickly into a confrontational tone, where a hierarchy of difference emerges among diverse 'mixed race' people. In such meetings, questions such as: 'Are you more "mixed race" than I am?' or, 'Will the real "mixed race" person please stand up?' are raised. At the heart of a productive 'mixed race' theory ought to be a clear articulation of various forms of political subjectivities forging alliances across difference. However, we have yet to contemplate creative alliances and the possibility of creating new collectives.

We find ourselves in good company as there are many other feminists who heed the importance of this call, like Chandra Mohanty, who insists that feminists should develop potential alliances across divisive boundaries in the creation of horizontal comradeship,[8] and Gillian Rose, a feminist geographer, who recognises the importance of alliances in struggle, where the spaces of separatism become spaces of interrelations.[9]

April: So how can we begin to create these new alliances? Our goal is to contemplate ways for 'mixed race' discourse to accommodate the experiences and views of individuals of a whole variety of 'mixes'. It is crucial to begin to address this issue now, as we witness greater partnering and intermarriage not only among black and white peoples, but also between various ethnic minority groups. We have entered into this discussion to see if unity is at all possible in 'mixed race' discourse. We must be able to participate in discussions about 'mixed race', valuing who we are as individuals, while bringing with us a respect for the many and varied experiences of 'mixed race' people. 'Who has it harder in society?' is not a productive question. Instead, we wish to ask: What kinds of oppression, and what kinds of experiences, more generally, have we shared? How can we create more liberating spaces?

Minelle: How can we come together, despite all of our wildly different experiences, as individuals who identify as 'mixed race', or as researchers who wish to delve into further explorations into 'mixed race'? Although it is important to recognise the variable experiences of mixed people, we wish to create some connections across our differences. How can we co-exist and at the same time avoid the potential pitfalls of reified categories? How can we fight stereotypes concerning the experiences of all 'mixed' people?

In approaching these difficult questions we have found the work of 'mixed race' researchers such as Michael Thornton and Cynthia Nakashima particularly compelling. Both authors have tried to open up the discourse on 'mixed race' identity. Thornton, himself of African American and Japanese descent, calls for a broadening of the research agenda to acknowledge that there is no single 'mixed race' experience.[10] Nakashima[11] also highlights the multiplicity within the 'mixed race' movement. She identifies three strands to its political activity. First, the struggle for inclusion within minority ethnic communities. Second, the sharing of a common identity and agenda among 'mixed race' people. Third, the struggle to develop a 'supraracial' discourse which creates connections across racialised boundaries, forging a common humanity. She ends by insisting that we listen attentively to all these voices to 'recognise and reflect the diversity of voices that make up the multiracial movement'.[12] We would emphasise the importance of producing theory and analysis which resonate with the experiences of diverse individuals of various mixes.

April: In order to move toward the generation of productive theorising, however, we must reshape the concept of 'mixed race'. Otherwise, the discourse of 'mixed race' is in danger of deteriorating through division, devaluation, exclusion, sadness and resentment. The title of our chapter is 'same difference' to reflect its dual emphasis. First, we acknowledge the commonality of being 'mixed race' and falling outside the prevailing racialised categories. Second, close reflection on our own experiences calls for a refinement of the emerging discourse on 'mixed race'. There are further dimensions added where one's ancestry is mixed, but not white. These complexities are largely unexplored in existing research which then feeds into a restricted conceptualisation of 'mixed race'.

We need to make further efforts to develop theory where all people who identify as 'mixed race' can contribute and share their experiences within the existing discourse. Although we have each discussed the personal and particular family experiences associated with our dual minority parentage, it would be erroneous to assume any clear-cut categorical differences in our experiences from those of other 'mixed' people. Nor should 'mixed' people conclude that their experiences are wholly different from those of monoracial minorities. In fact, Michael Thornton has questioned how distinct the experiences of 'mixed race' people are from those of monoracial minorities. These questions about areas of commonality and difference are complex and cannot be simply extrapolated from the particularities of individual, personalised accounts (though these are unquestionably important). Rather, such questions need more systematic empirical investigation.

Minelle: There are also many other issues that need further debate and study. For instance, what are the differences and commonalities between 'mixed race' identity and diasporic identity? How questions of nationalism tie in with 'mixed race' identifications also concern us. As North American citizens, April and I came to London to pursue our studies with a very different set of experiences involving particular ethnic and national identities. How does this affect our own interpretation of 'mixed race' in Britain? Future research also needs to interrogate gender differences experienced by 'mixed race' people. All of these questions require that we pay more attention to the specific contexts in which particular 'mixed race' identities are formed and experienced.

April: So although we will refold our map at this juncture, we want to emphasise that there are many more landscapes left to map. We only see this discussion as a point of departure. This map is in a continual state of process. We're constantly revising it, attempting to unveil the contours of 'race' and 'mixed race', emphasising certain roads, establishing landmarks and, most importantly, moving beyond the past discourse on race and 'mixed race' by establishing a new legend. And what would this new legend look like? We propose that it necessitates a new vocabulary – one which shatters the seemingly stable notion of 'race' to describe the varied and diverse terrain of multiracial experiences. This won't be an easy terrain to map, but in doing so, we can work toward revitalising and 'troubling' existing work on 'mixed race' identity.

Notes

1. Both authors are joint first authors.
2. We want to acknowledge an important debt here to Saloni Mathur, whose writing has inspired us to borrow the mapping metaphor she employs in her article, 'bell hooks called me a woman of color', in M. Silvera (ed.), *The 'Other' Woman: Women of Color in Contemporary Canadian Literature* (Toronto: Sister Vision Press, 1995).
3. See J. Ifekwunigwe, *Scattered Belongings* (London: Routledge, 1998); M. Root (ed.), *The Multiracial Experience* (London: Sage, 1996); N. Zack (ed.), *American Mixed Race* (London: Rowman & Littlefield, 1995); F. Twine, 'Brown Skinned White Girls: class, culture and the construction of white identity in suburban communities', in *Gender, Place and Culture* 3(2) 1996, pp.205–24.
4. M. Root (ed.), *The Multiracial Experience* (London: Sage, 1996), p.xvii.
5. Personal correspondence with Dr. Andrew Gotowiec, Research psychologist at the Centre for Addiction and Mental Health, Toronto, 27 July 2000.
6. J. Butler, *Gender Trouble* (London: Routledge, 1990).
7. A. Iwasaki Mass, 'Interracial Japanese Americans: the best of both worlds or the end of the Japanese American community', in M. Root (ed.), *Racially Mixed People in America* (London: Sage 1992).
8. C. Mohanty, 'Cartographies of struggle: Third World women and the politics of feminism', in C. Mohanty, A. Russo and L. Torres (eds), *Third World Women and the Politics of Feminism* (Bloomington: Indiana University Press 1991).
9. G. Rose, *Feminism and Geography* (Minneapolis: University of Minnesota Press 1993); see also Minelle Mahtani, Chapter 9, this volume.
10. M. Thornton 'Hidden agendas, identity theories and multiracial people', in M. Root (ed.), *The Multiracial Experience* (London: Sage, 1996).
11. C. Nakashima, 'Voices from the movement: approaches to multiraciality', in M. Root (ed.), *The Multiracial Experience* (London: Sage, 1996).
12. *Ibid*, p.97.

4
The Subject is Mixed Race: The Boom in Biracial Biography[1]

Paul Spickard

> Strange to wake up and realise you're in style. That's what happened to me just the other morning. It was the first day of the new millennium and I woke to find that mulattos had taken over. They were everywhere. Playing golf, running the airwaves, opening their own restaurants, modelling clothes, starring in musicals with names like *Show Me the Miscegenation!* The radio played a steady stream of Lenny Kravitz, Sade and Mariah Carey. I thought I'd died and gone to Berkeley. But then I realised. According to the racial zodiac, 2000 is the official Year of the Mulatto. Pure breeds (at least the black ones) are out and hybridity is in. America loves us in all of our half-caste glory.[2]

Multiracialism is all the rage. Golfer Tiger Woods proclaims he is 'Cablinasian' (Caucasian, Black, American Indian, Asian); singer Mariah Carey is alternately credited with being White, Black, and Latina; and no one seems to be certain of the racial identity of the artist formerly known as Prince. Even the White actor Kevin Costner claims some Native American ancestry.

Such claims of racial multiplicity are not just a celebrity avocation. In the past decade and a half, a multiracial movement has emerged in the USA. Although the movement is most active on the West Coast where it has taken such organisational forms as the Association of Multi-Ethnic Americans, Hapa Issues Forum and Multiracial Americans of Southern California, multiracialism has in fact become a national movement.[3] Responding to years of intense lobbying, the US Office of Management and Budget decided in 1997 to let people check more than one racial box on the 2000 census, in recognition of the desire of some people to acknowledge multiple ancestries.

Scarcely a textbook on race and ethnicity in the USA can be written these days without prominent mention of the multiracial phenomenon.[4] There is, in addition, a growing analytical literature on multiracial identity, led most prominently by two books edited by Maria Root, *Racially Mixed People in America* and *The Multiracial Experience: Racial Borders as the New Frontier*.[5]

No part of the multiracialist phenomenon is more striking than the 1990s' boom in biracial biography. Dozens of authors – many times more than in any other decade – have found publishers and readers for autobiographical and biographical treatments of the lives of people with multiple ancestries.[6] This chapter is an exploration of the shape of that publishing trend, and a contemplation of what it may mean for racial definitions and race relations in the USA as the century turns.

The Black Person in a White Body

To begin with, it must be said that most of these books are by or about people who mix Black and White ancestry, not other combinations. Of course, having mixed Black and White ancestry is not a new thing. Nearly all African Americans have at least some European, Native American or other ancestry; no one pretends otherwise. But the one-drop rule – one drop of Black blood, one known African American ancestor, makes one Black – has made mixed people Black in America for most of the last century and a half. It has unfortunately been an efficient tool for racial clarity and racial domination. What is new in this mixed-race memoir trend is that a large number of people are owning up to their mixedness. They are talking about their White ancestors as well as their Black ancestors, and about their mixed selves.[7]

There are discernible themes in this literature of Black–White mixedness. The first and most common is the Black person in a White body, in the case of mixed people who may appear to be White. Perhaps this perspective is common because this is the way some Black–White mixed people see their situations. Or perhaps it is simply that this construction of the issue does the least to undermine established racial binaries – both the White investment in there being only White and Black with White on top, and the Black investment in a Black–White binary as a clear-cut means of racial defence. Or, perhaps, such biographies may be popular because they are comfortable vehicles by which White readers can enter into the exotic and frightening world of Blacks in the company of a domesticated, half-White guide.

One such guide is Gregory Howard Williams, whose 1995 best-seller, *Life on the Color Line*, bore the subtitle: 'The True Story of a White Boy Who Discovered He Was Black.'[8] Williams is a great storyteller in simple prose, a sensitive observer, aware of his own feelings. Yet he does not question the received racial binary of Black and White. At the beginning of his story he is uncomplicatedly White: a young boy with a White mother, father, and little brother, living in family disharmony in rural Virginia, attending White schools, going to White theatres and swimming pools.

Then, in a traumatic revelation, he learns he is really Black. Abandoned by his White mother aboard a bus bound for his father's parental home in Indiana, Williams hears his father say: '"Remember Miss Sallie who used to work for us in the tavern? ... [S]he's really my momma. That means she's your grandmother." "But that can't be, Dad! She's colored!" ... I didn't understand Dad. I knew I wasn't colored, and neither was he. My skin was white. All of us are white, I said to myself. But for the first time, I had to admit Dad didn't exactly look white. His deeply tanned skin puzzled me as I sat there trying to classify my own father. Goose bumps covered my arms as I realized that whatever he was, I was. I took a deep breath. I couldn't make any mistakes. I looked closer. His heavy lips and dark brown eyes didn't make him colored, I concluded. His black, wavy hair was different from Negroes' hair, but it was different from most white folks' hair, too. He was darker than most whites, but Mom said he was Italian. That was why my baby brother had such dark skin and curly hair. Mom told us to be proud of our Italian heritage! That's it, I decided. He was Italian. I leaned back against the seat, satisfied. Yet the unsettling image of Miss Sallie flashed before me like a neon sign. Colored! Colored! Colored! ... I saw my father as I had never seen him before. The veil dropped from his face and features. Before my eyes he was transformed from a swarthy Italian to his true self – a high-yellow mulatto. My father was a Negro! We were colored!'[9] At that moment Greg Williams steps across the line from White to Black.

The rest of the story tells of his travails and ultimate personal triumph as a Black person in a White body. Initially, he is accorded an ambiguous welcome into an impoverished Black extended family and neighbourhood in Muncie, Indiana. Black playmates taunt him and his brother for being 'crackers', but gradually he makes a place for himself with a Black identity. He suffers deprivation on account of being Black and struggles with a murderous rage against all White people that is not fully extinguished until he is an adult. He is told by Blacks to stay away from White girls; their message is echoed by a White high school teacher: '"You better get it out of your mind that you're ever going to date any White girls. That kind of thing is just not done in our society. It's not going to be acceptable in my lifetime or yours, and it will never, ever happen here in Muncie! You have some potential. You could be a credit to your race."'[10] All of this Black racial signifying is laid on a young man who looks a good bit like Beaver Cleaver (an American television character from the 1950s who is unquestionably White in appearance). One way that *Life on the Color Line* appeals to White readers is that it takes them into a harrowing Black place, where there is a lot of poverty and some violence, where people live desperate lives on account of their Blackness; and yet those White readers can feel safe in the knowledge that their guide looks White and, by story's end (so the back cover tells us), will be a law school dean.[11]

The one issue Williams never raises is the possibility that he may be something other than simply Black. Perhaps it is where he was raised and when, in a sharply segregated town in the industrial Midwest. But he never explores any sense of racial twoness. Even though the book is founded on the anomaly of his Black and White ancestry, of his White appearance and his Black identity, racial mixedness is a question he does not take up. He is always, simply, really a Black person who is frequently mistaken for White.

An odd example of the Black-person-in-a-White-body is Lisa Jones's *Bulletproof Diva: Tales of Race, Sex, and Hair.*[12] Jones riffs in every direction, on subjects as diverse as women and men; genitalia and rear ends; hair cuts and hair colours; TV, movies, popular music and slick magazines. But everywhere the subject is race. Her essays on racial mixedness come down where Williams comes down: she sees herself as a racially mixed Black person. But there is a sharper political and intellectual edge to her account. She is not just telling a story; she has made a decision. She insists, 'That I'm a writer whose work is dedicated to exploring the hybridity in African-American culture and of American culture in general. That I don't deny my White forbears, but I call myself African American, which means to me, a person of African and Native American, Latin, or European descent. That I feel comfortable and historically grounded in this identity. That I find family there, whereas no White people have embraced me with their culture' even though she writes fondly of her close relationship to her White mother. 'We of the rainbow persuasion joke about Whites' inability to imagine why we would want to see ourselves as people of color and as African Americans – how connected this makes us feel ... I'm on the other side of the spectrum from race-neutral rainbow babies [like Mariah Carey] who claim a multitude of heritages but no race ... I ... never explored an option other than black, never wished to. Blackness has always been this wide and miraculous world of people and places and passions and histories and stances.'[13] Amid a more self-conscious acknowledgement of her racial mixedness than any of the authors noted above, Jones chooses to be politically Black. In 'White Like Me', a biographical treatment of Anatole Broyard written for the New Yorker,[14] Henry Louis Gates lays his confusion about Broyard at the top of his essay: 'Anatole Broyard wanted to be a writer, not a black writer. So he chose to live a lie rather than be trapped by the truth.' The first sentence is an accurate depiction of the feat Broyard set for himself; the second is where Gates makes his mistake, for what Broyard did cannot be captured with simplistic terms like 'lie' and 'truth'.

Broyard was one of the pre-eminent critics on the New York literary scene from the 1950s through the 1980s. Born to a very light-skinned, Black-identified family in New Orleans, after coming to New York Broyard passed as White, as had his father, in order to pursue his vocation. In the elder's case his vocation was carpenter; in Anatole's case it was man of letters. As Gates writes: '[H]ere is a man who passed for White because he wanted to be a writer, and he did not want to be a Negro writer. It is a crass disjunction, but it is not his crassness or his disjunction. His perception was perfectly correct. He would have had to be a Negro writer, which was something he did not want to be. In his terms, he did not want to write about black love, black passion, black suffering, black joy; he wanted to write about love and passion and suffering and joy.'[15] He did not want to be trapped, as were his contemporaries Richard Wright, Ralph Ellision, and James Baldwin, in being a Black writer, so he presented himself as White. And unlike them, he was not trapped.

Yet, if we are intellectually even-handed, why should Broyard's choice be construed as passing for something he was not? His appearance was White, his ancestry was mostly White, he functioned smoothly as a White man in the world without raising serious questions, his adult family and friends were White – in what meaningful sense was he not White? Why should some essentialist, one-drop notion of race, on Gates's part or ours, compel Broyard to identify himself as Black? If Lisa Jones can take solid comfort in a political and personal decision to be unambiguously Black in her mixedness, why should not Anatole Broyard be allowed the aesthetic and personal decision to be unambiguously White in his? Jones is of a different age, when a multiracial identity is a legitimate option, so she can own her mixedness and choose a Black identity. Broyard, just a few decades earlier, did not have the choice to acknowledge his mixedness, to note that his appearance and associations were White, and choose a mainly White identity. In his era, the rules were binary: either he could be Black despite his appearance, aspirations and associations, or he could pretend he had no African ancestry. He chose the latter option. Gates, trapped in the same binary, does not want to allow Broyard that option. He continually shrinks from the actual implications of Broyard's life, and uses terms like 'anguish' and 'lie' to describe Broyard's self-creation. He even implies – without offering any evidence – that Broyard's failure to complete a novel was caused by his denial of his Black authenticity.

Gates does point us in the direction of some understanding, however, when he notes that 'The thematic elements of passing – fragmentation, alienation, liminality, self-fashioning – echo the great themes of modernism.'[16] One might go a step further and say that the themes of multiraciality – constructedness, contingency, paradox, multiplicity – are among the themes of postmodernism. Broyard might have been the modernist soul that Gates paints, feeling himself Black and yearning to be White. But it just may be that somewhere within that very modernist literary critic – Broyard – lay the embryo of a postmodern racial consciousness. It just may be that it was that more complex, multiracial soul, longing to get out, that Gates fails to perceive.

A Tragic Mulatto Still

Gates's misportrayal of Broyard as a tormented individual who tried to hide his Black essence in a vain pursuit of Whiteness leads into the second theme of this biracial literature. That hoary metaphor, the tortured mulatto, is with us still, and might have influenced Gates's misunderstanding of Broyard. The light-skinned Black who tries to pass as White, and then lives tormented by private demons and the fear of discovery, is one of the oldest conventions of one-drop-rule American literary culture. It is near the heart of D.W. Griffiths's classic racist film *Birth of a Nation*, Nella Larsen's Harlem Renaissance novel *Quicksand*, the musical *Showboat*, and a hundred other stories.[17]

Now the tortured mulatto is alive in 1990s biography. The jacket blurb of Kathryn Talalay's erudite and gracefully-written biography of Philippa Schuyler, *Composition in Black and White*, sets the theme: 'The Tragic Saga of Harlem's Biracial Prodigy'.[18] Schuyler was the child of the brilliant and pugnacious Black journalist George Schuyler and his White wife Josephine Cogdell Schuyler. Philippa grew up in the public eye, was a prodigy pianist, and later had a second career as a foreign correspondent. Her parents raised her as an experiment in invigorating the races by hybrid mixing to produce gifted offspring, and they hoped she would be the herald of a new, mixed generation that would break down the colour line. Yet she was frustrated by the American classical music industry, which had no place for an artist they regarded as Black, and she was uncomfortable with her mixedness. For a time in her late twenties and early thirties she changed her name to Felipa Monterro y Schuyler in an attempt to pass as Iberian. In this identity, she denied having any Black ancestry and adopted an intensely conservative political posture, but still failed to find personal peace. Talalay – in contrast to a writer like Gates – does not fault Schuyler for choosing to deny the person she really was to some. Rather, she puts a positive spin on Schuyler's wandering spirit. She chooses to view Schuyler as one who took action to reinvent herself in order to clear the hurdles placed before her. That is a new way to view the tragic mulatto – as self-creation – but the mulatto here is still tragic. At the very least, multiraciality is a problem that must be fought, and that perhaps cannot be overcome.[19] Happily, the tragic mulatto is but a minor note in the rich symphony of current writing on racial mixedness.

Celebration of Mixedness

In contrast to the memoirs on these first two themes, which either deny racial mixedness or portray it negatively, there is a growing biographical literature that embraces the proposition that one can be unproblematically mixed. No book in this genre has attracted a wider audience than Shirlee Taylor Haizlip's *The Sweeter the Juice*.[20] There is no torment here, neither is there exactly a Black person in a White body. Rather, Haizlip and the branch of her light-skinned family that inhabits most of this memoir are not distressed by their racial mixedness. Mixing and its complications are the theme of the book, to wit:

> This is the story of a family that is black, White and Indian.
> This is the story of how color separated that family.
> This is the story of a family that accepted its color but rejected its race.
> This is the story of a family that accepted its race but rejected its color.
> This is the story of how the black family prospered and became visible.
> This is the story of how the White family fled and became invisible ...
> This is all one story.
> This is the story of my family.

Beyond that, Haizlip lays a larger claim: 'I am in all America. All America is in me.'[21] Haizlip thus asserts that the racial mixedness of her family is an emblem for the American experience.

The main branch of the family – Haizlip's – chooses to identify as Black throughout. Hence the title, recalling Leadbelly's lyric, 'The blacker the berry, the sweeter the juice'.[22] They have hard times on account of their Blackness, but in the end they prevail. Some relatives made another choice: they passed as White in search of a better life. The book's central irony is that the side of the family that embraced Blackness rose to considerable wealth and influence, while the branch that passed as White became 'a marginal family, broken and poor'.[23] Perhaps there is a cautionary aspect to this tale – those who fled a Black identity did not prosper. But the overall tone of the book is genial, it embraces mixedness and does not condemn those who make a different choice.

The many members of Haizlip's family took various paths to racial identity. Even more variety is to be found in Lise Funderburg's *Black, White, Other*. This is not an individual or family biography; rather, the fruit of several dozen interviews with people who have one Black-identified parent and one White-identified parent.[24] If there is a unifying theme to *Black, White, Other*, it is that there is no one way to be biracial. Each person has a story that is unique, even as that person's issues are related to those of other biracial people. Thus on the question of which side to date on, Jimmy Pierre says: '"I've never had any relationships with a White woman,"' while Mark Durrow answers: '"What's my dating history? White, White, White, White."' On whether there is a commonality among racially mixed people, Kyria Ramey says: '"For me, the same way black people have a sisterhood or a brotherhood, that's something that I felt towards this mixed guy who worked at the same restaurant I did – that we had this connection just because of who we were."' Yet Jacqueline Djanikian says: '"I don't really feel a particular connection to mixed people. I understand what they've gone through, but I don't necessarily say we are closer because we're both mixed."'[25] The sum is a look into the lives of some forty-six biracial people that stresses the variety of individual experience. It suggests that nothing so simple as the tragic mulatto stereotype does justice to the experience of multiracial people.

Monoracialist Reaction

There is a backlash against the celebration of mixedness. The most prominent book on that theme is Jon Michael Spencer's *The New Colored People*.[26] Because of its sharp political edge, it must be discussed here, although *The New Colored People* is neither biography nor social analysis but a diatribe against the multiracial movement.

There are two problems with *The New Colored People*. First, it is founded on the part-and-the-whole fallacy. One activity of the multiracial movement (agreed on by most active multiracialists but not the centre of the movement) has been an effort by some mixed people to get schools and government agencies to allow them to check all applicable boxes on forms, thus allowing a person to be publicly recognised as, for example, both Korean and Chicana, rather than having to choose just one – precisely what the US government decided to endorse in 1997.

There was a related campaign, by a very small number of multiracial people and by some White parents of multiracial children, to have instead a box marked 'multiracial' added to school and census forms. Spencer seizes on this last as the essence of the multiracial movement and the central issue for his book. He is simply mistaken. If he paid careful attention to the words of Maria Root, Reg Daniel, Carlos Fernandez, Susan Graham or Ramona Douglass – all of whom he lists in his bibliography – he would know two things:

1. While they and other multiracial activists support the check-all-that-apply option, they have much less interest in a multiracial category.
2. Census box-checking of any kind is not the highest issue on the agenda of the multiracial movement.[27]

They are more concerned with a host of other issues, from individual identity development and the dynamics of interracial families to the formation of mixed-race community institutions.

Census numbers are, however, at the top of the agenda for Spencer and some other monoracialists. They fear that, without the support of much evidence, if a multiracial option is allowed, monoracially-defined communities such as African Americans will lose numbers. Spencer writes: 'What would have happened if blacks such as Thurgood Marshall, Mary Church Terrill [*sic*], Adam Clayton Powell, Jr., and L. Douglas Wilder had been classified as multiracial rather than black? The answer is that there would have been a skimming off of tens or even hundreds of thousands of people from the black community.'[28] Daniel, Root, Douglass, and other multiracial activists have been sensitive to such concerns and supportive of the needs of America's monoracial communities of colour. Most multiracial activists recognise solidarity with their ancestral communities of color, and at the same time assert multiracial identities. Because of that sense of solidarity, they have eschewed a separate multiracial category in favour of the check-all-that-apply option, but Spencer does not notice. Spencer's construction of the issue betrays his lack of confidence in the attractions of Blackness. He seems unable to imagine an enthusiastic embrace of the Black community by a multiracial person like Lisa Jones. He assumes that anyone who could escape a monoracial Black identity would choose to do so. Therefore, we must by public agreement deny them the opportunity to choose. That Jones might note mixed ancestry and choose monoracial Blackness, or that Khanga and Haizlip might embrace multiracialism and Blackness at once is more than Spencer can fathom.

Spencer's fixation on the census question leads to the second problem with *The New Colored People*: its argument depends on unthinking adherence to a misplaced analogy between the American multiracial movement and racial politics in South Africa. He writes: 'The premise of this book is that the coloured people of South Africa and the proposed category of 'multiracial' people of the USA are parallel groups.'[29] That dubious premise is never justified, or even fully explained. Whenever Spencer encounters a rough spot in his argument against the multiracial category, he hits the default button and starts talking about South Africa. Yet he never demonstrates that the formal intermediate position of the Coloured population in apartheid-era South Africa is in fact like the fluid, multi-faceted situation of multiracial people in the USA.

A celebrated autobiography that echoes Spencer's monoracialism is an example of a special sub-genre of the biracial biography field: tales by White mothers about their lives with their Black children. Maureen Reddy, in *Crossing the Color Line*, writes evocatively of the betwixt-and-betweenness of people who marry interracially.[30] When Reddy is referred to by a friend as a White person who has assimilated into a Black community, she says: 'I don't think a White person can really assimilate; the color line doesn't work that way. I'm still White. I think I stand on the color line itself, not on one side of it. Or maybe I'm like a bridge, stretching across the line, touching both sides, but mostly in the middle somewhere.'[31] Reddy is clear that race is a social construction, not a biological fact, and she is articulate on the subject. She is sensitive to the social effects of colourism among African Americans and the negative impact on Black people of White preferences for light-skinned African Americans.

Reddy is also, and importantly, sensitive to the difficult racial dynamics her children face, dynamics for which she as a monoracial White woman believes she is not experientially well prepared. She is clear that her biracial children will be treated by most people in

American society as monoracial African Americans. She does her best to prepare her children for White racism, although she counts on her Black husband to take the lead in racial education. Reddy recounts uncomfortable stories of White incomprehension and race-baiting even in genteel upper-middle-class Providence.

This is a story well told, full of generosity, self-criticism, anti-racist fervour, and courage. But it is the story of the racial dilemma of a White mother, not of her children. There is in *Crossing the Color Line* a monoracial prescriptiveness that may not serve multiracial people so well as the author imagines. Although Reddy can critique essentialist ideas about race and lives daily in a manifestly multiracial family, in the end, like Spencer, she sees only monoracial Black and monoracial White. Thus, Reddy writes of 'Joanna, a very light-skinned black woman, who was often mistaken for White'.[32] Trapped in the binary even as she describes it with sensitivity, Reddy has no place for anyone who is not one or the other. The world of her racial analysis has no Asians, Latinos or Native Americans, and certainly no multiracial people.

Reddy expresses fear that her son will not be Black enough, and that his insufficient Blackness will reflect badly on her. When, at age six, he asserted at the dinner table that he was not just Black, but Black and White, she was thrown into a tizzy of self-doubt:

> Was Sean denying his blackness? Would he prefer to be White? What might have happened to lead him to this kind of statement? What kind of trouble was he facing down the line if he refused to see himself as black? Why wasn't he proud of his race? We'd been surrounding him with countless images of black achievement and black pride from infancy, he knew plenty of black people, we had always spoken positively about blackness ... what had gone wrong? I, in particular, was suffused with guilt and shame, perceiving Sean's assertion as an indictment of my mothering.[33]

Reddy also fretted that he and his sister did not look Black enough. All this seems part of Reddy's effort to make solidarity with African America by dethroning her own Whiteness:

> I love my children, and I have chosen to love blackness also, as I hope that Sean and Ailis will ... [T]he choice of loving blackness is open to Whites as well as to blacks ... Loving blackness is about refusing to put Whiteness at the center of everything, resisting White supremacist views of blackness, seeing the value of blackness.[34]

This is a political choice as clear and virtuous as Lisa Jones's. But is it helpful for multiracial people, or for others who are not White? Reddy does not see Asians, Native Americans, Latinos – any race besides Black and White – and she does not concede the possibility of meaningful multiraciality for people who have a Black parent. By insisting on a monoracial Black identity for her children (and by extension for other people of mixed parentage), Reddy constrains the issues and choices that may operate in their lives. Ultimately, *Crossing the Color Line* is Reddy's tale of how she deals with her own Whiteness. It is a White story, and is not particularly useful in charting a course for multiracial people.

Not Everyone is Part Black

By far the majority of the books in the biracial biography boom are about people who mix Black and White ancestries. That is odd testimony to the degree to which the Black–White encounter holds centre stage in the American racial imagination despite the presence of many other important racial dynamics. More than half the children born to a Native American parent in the 1990s also have one non-Native parent, and more than a third of Asian and Latino children also have mixed parentage. By comparison, less than 10 per cent of children with at least one Black parent are mixed. Yet the number of books on multiracial themes that address those non-Black populations is far smaller. Still, the existence of some such books reminds us that race in America is not now (nor has it ever been) about Black and White only. It is about Black and White and Red and Brown and Yellow, and multiple mixes of all of these.

Patricia Penn Hilden tells a story of her multiracial Indianness, coming of age in California and various academic outposts from the 1950s through the 1980s, in *When Nickels Were Indians*.[35] Her Indian identity is always mitigated by her blue eyes and sandy hair; her mixed blood is always Indian inflected. One striking difference from the Black–White biracial biographies surveyed above is the very different angle on race in *When Nickels Were Indians*. Penn Hilden will admit no racial binary. Chicanos, Chinese and other people of colour inhabit these pages along with Blacks, Whites and Indians. Maybe it is simply that Penn Hilden comes from the polyglot West Coast, or maybe her being Indian makes her sensitive to people who are neither White nor Black. But, unlike Gates, Spencer and Reddy, she always understands that the racial reality is multipolar.

Recent years have seen the birth of a cottage industry of scholarly writing about turn-of-the-century Chinese–British–North American writer Edith Maude Eaton (see also Chapter 5). The fullest treatment is *Sui Sin Far/Edith Maude Eaton*, a literary biography by Annette White-Parks.[36] Born in England in 1865 to a British father and Chinese–British mother, Edith Eaton came with her family to Canada when she was a young girl. She worked as a stenographer and journalist, travelled across North America and the Caribbean, and spent most of her adult years on the American West Coast. Turning to fiction as Sui Sin Far, she left a book of short stories, *Mrs Spring Fragrance*.[37] Those stories and Eaton's journalism take readers inside Chinese America, not with tales of dark and exotic Chinatowns as was the custom, but with sympathy. She portrays Chinese Americans as ordinary people with understandable emotions and aspirations. She also bends gender in stories like 'The Smuggling of Tie Co' and 'Tian Shan's Kindred Spirit'.

Unfortunately, White-Parks is less interested in the life of Edith Maude Eaton or the themes of her writing than in making points in the scholarly world of feminist literary criticism. The book is burdened with jargon and unconvincing arguments about dual fictional voices and trickster figures. Worse, White-Parks treats Eaton as a monoracial Chinese American, when Eaton manifestly lived on the White side of the line and entered Chinese America only as a sympathetic outsider. White-Parks relentlessly refuses to see the crossing of national, racial and gender boundaries that lies at the core of Sui Sin Far's fiction.

Finally, White-Parks sets up a cheap authenticity contest between Edith Eaton and her sister, Winifred Eaton Babcock.[38] Winifred was a much more successful fictionist of the same era. Where Edith took a Chinese-sounding pseudonym, Sui Sin Far, and wrote about Chinese America, Winifred adopted a Japanese-sounding pen name, Onoto Watanna, and wrote about Japan. White-Parks lauds Edith as the good sister for embracing Chineseness, and condemns Winifred as the bad sister for masking her Chineseness with another identity. She fails to recognise that both were seeking Orientalist literary identities. More important, she refuses to credit the betwixt-and-betweenness that is at the heart of the work of both these multiracial sisters.[39]

The best-seller in the multiracial Asian American bunch is *On Gold Mountain* by Lisa See.[40] This is a story not of personal identity but of family history. Lisa See grew up in and around her family's store in Los Angeles Chinatown. Her great-grandfather Fong See, an immigrant from Guangdong Province, married a White woman, Letticie Pruett, despite laws forbidding it. So did their son and grandson. Yet, despite the ever-Whitening gene pool, the pull of patriarchy and the push of White ostracism drew the family to the Chinese side. Lisa See tells the stories kept by the four See generations in America. She spreads them against the backdrop of Chinese-American history from building the railroads in the 1870s to the immigrant boat people of the 1990s. The Sees are a colourful family and their stories are memorable. The book's theme is the overwhelming importance of family.

Although Lisa See notes her generationally repeated mixedness, she chooses to assert an identity that is simply Chinese:

> Many of the Chinese I interviewed talked about Caucasians as lo fan and fan gway, as White people, 'White ghosts'. Often someone would say, by way of explanation, 'You know, she was a Caucasian like you.' They never knew how startling it was for me to hear that, because all those years in the store and going to those wedding banquets, I thought I was Chinese. It stood to reason, as all those people were my relatives. I had never really paid much attention to the fact that I had red hair like my grandmother and that the rest of them had straight black hair ... Though I don't physically look Chinese, like my grandmother, I am Chinese in my heart.[41]

Note that See's definition of Chineseness is cultural and familial, defined by how one behaves and whom one knows intimately.

Hawaii has long been advertised as a site for Asian-inflected multiracialism. The islands' intermarriage rate has been high for several generations, and people with no racial mixture by continental US measures are barely a majority in the islands. It has long been noted that the most important intergroup distinction in Hawaii is not between Hawaiian and Haole (White), Chinese and Japanese, or Korean and Filipino, although such differences are marked constantly in casual conversation. Rather, the salient difference in Hawaii is between people who are local and those who come from outside. A literary movement celebrating that distinction and promoting Pidgin, the local language, has illuminated Honolulu literary circles for some two decades. A Hawaiian word, *Hapa*, has been appropriated into Pidgin to stand for people of almost any racial mixture.[42]

Such a multicultural consciousness founded on racial mixing forms the base of Kathleen Tyau's autobiographical novel *A Little Too Much Is Enough*.[43] The main character Mahealani Wong grows towards maturity in a polyglot family, with members who are mostly this and some of that, mainly Chinese and Hawaiian, but also Haole and Japanese and Filipino. All are marked racially, but there is a fluidity to their racial identities. Mahealani is more Chinese with her Chinese relatives, more Hawaiian when with that side of the family. Everyone eats rice and pig, speaks Pidgin, knows to ask for red envelopes containing money from older Chinese relatives, uses the Japanese word for soy sauce, knows the Japanese stories of ghosts and the Hawaiian stories of volcano goddesses. If one identity prevails over the others it is Hakka Chinese, but only by a narrow margin.[44]

In all the Asian- and Native American-inflected biracial stories, unlike African American-inflected biracial stories, there is an understanding that race is multiple even when it is not mixed: that is, there are several races at work in the American scene, not just Black and White, and they have been meeting and mixing for a long time. That understanding of racial mixedness is most prominent in the biracial literature that is Latin inflected. Mexicans, Dominicans and other Latinos have long seen themselves as racially mixed peoples. The foremother of this literature is Gloria Anzaldúa. *Borderlands/La Frontera: The New Mestiza* is the ultimate expression of Hapa consciousness.[45] The mixedness extends even to the form of her writing. *Borderlands/La Frontera* is written in English and spattered with untranslated Spanish, for why should one translate Spanish? In poetry and prose it tells of Anzaldúa's childhood on the Texas–Mexico border. It also tells the story of the Mexican people as a multiracial and multicultural blend of Black, Indian and European, and of Chicanos as immigrants and first people. In *Borderlands/La Frontera,* Anzaldúa draws on a Mexican intellectual tradition celebrating *mestizaje* that goes back at least three-quarters of a century to José Vasconcellos's *La Raza Cósmica.*[46]

Interpretations

So far, this chapter and its notes have covered three dozen biographies and autobiogaphies all published in the 1990s, many times more than in any previous decade. What does this mean? Yes, there is a trend, but what does it signify?

A telephone poll of the editors who brought these books to print achieved mixed results. Some editors did not see their work as part of a multiracial trend. Ed Barber, who edited *Soul to Soul* for Norton, said he thought Khanga's was 'just the most fantastic story, the marriage of those different cultures' – Russian and African and American Jewish. At Dutton, Deborah Brody did not see *Life on the Color Line* as a mixed-race story; rather, a Black story: 'It's not so much multiracial as African American publishing. It's just taken off in the last six years or so. It took publishers a long time to realise that African Americans read books and that non-African Americans are interested in reading them. These books are really popular. They have a voyeuristic appeal.' As for *The Color of Water*, Cindy Spiegel at Riverhead Books did not mark the multiracial issue, or even particularly note the author and narrator, James McBride. Rather, it was his mother's voice that held her in a trance: 'I just fell in love with that voice. It's a weird amalgam of Yiddish, Southern, Black.'[47]

Other editors, however, did see a multiracial publishing trend. Sandy Thatcher, who edited two books on multiracial themes for Pennsylvania State University Press, talked about the growing recognition of the constructedness of race and 'the currents in a lot of disciplines now that permit blending of the analytical and the autobiographical'. Jennifer Hammer, as the editor of *The New Colored People* for New York University Press, was no friend to multiracialism, yet she saw a trend toward publishing books addressing multiraciality. Sharon Toorian at Duke University Press agreed. Even though Jane Lazarre, author of one of her multiracial autobiographies, took a monoracialist position, Toorian said of the multiracial issue: 'We just felt this can be a hot topic. A lot of people will buy it. And it just took off. People are no longer just taking what they were given. In the past these people were held in the closet, but nowadays, because so many young people are multiracial, they're being it in public and everybody has to acknowledge it ... They don't want to be called just Black or White, but both. We are all of those. Now there's room for somebody to be Black and something else.'[48]

Some might regard this publishing trend as little more than a nervous exercise in titillation. From time to time in American letters there has been a brief vogue of novels, short fiction, movies, and magazine articles exposing 'passing': racially mixed people with some African ancestry presenting themselves as unmixed Whites. Some have attributed the interest in this literature to fear on the part of some Whites that they might wake up some morning and find out the person in bed next to them is Black.[49]

Does the boom in biracial biography reflect a boom in interracial marriage? Not exactly. Intermarriage numbers for Asian–White couples increased steadily from the 1960s through the 1990s and, by century's end, a solid minority of Asians were marrying non-Asians. Black outmarriage also increased, but the numbers were still small – less than 10 per cent – although, as in other eras, interracial mating outstripped formal intermarriage between Blacks and Whites. Other sorts of intermarriages – between Latinos and Anglos, between Native Americans and non-Indians – were common, but not much more so than in previous eras. In any case, as is often noted these days, race is just a social construction anyway, and the idea of pure races is a myth discredited outside skinhead circles. Not only are Blacks a mixed multitude; so, too, are Native Americans, Chicanos and even most Asian American populations. White Americans, in fact, are not nearly so racially pure as they once believed themselves to be. Intermarriage has always been with us. Although the intermarriage numbers for certain groups rose dramatically in the last third of the twentieth century, the total number of people with a living memory of mixed heritage probably has not increased much in recent decades.[50]

So the boom in biracial biography does not reflect a sudden upsurge in the number of biracial people. But it may reflect a wide-spread recognition that people have multiple ancestries, and a concession that they are free to express them. Books have been published in this decade with titles like *Ethnic Options* and *Making Ethnic Choices*, detailing the ways that people choose among their ethnic possibilities.[51] More broadly, one may interpret the boom in biracial biography as one more evidence that the American racial category system is breaking down. Between 1950 and 1990, the US census's racial designations went from three (Negro, White, Other) to forty-three.[52] In the millennial census, respondents will be able for the first time to choose as many racial identities as they feel apply.

Granted that multiraciality is a topic of increasing interest, why do so many people choose to write autobiography rather than some other genre? Certainly, there are plenty of monoracial autobiographies. But Claudine Chiawei O'Hearn suggests that multiraciality may inevitably be autobiographical in that it is an identity that draws its life-force from fashioning and refashioning the story of the ethnic self:

> Because most people didn't know where to place me, I made up stories about myself. In bars, cabs, and restaurants I would try on identities with strangers I knew I would never meet again. I faked accents as I pretended to be a Hawaiian dancer, an Italian tourist, and even once a Russian student. It always amazed me what I could get away with. Being mixed inspired and gave me license to test new characters, but it also cast me as a foreigner in every setting I found myself in.

Every multiracial person I have gotten to know well can tell a similar story. In trying on labels and telling stories, O'Hearn reaches toward identity, 'inconstant and shifting' as she admits, but intensely meaningful nonetheless.[53]

The telling of one's ethnic story, often a story of trying on various identities, is especially important in the case of the multiracial person, who frequently operates at a point of rupture between two or more taken-for-granted identity possibilities. Autobiography – the narrative that says 'I am the person who ... ' – gives multiracial people a means of fashioning a coherent ethnic narrative for themselves. As Reg Daniel says: 'Most single racial identities are given. For multiracial people, you live your racial narrative by creating it. The created element is particularly strong in the case of multiracial people. There is an element of fictionalising to it, but it's not falseness. It is choosing the proportions and the proper fit of the various ethnic elements one possesses.'[54]

Multiplicity in a Postmodern Context

For readers, the boom in biracial biography may reflect a spreading wonderment at how to deal with all the multiplicity that surrounds them. We may surmise that an individual who lives in a context that questions the simple durability of a particular monoracial identity may experience uncertainty and fear inauthenticity. One way to cope with that uncertainty and fear is to read the stories of others in a similar situation and develop coping strategies based on their experiences along with one's own. Simply put, these books have an audience, not because there are dramatically more mixed people now, but because Americans of many racial identities have a new sense of the multiplicity around them and an interest in learning about the mixedness that is us all.

In academic circles, this impulse is found in a fascination with hybridity and categorical instability in certain poststructuralist and postcolonial circles. Homi Bhabha writes of 'cultural hybridity' as 'liminal space, in between the designations of identity ... the connective tissue that constructs the difference between upper and lower, black and white. The hither and thither ... this interstitial passage ... that entertains difference without an assumed or imposed hierarchy'. Like many of his colleagues, Bhabha is not very clear about what he means by hybridity and assumes that this amorphous mixedness is antihierarchical, revolutionary, and therefore good.[55] Pnina Werbner writes of: 'The current fascination with cultural hybridity ... the [oft-presumed] transgressive power of symbolic hybrids to subvert categorical oppositions and hence to create the conditions for cultural reflexivity and change'. Like Bhabha and most other writers, Werbner does not define what 'hybrid' means.[56] Such writers imply that hybridity confounds classification and undermines established structures of ideas and power, which, they further imply, is a good thing.

Robert Young, however, cautions us that in history – in the American adventure in the Pacific and the British imperium in Asia – powerful White people's fascination with hybridity was always an undercurrent in racial marking and the creation, not the destruction, of colonial hierarchy. In fact, Young sees White fascination with the racial and cultural hybrid, and fantasising about interracial sex, as key tools in creating and maintaining racial hierarchy. For Young, the desire for transracial sex and fascination with the hybrid are fundamental to the establishment of racial hierarchy. He refers to postmodern scholars' assumption that they are free of such thinking as 'fantasy.'[57]

Perhaps Bhabha is right: hybridity is revolutionary and necessarily overturns hierarchy; or, conversely, Young, who says hybridity is implicated in the creation of colonial hierarchy. I cannot agree fully with either. Young may be right that European hegemonists fantasised about interracial sex, but I do not see multiracial people at the heart of colonial oppression. And Bhabha's and Werbner's assertions that hybridity overturns hierarchy are just that: assertions. In any case, neither Young nor Bhabha is very clear about what he means by hybridity. Nonetheless, their postmodern musings on hybridity bring us back to the difference between Henry Louis Gates's take on Anatole Broyard as modern man and my own view of Broyard as incipiently postmodern. Gates saw in him a Black man passing as White, and wrote: 'The thematic elements of passing – fragmentation, alienation, liminality, self-fashioning – echo the great themes of modernism.'[58] I see in Broyard, and in the other multiracial figures described here, mixed individuals choosing among bouquets of racial possibilities, not without political consequences, but in full knowledge of their situations. I see in Broyard and the literature of multiraciality the themes of postmodernism: constructedness, contingency, paradox, multiplicity.

The Hapa, the multiracial person, then, may be the acme of a postmodernist age. The biracial biography publishing trend may reflect a transition in the reading public's mind from the stable categorical thinking of the modern era to the multi-faceted and contingent thinking of the postmodern.

Notes

1. Some of the observations and insights written here first came from the minds of Reg Daniel, Naomi Spickard, Laurie Mengel, Patrick Miller and the students of Asian American Studies 137 at the University of California, Santa Barbara. Thanks.

2. Danzy Senna, 'The Mulatto Millennium', in Claudine Chiawei O'Hearn (ed.), *Half and Half: Writers on Growing Up Biracial and Bicultural* (New York: Pantheon, 1998), p.12.
3. Nancy G. Brown and Ramona E. Douglass, 'Making the Invisible Visible: The Growth of Community Network Organizations', in M. Root (ed.), *The Multiracial Experience* (Thousand Oaks, Calif.: Sage, 1996), pp.323–40.
4. Becky Thompson and Sangeeta Tyagi (eds), *Names We Call Home: Autobiography on Racial Identity* (New York: Routledge, 1996); Stephen Cornell and Douglass Hartmann, *Ethnicity and Race: Making Identities in a Changing World* (Thousand Oaks, Calif.: Pine Forge Press, 1997).
5. M. Root (ed.), *The Multiracial Experience* (Thousand Oaks, Calif.: Sage, 1996); M. Root (ed.), *Racially Mixed People in America* (Newbury Park, Calif.: Sage, 1992).
6. For a fairly comprehensive listing of biracial biographies and other 'interracial literature' before the 1990s, see Werner Sollors, *Neither Black Nor White Yet Both: A Thematic Analysis of Interracial Literature* (New York: Oxford, 1997), pp.361–94.
7. Few are talking about mixedness in themselves that is based on interracial mating that took place further back in family history, in the manner of W.E.B. Du Bois in *Dusk of Dawn* (New Brunswick, N.J.: Transaction, 1997 [1940]). One exception to that rule is Adrian Piper, 'Passing for White, Passing for Black', in *Transition* 58 (1992), 4–32.
8. Gregory Howard Williams, *Life on the Color Line* (New York: Dutton, 1995).
9. *Ibid*, pp.32–4.
10. *Ibid*, p.182.
11. Cf. Mika Tanner, 'Mirror Mirror On the Wall', *Rafu Shimpo* (March 1998), 1, 4.
12. Lisa Jones, *Bulletproof Diva: Tales of Race, Sex, and Hair* (New York: Doubleday, 1994).
13. *Ibid*, pp.31, 32, 202.
14. Henry Louis Gates, Jr, 'White Like Me', in *New Yorker* (17 June 1996), pp.66–81.
15. *Ibid*, p.78.
16. *Ibid*, p.75.
17. Paul R. Spickard, *Mixed Blood: Intermarriage and Ethnic Identity in Twentieth-Century America* (Madison: University of Wisconsin Press, 1989), pp.329–39; Judith R. Berzon, *Neither Black Nor White: The Mulatto Character in American Fiction* (New York: New York University Press, 1978).
18. Kathryn Talalay, *Composition in Black and White: The Life of Philippa Schuyler* (New York: Oxford, 1995).
19. See also Lori Andrews, *Black Power, White Blood: The Life and Times of Johnny Spain* (New York: Pantheon, 1996); Danzy Senna, *Caucasia* (New York: Riverhead, 1998).
20. Shirlee Taylor Haizlip, *The Sweeter the Juice: A Family Memoir in Black and White* (New York: Simon and Schuster, 1994).

21. *Ibid*, pp.8, 16.
22. Lawrence W. Levine, *Black Culture and Black Consciousness* (New York: Oxford, 1976), p.288.
23. Shirlee Taylor Haizlip, *The Sweeter the Juice: A Family Memoir in Black and White* (New York: Simon and Schuster, 1994), p.248.
24. Lise Funderburg, *Black, White, Other: Biracial Americans Talk About Race and Identity* (New York: Morrow, 1994). In some cases, the mixing took place in an earlier generation.
25. *Ibid*, pp.192, 319.
26. Jon Michael Spencer, *The New Colored People* (New York: New York University Press, 1997). Some parts of the analysis presented here appeared in my review of *Neither Black Nor White Yet Both* and *The New Colored People* in the *Journal of American Ethnic History*, 18.2 (1999), pp.153–6.
27. M. Root, 'Within, Between, and Beyond Race', in *Racially Mixed People in America* (Newbury Park, Calif.: Sage, 1992); G. Reginald Daniel, 'Beyond Black and White: The New Multiracial Consciousness', in *Racially Mixed People*; Carlos Fernandez, 'Government Classification of Multiracial/Multiethnic People', in M. Root (ed.), *The Multiracial Experience* (Thousand Oaks, Calif.: Sage, 1996), pp.15–36; Susan Graham, 'The Real World', in *The Multiracial Experience*, pp.37–48; Nancy G. Brown and Ramona E. Douglass, 'Making the Invisible Visible: The Growth of Community Network Organizations', in *The Multiracial Experience*. For a fuller account of this movement, see G. Reginald Daniel, *Multiracial Identity in the New Millennium* (Philadelphia: Temple University Press, forthcoming).
28. Jon Michael Spencer, *The New Colored People* (New York: New York University Press, 1997), p.84.
29. *Ibid*, p.11.
30. Maureen T. Reddy, *Crossing the Color Line: Race, Parenting, and Culture* (New Brunswick, N.J.: Rutgers University Press, 1994). See also Jane Lazarre, *Beyond the Whiteness of Whiteness: Memoir of a White Mother of Black Sons* (Durham, N.C.: Duke University Press, 1996).
31. Reddy, *Crossing the Color Line*, p.5.
32. *Ibid*, p.77.
33. *Ibid*, p.68.
34. *Ibid*, p.172–3.
35. Patricia Penn Hilden, *When Nickels Were Indians: An Urban, Mixed-Blood Story* (Washington: Smithsonian Institution Press, 1995). See also Janet Campbell Hale, *Bloodlines: Odyssey of a Native Daughter* (New York: Random House, 1993); William S. Penn (ed.), *As We Are Now: Mixblood Essays on Race and Identity* (Berkeley: University of California Press, 1997); Drew Hayden Taylor *Funny You Don't Look Like One: Observations from a Blue-Eyed Ojibway*, revised ed. (Penticton, B.C.: Theytus Books, 1998).
36. Annette White-Parks, *Sui Sin Far/Edith Maude Eaton* (Urbana: University of Illinois Press, 1995). See also Amy Ling, 'Pioneers and Paradigms: The

Eaton Sisters', in Ling, *Between Worlds: Women Writers of Chinese Ancestry* (New York: Pergamon, 1990), pp.21–55.

37. Sui Sin Far, *Mrs Spring Fragrance and Other Writings*, Amy Ling and Annette White-Parks (eds), (Urbana: University of Illinois Press, 1995 [1912]).
38. White-Parks follows Ling, 'Pioneers and Paradigms'; S. E. Solberg, 'Sui Sin Far/Edith Eaton: First Chinese-American Fictionist', in *MELUS*, 8 (Spring 1981), pp.27–39; Jeffrey Paul Chan and Frank Chin, Lawson Fusao Inada and Shawn Wong (eds), *The Big Aiiieee!* (New York: Meridian, 1991), p.111.
39. Winifred Eaton, *Me: A Book of Remembrance* (Jackson: University Press of Mississippi, 1997 [New York: Century, 1915]).
40. Lisa See, *On Gold Mountain: The One-Hundred-Year Odyssey of my Chinese-American Family* (New York: Vintage, 1995). See also Aimee E. Liu, *Face* (New York: Time-Warner, 1994); Heinz Insu Fenkl, *Memories of My Ghost Brother* (New York: Penguin, 1996); and Patricia Justiniani McReynolds, *Almost Americans* (Santa Fe: Red Crane Books, 1997).
41. See, *On Gold Mountain*, p.xx.
42. Eric Yamamoto, 'The Significance of Local', in Peter Manicas (ed.), *Social Process in Hawai'i: A Reader* 2nd edn (New York: McGraw-Hill, 1995), pp.138–50; Jonathan Okamura, 'Why There Are No Asian Americans in Hawai'i: The Continuing Significance of Local', in Manicas (ed.), *Social Process*, pp.243–57; Paul Spickard and Rowena Fong, 'Pacific Islander Americans and Multiethnicity', in *Social Forces*, 73 (1995), pp.1365–83.
43. Kathleen Tyau, *A Little Too Much Is Enough* (New York: Norton, 1996).
44. See also Carolyn Lei-lanilau, *Ono-Ono Girl's Hula* (Madison: University of Wisconsin Press, 1997); Teja Arboleda, *In the Shadow of Race* (Mahwah, N.J.: Lawrence Erlbaum Associates, 1998).
45. Gloria Anzaldúa, *Borderlands/La Frontera: The New Mestiza* (San Francisco: Aunt Lute Books, 1987).
46. José Vasconcellos, *La Raza Cósmica/The Cosmic Race* (Los Angeles: Department of Chicano Studies, California State University, 1979 [1925]).
47. Ed Barber, W.W. Norton and Company, New York, interviewed by the author, 28 January 1998; Deborah Brody, Dutton, New York, interviewed by the author, 28 January 1998; Cindy Spiegel, Riverhead Books, New York, interviewed by the author, 15 January 1998.
48. Sandy Thatcher, Pennsylvania State University Press, State University, Penn., interviewed by the author, 15 January 1998; Sharon Toorian, Duke University Press, Durham, N.C., interviewed by the author, 15 January 1998; Jennifer Hammer, New York University Press, interviewed by the author, 15 January 1998.
49. Paul R. Spickard, *Mixed Blood: Intermarriage and Ethnic Identity in Twentieth-Century America* (Madison: University of Wisconsin Press, 1989), p.329–39; James E. Conyers, 'Selected Aspects of the Phenomenon of Negro Passing' (PhD. diss., Washington State University, 1962).

50. Spickard, *Mixed Blood*; Larry Hajime Shinagawa and Gin Yong Pang, 'Asian American Panethnicity and Intermarriage', *Amerasia Journal*, 22.2 (1996), pp.127–52.
51. Mary C. Waters, *Ethnic Options* (Berkeley: University of California Press, 1990); Karen I. Leonard, *Making Ethnic Choices* (Philadelphia: Temple University Press, 1992).
52. Paul Spickard, Rowena Fong and Patricia L. Ewalt, 'A Multiracial Reality: Issues for Social Work', *Social Work*, 40:6 (1995).
53. Claudine Chiawei O'Hearn, 'Introduction', in O'Hearn (ed.), *Half and Half: Writers on Growing Up Biracial and Bicultural* (New York: Pantheon, 1998), p.ix.
54. G. Reginald Daniel, private communication with the author, Goleta, Calif., 8 June 1999. See also Daniel, 'From Race to Metarace: A Personal Odyssey Through the Twilight Zone', in Ken Wilber (ed.), *Kindred Visions*, (Boston: Shambhala, 1999).
55. Homi Bhabha, *The Location of Culture* (New York: Routledge, 1994), p.4; also pp.7, 13, 38, 114, 118, etc. Bhabha takes off from M.M. Bakhtin's work on linguistic hybridisation in *The Dialogic Imagination*, trans. Caryl Emerson and Michael Holquist (Austin: University of Texas Press, 1981), esp. p.358ff.
56. Pnina Werbner, 'Introduction: The Dialectics of Cultural Hybridity', in *Debating Cultural Hybridity*, ed. Pnina Werbner and Tariq Modood (London: Zed, 1997), pp.1–26. Werbner sees the contradiction, and attempts to resolve it by presenting hybridity not as an item or an attribute but as a process.
57. Robert J.C. Young, *Colonial Desire: Hybridity in Theory, Culture and Race* (New York: Routledge, 1995), pp.180–82.
58. Henry Louis Gates, Jr, 'White Like Me', in *New Yorker* (17 June 1996), pp.75.

5

Triples – The Social Evolution of a Multiracial Panethnicity: An Asian American Perspective[1]

Laurie M. Mengel

The Arbitrariness of Race

It is commonly accepted today that race is a social and not a biological construct. Once based on a pseudoscientific notion of biology, race is now realised to be a grouping of dissimilar peoples by those in power to impose a social and economic hierarchical structure based on skin tone and country of origin.[2] The construction of Whiteness emerged from groups previously considered separate to create a commonality in opposition to those deemed inferior.[3]

The boundaries between racial groups have been historically defined according to the conveniences and political and economic advantages of the dominant group. Arbitrary geographical boundaries are often used to distinguish between the races, regardless of a common culture or group identification. This process not only lumps together groups that would consider themselves distinct and separate, such as the Punti and the Hakka, or Naichi and Okinawan, not only as Chinese and Japanese respectively, but as Asians, inclusively, and differentiates them from Haitians and Ethiopians, for example, who are lumped together as Black. The geographical dividing line, while sometimes uniting separate peoples and land bodies, can alternately run through continents. In 1995 the category 'Black', according to the US Office of Management and Budget's Directive 15, encompassed anyone 'having origins in the Black racial groups of Africa' – peoples who consider themselves separate and distinct – but excluded people from North Africa, who were considered White.[4]

Race, however seemingly arbitrary, continues to play an important role in the lives of Americans. The statement 'race isn't real – racism is' is commonly held to be true.[5] Nevertheless, Michael Omi and Howard

Winant point out that, as with gender, race is one of the first things observed in meeting a person. Racial identity is so integral to this society, they assert, that without a racial designation one is left without a complete identity.[6]

This chapter explores the evolution of the social groupings of people of mixed racial descent in the USA. Much of the contemporary literature on mixed race identity is focused on the duality of hybridity. In this model, people of two or more racial groupings are said to be able to embrace, and be embraced by, both (or more) of his or her racial communities. Adherence to this theory would suggest that a mixed race person of Japanese American and Irish American descent, for example, could participate and identify with both ethnic communities, and thus possess a racial identity that is both White and Asian. Yet this theorising of mixed identity does not explain the growing association of mixed race people on the basis of mixedness *per se*.

The life experiences and histories of mixed race people do not adhere to the racial constructions defined by dominant groups. Instead, as this paper's title suggests, their experience is more accurately expressed as 'triple', for it reveals the existence of a 'third space' which multiracial people inhabit.[7] This third space recognises mixedness as a panethnic link between people, which is different from linkages between mixed race people and monoracials who share a common ancestry.

The study of race, to paraphrase Frantz Fanon, must inherently be interdisciplinary, and this paper necessarily reflects this perspective.[8] I therefore draw on such disciplines as philosophy, sociology and literature. The voices, observations and life experiences of multiracial people will be analysed through literary references and gathered data.

Fractional Representation of Mixed Race People

Mixed race people of all backgrounds and histories have tended to have similar characteristics attributed to them. The most common designation imposed on mixed race people of all ancestries is the inference that they are fragmented beings. Words such as 'mulatto' and 'octoroon' have referred to those having origins in Africa, while for Native Americans, 'mixblood' or 'half-breed' is more commonly used. In Latin America, and among US Latinos, 'mestizo' refers to Indian/White mixes. For those with mixed origins among Asians, the Hawaiian derived 'Hapa' is used, or, for those with roots in Japan, 'Haafu' (both generally meaning 'half'). Regardless of the reference, however, all of these terms perpetuate notions of blood division that can be quantified in fractional terms, and, in a race-conscious society, serve to reinforce the ideology that the mixed race individual is somehow less than a whole person.

Based on their mixedness, mixed race people of all combinations have been subjected to these representations (see Chapter 1). Pathologies of ill-fitting body parts and psychological deviancy have been attributed to the alleged incompatibility of different racial types coursing throughout a fragmented body. At the height of America's eugenics movement in the late 1920s, for example, Harvard University President Francis Graham Crookshank proposed a theory to explain why a White couple would give birth to a Down's Syndrome child. Somewhere in the couple's ancestry, he concluded, miscegenation between a 'Mongol' and a 'Caucasian' must have taken place, resulting in the birth of a mutant baby orangutan.[9] Although this type of 'science' is now considered absurd, and its social consequences entirely discredited, especially following the German holocaust, the representation of all mixed race people as ill-fitting and fractional continues.[10]

The references to mixed race people cited above tend to express what percentage of a person is 'of colour'. For example, 'half-breed' refers to the half that is Indian, 'octoroon' refers to the one-eighth of Black blood, and so on. In this way, the notions of Whiteness as normative and being a person of colour as deviant or pathological are perpetuated. Moreover, because Whiteness is a racial construction based on notions of unalloyed purity, by definition, mixed race people cannot be White.[11]

Yet, the historical reduction of whole people into terms representative of pieces and parts subjects the mixed race person to questions about ethnic authenticity within some communities of colour.[12] A person of Japanese and Irish origins, for example, might elicit responses such as, 'What part of you is Japanese – your big toe?'[13] from a monoracial member of a Japanese American community.[14] Comments such as this, along with the fractional terminology, not only challenge a person's full membership in a community of colour, but they also reinforce pseudoscientific ideas about distinct biological racial components that may be separated out within a person's anatomy. In other words, if only a toe is Japanese, the rest of the body must be rendered suspect. Fractionalising blood, then, precludes Whiteness, yet simultaneously prohibits full inclusion within the perimeters of some monoracial groups of colour.[15]

Newer scholarship has done much to challenge this type of thinking. Mixed race people are now understood to be complete individuals, and encouraged to participate fully, and identify wholly, in both or more of their racial or ethnic heritages. 'Doubles' is a term that is used to illustrate this growing awareness of a possible multiracial identification with, and perceived standing in, both (or more) of his or her racial communities and heritages.[16] However, even this term, and the ideas that accompany it, are inadequate in addressing the complexities of mixed race experiences. This 'embraced by both' ideology posits Whiteness as an ethnic grouping, rather than as the top rung of a hierarchical system of power, and ignores forms of racial antagonism stemming from communities of colour. Put simply, the 'embraced by both' ideology suggests that an individual can easily pick and choose their ethnic affiliations and be embraced by various ethnic groups unproblematically.

Although community dynamics regarding racial mixture differ according to group, time, and place, this essay mainly looks at the way in which racial mixture functions from the perspective of people with some degree of Asian ancestry in the USA.

Asian American Panethnicity

People from different locations, classes and histories acknowledge the importance of racial groupings, not only for identity, but also for political representation. Many people within the Asian racial grouping object to the term 'Asiatic', but politically and socially unite within the panethnic category 'Asian' in opposition to the dominant racist discourse. In the USA, the category 'Asian American' includes diverse groups of people, including Japanese, Chinese, Korean, Indian and Vietnamese, and others.

Yen Le Espiritu defines Asian American panethnicity as evolving from the 'racialization of Asian national groups by dominant groups, as well as in response to those constructions by Asian Americans themselves.' She further states that by 'adopting the dominant group's categorization of them, Asian Americans have instituted pan-Asianism as their political instrument – thereby enlarging their own capabilities to challenge and transform the existing structure of power'.[17] Lisa Lowe identifies the locus of Asian Americans, the defining point that unites different people into a single grouping, through the Asian-specific exclusion policies of US immigration. That Asians have been, and continue to be, defined as 'immigrant' or 'alien', juxtaposed to the White 'citizen', is, according to Lowe, the defining characteristic of the pan Asian American experience.[18]

The grouping of a people as different from the majority, based on imposed racial boundaries, creates political alliances. This has expressed itself in Asian American and pan Asian political groups such as the Asian Law Caucus and the Asian Immigrant Workers Association, both located in San Francisco. Regardless of distinct ethno-national backgrounds, Asian Americans are treated as being racially similar, as demonstrated by anti-Asian hate crimes and typified by the murder of Vincent Chin in 1982. Vincent Chin, a Chinese American, was brutally beaten and killed by disgruntled White auto workers in Detroit, who targeted all Asians and Asian Americans for the success of the Japanese auto industry. Chin's murderers justified their crime on the grounds that they thought he was Japanese. This heinous crime illustrates the perception of the interchangeability of all Asians by the dominant group, and it became a rallying call to Asian Americans.

This panethnic unity and identification is expressed in many ways, including a dramatic rise in interethnic marriage within the Asian American community,[19] and fourth-generation Americans of Japanese ancestry rushing home to watch, and identify with, *American Girl* – a now defunct television sitcom revolving around an immigrant Korean family. In sum, people who are similarly racialised by a dominant group who seek to maintain and justify their subordination may organise themselves within a panethnic grouping in order to challenge and resist structures of domination.

In this essay, I examine the parallels between the formation of multiracial panethnicity and Asian American panethnic formation, although comparisons with other panethnic groups can also be made. Both Asian Americans and multiracial people are comprised of dissimilar peoples with differing linguistic, cultural, geographical, and historical interactions, and yet they are seen as having similar characteristics to one another. Furthermore, as in the case of many mixed race people, questions of ethnic authenticity and group belonging are often integral to the experiences encountered by Asian Americans.

The primary sources for this research are derived from fifty interviews and survey responses taken in Los Angeles in 1997 – at a Nisei week celebration in Little Tokyo, at a Multiracial rally, an Asian-descent mixed race Internet group, and from responses taken from university mixed race groups in Rhode Island.

Political Organisations

Political organisations rallying around a mixed race identity in the US began to emerge in the 1970s. Unlike the Asian American panethnic groups, these new groupings were overwhelmingly initiated by monoracial Whites and, however unwittingly, served to impose a White agenda upon multiracial people.

After the Supreme Court overturned anti-miscegenation laws (in the case Loving *v.* Virginia) in 1967, some Whites began to enter into romantic relationships with people of colour, in a way that had not been socially or legally permitted previously.[20] Racisms which such White people had previously been able to ignore now entered their bedrooms and living rooms, and they were ill-equipped to deal with the repercussions. In an effort to combat this type of racism, these White people began forming interracial social and political groups, in which White people romantically involved in interracial relationships could get together and locate commonalities and establish political agendas. It is important to distinguish these groups, which I refer to as *interracial*, from groups initiated by mixed race people, which I refer to as *multiracial*. These interracial groups tended to create and propagate a monoracial agenda, frequently subordinating the voices and experiences of mixed race people.

Nancy Brown and Ramona Douglass document the largest six multiracial organisations.[21] They chronicle the founders and purposes of I-Pride in San Francisco, The Biracial Family Network of Chicago, The Interracial Family Circle of Washington DC, Multiracial Americans of Southern California (MASC), PROJECT RACE (Reclassify All Children Equally) in Georgia and the Association of Multiethnic Americans (AMEA) in Berkeley, California. Of these groups, four were primarily what the authors refer to as 'support groups', while two, PROJECT RACE and AMEA, were politically based. The latter two political organisations grew from the need to accurately record mixed race people on school, medical, employment, state and federal forms requiring racial accounting.

Of the six groups, only two (I-Pride and AMEA) were initiated by people of mixed race to respond to and express their experiences. The remaining four groups were founded mainly by monoracial White women, who were in interracial marriages and who had difficulties in dealing with the racism they encountered. While support groups for monoracial people learning how to cope with their interracial dating and marriage choices may be helpful for some, there is little commonality between such organisations and those established for the needs of mixed race people. The life experiences of a mixed race person, and his or her choices, experiences and world views, encompass significant complexities that cannot be addressed solely by issues concerning relationships between Whites and monoracial people of colour.

The 'You Are Both' Fiction

Much of the rhetoric espoused by monoracials in the interracial groups discussed above revolved around the construction of a dual identity for the multiracial person. Intended to confront the 'choose one' categorisation in the US census (as dictated by the Office of Management and Budget's Directive 15), monoracial parents began advocating a 'you are both' philosophy. In this model of racial utopia, a multiracial person could embrace, and be embraced by, both (or more) of his or her heritages, and in the process become a bridge for monoracial groups to come together with greater understanding. However welcoming this idea might be to some, it is overly simplistic and confuses race – which is an ideology that upholds a power hierarchy – with cultural heritage.

By disregarding the power discrepancies and privileges of racial assignment and meaning, advocates of the 'you are both' fiction revealed their motivations to be personally self-serving. Rather than attempting to understand and address the complexities of ethnic identity for mixed race people, many White parents imposed their choices of identification on their multiracial children. One Black/White woman remembered finding a positive racial identity through James Brown's song 'Say it Loud, I'm Black and I'm Proud'. Her White mother revealed her own self-absorption with regard to her daughter's racial identity by reprimanding, 'Why do you have to refer to yourself that way? Calling yourself black makes me feel like I'm invisible. Like I don't exist. Like I don't count.'[22] The mother here appears to be more concerned with her inclusion in her daughter's identity, than in the evolution of her daughter's identity, or her daughter's understanding of race in a racist society.

Following the lead of various interracial groups, some White women began to write about their experiences in 'crossing the colour line.'[23] Maureen Reddy and Jane Lazarre exemplify the trend of monoracial Whites who act as the authorities for mixed race folks. Lazarre, a White woman married to a Black man, writes that she is 'an ex-white person',[24] explaining that by giving birth and awakening to a racial consciousness: 'I am no longer white … I am a person of color now.' Reddy, also married to a Black man, relates a story in which her first-grade [first year in primary school] son comes home from school proclaiming a Native American identity. Like many other mixed race people, it appears that her son is articulating an identity that is neither White, nor Black, but positioned somewhere between the two, and in a grouping all of its own. His mother, however, is appalled at this choice. 'Another crisis!' she exclaims, and reflects: 'I wonder how much of this desire to be "special" was rooted in a wish to be "not black".' Not only does she not interrogate the possibility that he might be choosing to be 'not White' (or recognises his social inability to be White), she cannot fathom the notion of an altogether different ethnic identity, and condescendingly refers to this action as his 'need to be special'.[25]

Other mixed race people, like Reddy's son, have employed similar methods to articulate an awareness of a third space. For example, in the late 1800s, sisters Winifred Eaton Babcock and Edith Maude Eaton, writers of Chinese and English origins, adopted, respectively, the *noms de plumes* of Onoto Watanna and Sui Sin Far. Both of these pen names are clearly playing with oriental-sounding names – one Japanese, and one Chinese.[26] A separate space is invented to address this third-ness. Watanna's choice to adopt a fictitious Japanese name (her name choice is 'Japanese-sounding' but entirely made up), reveals her identification with being in-between, rather than having any real affinity to Japanese or Japanese-American culture. Like Reddy's son, Watanna is articulating a third space.

Organisations, such as RACE (Reclassify All Children Equally), Multi Racial Family and Youth Network, Interracial Family Support Network, BRANCH (Biracial and Natural Children), Child International, Interracial Family Circle, Society for Interracial Families and countless others bearing similar names, are cited as the authorities on matters of racial mixedness. Yet these organisations do not seem to have a place for the person who is not overly concerned with parent/child issues. Single people without children, gay people without children, attached people who choose not to have children and adults who are at either pre- or post-childrearing stages, do not seem to have a place in these organisations. Nor are the experiences of mixed race people who were not raised in heterosexual, dual-biological parent-nuclear families addressed in these organisations.

While some of the work done by White monoracials has given some mixed race people the tools and vocabularies from which to work and explore a collective voice, these organisations all characterise multiracial individuals as voiceless, disempowered, unformed persons – children – who need the authority of a White monoracial adult to speak for them. As a historical grouping of people who have shared similar histories of racial formations and exclusion, they have existed since the idea of 'race' was formulated. They have existed despite anti-miscegenation laws. These family-oriented groups reinforce the ideologies of nuclear families as normative, and mixed race people as children – further marginalising both mixed race people and all people who are not part of such familial systems.

Monoracials privileged by Whiteness and who have 'crossed the colour line', then, may not be the best authority to represent those who *are* the colour line. R. Radhakrishnan describes the first American-born Asian Indian generation as being caught up in a similar 'you are both' fallacy. They are not 'really' Indian as they have never been to India, yet are not perceived as American due to skin colour (not White) and 'cultural behaviors' that are not perceived as American (not White).[27]

Monoracial parents may experience racially motivated antagonism due to their relationships with other (racially different) monoracials. However, the parents of the mixed race individual, unless multiracial themselves, simply cannot be the authorities through which this shared history can be passed. Put simply, two monoracial experiences do not a multiracial experience make.

Acceptance from Monoracial Minorities?

Being seen as 'not really American' is similar to many multiracial people's experiences of their ethnic authenticity and membership being questioned within communities of colour. Perhaps because Asian American panethnicity developed in response to White oppression, their collective act of unity and resistance can be partly manifest in hostility toward the 'White blood' coursing through the veins of the multiracial of White and Asian ancestry – whether or not they have any access to White privilege. If a mixed race Asian American has ancestry in non-White, non-Asian groupings, they may be similarly denied acceptance, due to the perceived inferior status of these groups.[28]

Having access to a community, usually through the associations of parents, appears to be vastly different from being perceived as a full member of that community. One survey respondent replied: 'I don't feel that I can ever be fully and completely accepted by one ethnicity or the other of my heritage[s]. There will always be someone who will find fault in the fact that I am only half, and can never be as "ethnic" as someone who is full.' Several respondents explained that their relatives considered them as being primarily of one race – but always the one that that family member was not. A Korean–Scottish woman wrote: 'I feel that both sides of the family seem to regard me as a member of the opposite race.' A woman of Spanish and Japanese descent confirmed that her family viewed her as primarily monoracial, but 'always as the other' race.

When historically antagonistic groups, such as the Koreans and Japanese, unite under the umbrella of panethnic Asian resistance, they can exclude the multiracial person with ancestry outside the racial grouping – sometimes with brutal results. A college student's experiences typify, with a degree of horror, the repercussions of such exclusion.

Ron, a mixed race person of Japanese and White American ancestry described his experiences in Japantown, San Francisco, one night after an evening of karaoke.[29] Wearing a fuku charm on his necklace, he left the club at about 4:30a.m. with some friends and subsequently encountered some acquaintances – one of Indonesian descent, one Chinese and one Vietnamese.[30] Ron described his experience in an Internet posting this way:

> [They] decided that I shouldn't be wearing [the charm] because I don't even know what it means [they said]. They just saw I wasn't full Asian ... I don't know if they thought I was Latino or what, but my friend told them I was half Japanese. This didn't matter though, they didn't like my presence there [because] I don't have jet black hair [and] eyes that are as slanted as theirs.

As Ron made his way to his car, the men tore off his necklace and began to brutally attack him. Later, sitting in his hospital room, Ron articulately summed up the experiences and voices of many mixed race people:

> This happened in Japantown. The place where I have felt the most comfortable. I am Japanese and I have a right to do whatever I want to, especially to wear my necklace. I have heard just about every derogatory, oppressive, and offensive comment from just about every full Asian or Pacific Islander person that I have ever met, and these people are usually supposed to be my 'friends'. Many ask me 'why do you want to be a Real Japanese so bad?' Ya know, I don't want to be anything. I am who I am. My culture that I have grown up with is Japanese American. What the hell am I supposed to do? I can't be White. I have had White people start fights with me because they think I am Mexican. I can't be full Japanese [because] shit like this happens to me all the time. I can't be Latino [because] I'm not Latino. I'm Hapa. But barely anybody I talk to knows what that is. And anyway, when I am myself – doing many Japanese things – people criticize me and say that I can't do that – I am only trying to be Japanese.

Ron's authenticity as a Japanese American or Asian American is challenged by the taint of White blood:

> This girl always asks me why I am in the Japan Club. She says that I am not Japanese and that I shouldn't be in it. She herself is mixed Malaysian and Chinese, but since she has black hair and slanted eyes, she feels that she has more of a right to be in the club than me. Then there are my friends who hang out with me when I am by myself, but when they get around [other] Asian people, they don't talk to me. When I sit next to them, even though I know all of them well, they stop talking and look at me awkwardly.

The Malaysian/Chinese woman's participation in the Japanese club, although she has no Japanese roots, demonstrates her inclusion within a monoracial Asian American identity and allows her to feel a right to membership in a panethnic organisation – to the exclusion and ostracism of Ron, who is Japanese American. In doing so, she perpetuates notions of 'right to membership' based on blood quantum and phenotype, rather than equal citizenry, and in effect upholds racial ideologies. That her parents have ancestry in two distinct ethnic groupings (Malaysian and Chinese) is insignificant. The common racial umbrella under which they fall (Asian) is sufficient to validate her membership and authenticity in the Japanese club and other similarly race-based communities and organisations. While in White America, Ron's Asian blood prevents him being White, in Asian America, his White blood prevents him being Asian.

Ron's story and experience is not unlike that experienced by many mixed race people within their racial/ethnic minority communities.[31] Their access to a minority community is often limited and their membership in the group tends to be conditional, based on a strict adherence to social rules that apply differently for mixed race individuals and for monoracial individuals (though there can also be similar pressures which bear on both multiracial and mononracial individuals). Survey responses taken in California, Rhode Island, and through a mixed race Internet list server, showed that 45 per cent of people who had families participating in monoracial minority communities and organisations did not feel accepted by these groups. One respondent replied that acceptance 'depends on the situation'. In order to maintain access to minority communities, whether or not it is the only community the mixed race person has known, the mixed race person must suppress his feelings about his experiences of racial antagonism and rejection. Venting his anger, and exposing the intra-group racism, would violate social codes and prohibit his inclusion within that community. He is thus forced to choose between expressing his sense of injustice about his treatment by some monoracial minorities (and thus endangering his ties with them), and remaining silent to maintain an allegiance with monoracial minorities.

While Ron is unable to be 'fully white' in the USA or 'fully Asian' in Asian America, it is also likely that the same people who tormented him about his claim to Japanese identity and heritage would have subjected him to racial slurs, such as 'banana' and 'whitewashed', if he had joined a 'White' group. It is also likely that his 'Japaneseness' would have had to be concealed in a White group as well. This dual silencing reinforces feelings of dishonesty and 'passing'. As purportedly inauthentic and suspected members of their own families, neighbourhoods and communities, the Asian-White person is often compelled to demonstrate their authenticity and encounters continual challenges to their claims to group membership.

Multiracial Collectivity

Multiracials have been grouping themselves in spite of, and because of, the marginalisation resulting from the dominant White society, interracial groups and monoracial minority communities. In response to the similarities in treatment, policies, voicelessness and stereotypes attributed to mixed race people through common racial constructions and exclusions, individuals of different ethnic backgrounds, interests and political affiliations began to organise around the issue of multiraciality.

Many of these collectives began in universities. Classes like 'People of Mixed Racial Descent', held as a result of student demand at the University of California at Berkeley, continue to be some of the most requested elective courses, often holding waiting lists of three hundred students. Multiracial groups, by, for and about multiracial people continue to crop up on college campuses across the nation, such as Students of Mixed Heritage (Santa Cruz, California); Hapa Issues Forum (Berkeley, California); and Brown University's Organisation for Multiracial and Biracial students (Providence, Rhode Island).

While some of these groups have defined political agendas, they are not based on any one political agenda, but on the basis of being multiracial. Many groups choose not to organise on a political level, but unite purely for social purposes. One leader of an east coast multiracial group laments: '[The members] seem to run from anything remotely political! All they want to do is sit around and talk and eat!'[32] In this group, the members are all multiracial, but come from a diversity of racial backgrounds. Some are interested in ethnic studies, some in engineering. Some come from families of class privilege, some are the first generation in their families to obtain a college education. They also come from widely varying geographical locations. Yet they socialise collectively on the basis of a multiracial experience.

Through the evolution of a group consciousness, which may be described as a 'third space', we can locate common processes of group formation for those of mixed racial descent. In this collective space, multiracial people can relieve themselves of their oppressive 'two-ness'[33] in favour of wholeness. Based on the commonality of being multiracial, and also transcending racial boundaries, these people are choosing to construct a new grouping to define themselves and to spend their social energies.

The lack of access to, or knowledge of, multiracial organisations does not prevent people from grouping themselves among other mixed race people. Certain groups, although traditionally defined in terms of a single racial category are, in fact, comprised of multiracial people with a history of multiraciality. Filipinos, for example, have a 400-year history of racial mixing, although they have now been racialised into a singular group.[34] The same can be applied to many Latino, Native American and Pacific Islander groups.[35] Racially mixed people whose ancestry is not apparent are frequently assumed to be a member of one of these traditionally mixed, but singularly racialised, groups.[36] Conversely, some mixed race people with or without a distinct mixed race community or vocabulary sometimes gravitate towards these racially mixed but singularly labelled groupings. By doing so, they seem to be seeking a shared understanding and experience of mixedness *per se*.

Some mixed race folks completely 'disappear' from either of their monoracial communities to be absorbed into various mixed race ones. Author Sui Sin Far described this phenomenon in 1909. She wrote: 'It is not difficult, in a land like California, for a half Chinese, half white girl to pass as one of Spanish or Mexican origin.'[37] Other mixed race people are locating themselves within culturally different, but similarly mixed, racial groups. One Welsh/Cherokee/Chinese man writes: 'I find myself most comfortable among Filipinos, Native Americans and Mexicans.'

This sort of group affiliation cropped up in 50 per cent of the survey respondents, particularly from older respondents who grew up mainly within their monoracial minority communities and who had no previous knowledge of a multiracial option or vocabulary. A 39-year-old Japanese/European woman who took the survey in Little Tokyo, Los Angeles, stated that she was not aware of mixed race groups, and had not been exposed to mixed race people while growing up. She 'sorta' felt comfortable within the Japanese American community, but did not feel accepted by them. She felt an affinity with other mixed race people with whom she did not share a common racial/ethnic heritage, frequently passed for Filipina and Latina, and participated within a Latino community grouping. Even when some respondents felt accepted by monoracial groups with whom they had a common ancestry, they tended to gravitate towards other mixed race groupings. A 23-year-old man of Japanese/European origins, for example, while feeling comfortable within the Japanese and Europeans groups from his childhood, reported that he now participated in Filipino-based community groups. In families or racial communities in which members come in a variety of hues and ethnic backgrounds, such as these, there is perhaps more tolerance and historical acceptance of difference both within and outside the community.

The recognition, however, of the power hierarchy and privileges of Whiteness is not lost among these people. Many mixed race people understand the impossibility of embracing Whiteness. In addition to their multiracial affiliations, many also remain firmly dedicated to their communities of colour. One respondent, who started up a mixed race group at his university, was asked if this affiliation precluded his involvement in 'traditional' minority groups. 'Hell, no!' he responded, 'I started the university's first Black fraternity, too!'

There appears to be a commonality, a level of comfort, a place where one does not have to code-switch, a level of unspoken understanding, that is experienced by mixed race in the company of others like them that is not found in their experiences with monoracial people. This commonality is not limited to national borders, but is located globally with mixed race persons reaching across national boundaries. A Cambodian transnational writes: 'I am Chinese, Cambodian and a bit of East Indian ... I have a tendency to hit it off with people of biracial backgrounds. I have never been completely comfortable in a Chinese community, or a Cambodian environment, or any other monoracial environment.'

There are currently mixed race groups in England, Japan, Canada, Hong Kong and Australia, as well as the USA. In these countries, mixed race people from all backgrounds are acknowledging their common status as mixed race people, and are creating a collective identity that crosses racial boundaries. Subjected to racially based representations, paternalism, violence and exclusions, many people are choosing to embrace a multiracial identity. This identity resists White racial hegemony which imposes racial categories, yet also resists notions of purity from within their monoracial communities of colour.

Multiracials are locating a commonality with other multiracial people – regardless of their particular racial ancestries – that is different from their groupings with monoracials with whom they share a common racial or ethnic ancestry or family bond. This commonality functions as a newly emerging ethnic and racial grouping based on similar historical continuities and life experiences that transcend traditional racial/ethnic categorisation. Multiracial people are creating a panethnic identity which is based on mixedness *per se*.

Notes

1. Thanks are due to those who have helped me with varying drafts of this paper. In no particular order, Miri Song, Suzanne Oboler, Maria Root, Mark Helbling, Teresa Kay Williams, Paul Spickard and Allison Hartle have listened, suggested revisions and offered encouragement. A special thanks goes to Angelo Ancheta.
2. M.Omi and H. Winant, *Racial formation in the USA: from the 1960s to the 1990s* (New York: Routledge. 1994); see also D.R. Roediger, *The Wages of Whiteness: Race and the Making of the American Working Class* (London; New York: Verso, 1991).
3. W.D. Jordan, *White over Black: American Attitudes Toward the Negro, 1550–1812* (New York: Norton, 1977).
4. Office of Management and Budget Federal Register, 28 August 1995.
5. M.Omi and H. Winant, *Racial formation in the USA: from the 1960s to the 1990s* (New York: Routledge. 1994), p.55; see also Frantz Fanon *Black Skin, White Mask* (New York: Grove Press, 1967), p.11.
6. Omi and Winant, *Racial Formation in the USA*, p.59.
7. For discussion on third space and hybridity see H. Bhabha 'The third space: Interview with Homi Bhabha', in J. Rutherford (ed.), *Identity: Community, Culture, Difference* (London: Lawrence & Wishart, 1990), pp.207–21.
8. Frantz Fanon *Black Skin, White Mask* (New York: Grove Press, 1967), pp. 11–12. For methodological problems in research on mixed race people, see M.P.P. Root 'Back to the Drawing board: Methodological Issues in Research on Multiracial People', in M.P.P. Root (ed.), *Racially mixed people in America* (Newbury Park, Calif.: Sage Publications, 1992), pp.181–9.
9. F.G. Crookshank, *The Mongol in Our Midst: A Study of Man and his Three Faces* (New York: E.P. Dutton, 1924). Francis Galton's Hereditary Genius was published in London in 1869 advocating the creation of a genetically superior race of man. The USA quickly embraced this notion and by 1926 the American Eugenics Society was created to prevent racial mixing and to sterilise those deemed inferior.
10. See, for example, *The San Francisco Examiner*, 14 January 1996, B1. In this news story, a journalist blames the pathology of a murderer on his Mexican/Black heritages, calling him 'ethnically confused'.
11. See, for example, L.R. Gordon, 'Sex, Race and Matrices of Desire', in L.R. Gordon, *Her Majesty's Other Children: Sketches of Racism From a Neocolonial*

Age (Lanham, Md: Rowman & Littlefield, 1997). For an American legal construction of Whiteness based on purity, see I. Haney-Lûpez, *White by Law: the Legal Construction of Race* (New York: New York University Press, 1996).

12. This paper focuses on studies being conducted within Asian American and multiracial communities. Within other communities, some African American and Pacific Islander American communities at varying places and times, for example, the histories of colonisation and the miscegenation and its progeny that result, are often absorbed within the community. See, for example, P. Spickard and R. Fong 'Pacific Islander Americans and Multiethnicity', in *Social Forces* 73, 4 (June 1995), pp.1365–83; and L.R. Gordon, *Her Majesty's Other Children: Sketches of Racism From a Neocolonial Age* (Lanham, Md: Rowman & Littlefield, 1997).
13. P. Spickard 'What Must I Be?', in *Amerasia Journal* 23, 1 (1997), pp.53.
14. The term 'monoracial' refers to a person whose racial ancestries fall neatly within one racial grouping.
15. The usual exception to this is the 'one drop rule' applied to those of African descent. That is, any amount of 'Black blood' makes one Black. See C. Nakashima 'The Invisible Monster: The Creation and Denial of Mixed-Race People in America', in M.P.P. Root (ed.), *Racially Mixed People in America* (Newbury Park, Calif.: Sage Publications, 1992), pp. 162–78. Yet, as illustrated by Kathy Russell in K. Russell, *The Color Complex: the Politics of Skin Color Among African Americans* (New York: Harcourt Brace Jovanovich, 1992), a person of 'Black:other' mix is not always fully embraced by Black communities.
16. *Doubles: Japan and America's Intercultural Children* (Hohokus, NJ: Doubles Film Library, 1995) [videorecording].
17. Y.L. Espiritu, *Asian American Panethnicity: Bridging Institutions and Identities* (Philadelphia: Temple University Press 1992), p.vii.
18. L. Lowe, *Immigrant Acts: on Asian American Cultural Politics* (Durham: Duke University Press, 1996), pp.1–36.
19. L.H. Shinagawa and G.Y. Pang, 'Asian American Panethnicity and Intermarriage', in *Amerasia Journal* 22, 2 (1996), pp.127–52. This article documents the rise in interethnic and intraethnic marriages within the Asian American community during 1980 to 1990. The rise corresponded with a dramatic decline in interracial marriages involving Asian Americans. Its analysis falls short, however. The federal over-turning of anti-miscegenation laws in 1967 and the US military presence in the Pacific did increase the rate of interracial marriages between Asian racial groups and White Americans. But, as a trend to locate mixed race people, and interracial unions, marriage statistics are inadequate. Anti-miscegenation laws only prohibited 'Negroes, Mulattos and Mongoloids [Asians]' from marrying Caucasians. As interracial marriages between Negroes, Mulattos and Mongolians were of little concern to the dominant group (Caucasians), records of those unions were not often kept. Likewise,

interethnic marriages, such as Chinese/Korean unions were not accurately counted. Some of these unions were long lasting and committed 'marriages', but would not show up in statistics. For discussion, see also L. Mengel 'Issei Women and Divorce in Hawaii: 1885–1908', in *Social Process in Hawai'i*, 39 (1997), pp.18–39.

20. These Whites were predominantly women. White men have always entered into sexual relationships with women of colour, although not usually consensual, nor legally sanctioned.
21. N. Brown and R. Douglass, 'Making the Invisible Visible: The Growth of Community Network Organisations', in M.P.P. Root (ed.), *The Multiracial Experience: Racial Borders as the New Frontier* (London; Thousand Oaks, Calif.: Sage, 1996), pp.323–40.
22. L. Funderburg, *Black, White, Other: Biracial Americans Talk About Race and Identity* (New York: W. Morrow and Co., 1994), pp.20–21.
23. See also S. Benson, *Ambiguous Ethnicity: Interracial Families in London* (Cambridge; New York: Cambridge University Press, 1981).
24. J. Lazarre, *Beyond the Whiteness of Whiteness: Memoir of a White Mother of Black Sons* (Durham: Duke University Press, 1996), p.128.
25. M.T. Reddy, *Crossing the Color Line: Race, Parenting, and Culture* (New Brunswick, NJ: Rutgers University Press, 1994), pp.70–71.
26. S.S. Far, *Mrs Spring Fragrance and Other Writings*, Amy Ling and Annette White-Parks (eds), (Urbana: University of Illinois Press, 1995).
27. R. Radhakrishnan, 'Is the Ethnic "Authentic" in the Diaspora?', in K. San Juan Aguilar (ed.), *The State of Asian America: Activism and Resistance in the 1990s* (Boston: South End Press, 1994).
28. Alternatively, Nakashima's 'Claim us if you're famous' theory – a recognition of the mixed race person's membership in an ethnic community if the person has accomplishments that the community would like attributed to them – also works here. A recent *Pacific Citizen* report glorifying Tiger Woods, referred to the mixed race golf pro as 'Asian American', with no reference to his African roots. See Nakashima 'Invisible Monster', in M.P.P. Root (ed.) *Racially Mixed People in America* (Newbury Park, Calif.: Sage Publications, 1992), pp.162–78.
29. A pseudonym.
30. A character meaning 'good fortune' in Chinese and 'happiness' in Japanese.
31. For a dialogue on skin colour in African American communities, see K. Russell, *The Color Complex: the Politics of Skin Color Among African Americans* (New York: Harcourt Brace Jovanovich, 1992).
32. Private conversation with author.
33. W.E.B. Du Bois originated this notion in reference to African Americans in 1903 in *The Souls of Black Folks* (New York: New American Library 1969), p.45. A multiracial choosing an African American identity, he writes: '[America is] a world which yields him [the Negro] no true self-consciousness, but only lets him see himself through the eyes of others, of

measuring one's soul by the tape of a world that looks on in amused contempt and pity. One ever feels his twoness – an American, a Negro; two souls, two thoughts, two unreconciled strivings, two warring ideals in one dark body, whose dogged strength alone keeps it from being torn asunder.'

34. Unfortunately, adopting the language of the coloniser, many Filipino Americans are choosing to ignore this history in favour of problematising Filipino/White American people. For discussion, see M.P.P. Root in M.P.P. Root (ed.), *The Multiracial Experience: Racial Borders as the New Frontier* (London; Thousand Oaks, Calif.: Sage, 1996), pp.80–94.
35. M.P.P. Root (ed.), *Racially Mixed People in America* (Newbury Park, Calif.: Sage Publications, 1992), p.9.
36. S.Oboler, *Ethnic Labels, Latino Lives: Identity and the Politics of (Re)presentation in the USA* (Minneapolis: University of Minnesota Press, 1995).
37. S.S.Far, 'Leaves from the Mental Portfolio of an Eurasian', in *Mrs Spring Fragrance and Other Writings* (Urbana: University of Illinois Press, 1995), p.227.

6

Colour, Culture and Class: Interrogating Interracial Marriage and People of Mixed Racial Descent in the USA

Stephen Small

The key public arena in which explicit discussions of 'race mixture' occur in the USA today is the debate around the inclusion of a 'mixed race' category in the US census 2000. Over recent decades individuals, groups and organisations have mobilised to push for recognition of their multiple heritages and have identified the census as one medium through which their goals might be advanced. They object to the despotism of the 'one drop rule' (which insists that any person with a single drop of blood from a racialised group other than White must be classified as 'non-White') and seek institutional mechanisms for the recognition of their diverse ancestries. In presenting their platform, members of this so-called 'Mixed Race Movement' proclaim the end of 'race' as we know it.[1]

In this chapter I discuss the changing nature of racialised sexual relations and marriage, the dramatic increase in the numbers of people of mixed origins and the organisation and demands of the 'Mixed Race Movement' in the USA today.[2] I identify and describe a range of discursive terrains and institutional domains in which notions of 'race' and 'race mixture' are both endemic and salient. My goal is to illustrate the ways in which notions of 'race mixture' remain central to broader patterns of racialisation.[3] I demonstrate how historically entrenched ideas and images of 'race' and 'race mixture' reiterate themselves in the social fabric of the USA today, and I urge a critique of the common sense and antiquated concepts that continue to insinuate themselves in our analysis. I argue that an understanding of the pervasiveness and depth of notions of 'race mixture' will derive best from an appreciation of the structural contexts, institutional patterns and ideological articulations that imbricate themselves in the racialised social formation of the contemporary USA. The 'Mixed Race Movement' is only one institutional domain among many – each revealing its own organisational vectors and discursive idioms – that compete for the attention of the American public over the meaning and significance of 'race mixture'.

Patterns of Racialised Dating, Marriage and People of Mixed Origins[4]

People in the USA are far less likely to marry today than they were in the past, they marry at a later age, and the marriages do not last as long. At the same time, divorce rates are as high as 50 per cent.[5] But among those who do marry, marriage across racialised groups is on the rise, with the highest patterns occurring for Asian Americans, Native Americans and Latinos, all of whom have rates of marriage to members of a different racialised group of over 50 per cent. It is the women in these groups who are far more likely to intermarry – usually to a White man. While the rates are much lower, the percentage of Black people married to non-Blacks has also steadily risen. In 1940, 1 per cent of Black people who were married were married to a non-Black; in the 1990s, 3 per cent of Black people who married, married non-Blacks. For Black people it is the men rather than the women who intermarry – 3.6 per cent of men compared to 1.2 per cent of women. While Black women display the lowest rate for any racialised gender category; their numbers have doubled in the last five years, and are likely to continue rising faster than other groups given the shortage of economically active Black men, and the lower rates of economic disparities between Black women and Black men.[7] While Black people reveal the lowest rates, they constitute the highest absolute numbers (Black people amounted to 48 per cent of all people of colour in 1990). This will change shortly as Latinos soon become the largest racialised minority group in the country – as early as 2005 by some estimates.[8]

Marriages across racialised groups are lowest in the South, and highest on the West Coast. The 1990s saw rates of around 10 per cent in California, with some cities (Los Angeles and the San Francisco Bay area) around 20 per cent. Similarly, cities like New York, Chicago, Denver, Seattle have rates several times higher than the national average. No State beats Hawaii, which has a rate of 85 per cent.[9] Intermarriage is more common among the middle-class, particularly those with a university education, than it is for other groups. The numbers are far higher among younger people and interracial marriage is far more likely, almost by definition, when it comes to people of mixed descent. Today, the higher the educational level of those getting married, the more likely the marriage lasts, without regard to racialised group identity.[10] The highest rates of marriage are for Asian American women who marry non-Asian American men (usually Whites). Patterns are equally high among Native Americans and Chicanas.

These patterns indicate that women refuse to submit any longer to the dictates of men over the nature, control and expression of their sexual choices. And marriage is only the tip of the iceberg. Far more interracial dating occurs than marriage – it involves less pressure, is more fleeting, and motivated by different factors – and all the evidence suggests it continues to increase. Surveys reveal increasingly larger numbers that have dated across racialised groups, or who say they would consider doing so. In a recent survey at least 30 per cent of the population said they would do so, with dramatic variations among racialised categories (90 per cent of 'Hispanics', 60 per cent of Black people and 47 per cent of Whites).[11]

These numbers, of course, are reflected in the growing size of the population of mixed racial descent. In the 1990 census almost 10 million people checked the 'other' box, a number which just about every one accepts is a dramatic understatement of the size of the population knowledgeable of its mixed ancestry. We know that very large proportions of the American population are mixed, though millions choose to deny that mixture for a variety of reasons, particularly the salience of the distinction between 'White' and 'non-White' and the dominance of 'hypodescent' in their lives.[12] The rule of 'hypodescent' means that Americans of all racialised groups continue to genuflect to the idea that anyone with a single drop of 'non-White' blood should be regarded as 'non-White'.

These patterns have been explained by changes in law, educational and occupational mobility, increased levels of social interaction (especially in colleges and the work place), changing patterns of demography and immigration, the increasing independence of women and a changing social climate. In 1967 the Supreme Court ruled 'anti-miscegenation' laws unconstitutional, as it had done in the 1950s for the racist exclusions of Jim Crow segregation. Recent decades have seen the unprecedented access of African Americans, Latinos and Asian Americans to higher education and professional occupations. Changes in immigration legislation have led to far higher proportions of people of colour immigrating into the nation than ever before. Women have achieved unprecedented levels of formal progress, and expectations about gender roles – at home and in the work place – have allowed for far more opportunities and successes by women. The social climate of California and other western states, and of some bigger cities, is far less hostile to such relationships than elsewhere in the nation. And we now enjoy increased representations of such relationships throughout the media. These factors operate together and reinforce one another.

But before we get the idea that all the barriers are down, we should not forget that the vast majority of all marriages in the USA – over 97 per cent – occur between people within the same racialised group – and this in a nation where people of colour amount to around 25 per cent of the population (with much higher proportions among the young and those of marriageable age).[13] Continuing levels of housing, educational and occupational segregation, and the prevalence of stereotypes, will sustain such patterns. Besides, antiquated ideas and images of 'race mixture' have a far greater currency in a much wider range of American institutions than is suggested by the numbers.

The Discursive Terrains of 'Race Mixture'

Over the course of American history, the attitudes of powerful White men towards 'race mixture' have been clearly stated and almost invariably hostile. Under colonialism and slavery, laws were introduced to prohibit 'amalgamation' and to prosecute those that practised it; after the Civil War, laws were introduced against 'miscegenation'; White politicians deprecated it, while presidents condoned lynching; films were loath to show scenes of intimacy across racialised groups, and Hollywood had its code against it, especially for Blacks and Whites; professors and medical doctors offered scientific evidence that 'race mixture' contaminated Europeans, biologically, and culturally, and gave rise to a population of mixed origins that was physically inferior and psychologically unstable (see Chapter 1). Literature generally provided the creative analogues of such views.[14] At the same time, the vigour with which White men opposed 'race mixture' officially, especially for men of colour, was exceeded only by the fervour with which they practised it privately.

Today, we are far less likely to hear the views on 'race mixture' of politically and socially powerful White men, and one would be hard pressed to locate statements by national or local politicians, or key social agencies, other than platitudes about personal choice. Despite such evasions and silences, attitudes towards 'race mixture' pervade American society. These attitudes are articulated through the varied idioms of distinctive discursive terrains. Discursive terrains are social idioms predicated on expected and accepted principles that provide the context for interpreting and evaluating social concerns, and they are defined by appeal to long established ideas and notions. They serve as conceptual corridors through which 'race mixture' is defined and understood, and they invoke the criteria by which 'race mixture' is to be evaluated. While such discourses are not restricted to specific institutional sites, nevertheless, it is possible to identify several that have unique vectors in particular institutional sites.[15] I call these sites social domains. They are characterised by institutional structures, particular social constituencies, and elaborate modes of articulation. When we examine these domains and terrains we find explicit and detailed articulations of 'race mixture' and hybridity, articulations which reflect and infect public and individual discourses and beliefs. I suggest that these discursive articulations are irreconcilable.

I have identified five main discourses which frame debates about 'race mixture'. At one end of the continuum of discourses is the discourse of race purity (which argues staunchly against 'race mixture'); at the other end are the discourse of carnal delight and that of individualism and personal rights (both of which argue staunchly in favour of 'race mixture'). Occupying a space between them are discourses of economism and bureaucracy, and the discourse of consumerism. I discuss these five discourses in turn.

Race Purity

The discourse of race purity is prevalent among White supremacist groups, and their followers. The articulation is good old-fashioned racism (crude, vulgar, brazen-faced and brutal). This is based on presumed biological truth, race purity, and the avoidance of degeneracy, mongrelisation and cultural and intellectual decay. The motivation is physical, mental and cultural purity, the ascendancy of the White race and the avoidance of pollution and contamination. The advocates see themselves as the 'real leaders' of the White race in a constituency largely comprised of good-for-nothing White men, intellectual and educational failures, those who were near-misses politically, as well as a whole array of marginals driven to the extremes. The goals are preservation of racial purity and civilisation, and the retaking of the White House and government. The designated methods are legal, extra-legal and illegal; laws against the wanton irresponsibility of dating and marriage across racialised groups, the expulsion of immigrants of colour, and extermination of inferiors, along with violence and terror. Information is disseminated via newsletters, marches and websites. Today, many supremacists refer to the Bible for rationalisation, one website entitled 'God's Order Affirmed in Love: Reference Library for Reconstructing a National Identity for Christian Whites' firmly opposed race mixing because it ends up 'destroying the races as

God created them'.[16] Others seek authority in science arguing that 'hybridized recombinations of racial-genetic traits actually reduce, and are destructive of, biological racial diversity to the extent that they replace or deplete the parent "racial stocks"'.[17]

Economism and Bureaucracy

The discourse of economism and bureaucracy is prevalent among agencies of the state, with the Office of Management and Budget (the agency primarily responsible for the census) reluctantly acting as institutional fulcrum. In this institutional domain, government has been pressed to provide a census and monitoring of people of mixed origins so their existence might be acknowledged and their demands responded to. The articulation is rationality and efficiency (cost effectiveness, bureaucratic containment and efficacy, reasonableness in the face of an infinitely expanding workload). The motivation is cost reduction and bureaucratic efficiency in a world of heterogeneous, uncontainable and infinitely multiplying categories. The constituencies are the bureaucrats of the federal government. The goal is to fulfil one's public service, while keeping racialised categories to a minimum, and yourself in a job. The designated method is the formulation of decisive rationalistic criteria – via meetings, forums, consultation of experts, memos, discussion and working papers, dissemination of options under consideration, decisions made and defended. The primary audience is academics, policy makers, state and private agencies. Debates on the inclusion of a 'mixed' category in the census date back decades and have commanded considerable time and resources from the Office of Management and Budget, involving consultations with specialists, seminars, working papers and decisions. The 'check all identities' option for people of mixed descent in the US census 2000 will further tax the administrative capacity of government bureaucrats (see Chapter 7 for related debates on the British census).

Consumerism

The discourse of consumerism is prevalent in the media (including film, television, adverts and music). This discourse is expressed through linguistic and visual creativity, artistic innovation and poetic licence. The motivations are multiple – sell goods and advertising space, and support American liberal democracy and individualism. The constituencies are the writers, producers and directors of films, videos, advertising and literature, and the corporations that sell goods. The underlying goal is to get the products sold, especially by promoting a way of life that looks cool (as in Hip Hop videos), while the designated media are air space and air waves, huge billboards (as in the distinctive cartography of Los Angeles), and images and photos. The audience is the American consumer, especially the young, hip ones. Films are paramount here. In *Jungle Fever* (1991) an African American architect commits adultery with his Italian American secretary. They attempt to develop a relationship together but succumb to the pressures of racialised family and community. In *Lone Star* (1996), mystery and the legacy of the past – told through the lens of an aborted adolescent sexual adventure – reveals itself in the transgressive relationship of adulthood, in southern Texas. This time it is made poignant and ridiculous through the accidental discovery of kinship and incest. Even James Bond in *Tomorrow Never Dies* (1998) ultimately gets his Asian woman, though she may be smarter, and more reluctant, than her predecessors. Topping all films for the deep and pervasive reverberations of 'race mixture' is *Blade* (1998). Ostensibly about vampires, the film is an allegory for purity of blood, in which Blade, half-human, half-vampire, phenotypically Black (Wesley Snipes), fights Deacon Frost, half-human, half-vampire, phenotypically White (Stephen Dorff), for the future of the human race. Frost is rejected by the pure vampires (those born as vampires, rather than 'turned' by a bite on their neck) who organise their activities through a council of elders. 'Who are you to challenge our ways?' asks Quinn, the leader of the vampire council. 'You're not even a pure blood!' Frost seeks an alliance with Blade, but is rejected by him, as Blade aligns himself with the humans. Frost taunts: 'You think the humans will ever accept a half-breed like you? They can't. They're afraid of you. And they should be. You're an animal.' In the film neither man fits into a world of racialised purity, and they can only exist in its interstices.

The discourse is reproduced on television. One of American television's most popular shows, *ER*, featured a sexual relationship between a Black man and a White woman in Spring 1999. At that time it generated a controversial debate, when the actor who plays the lead character protested off-screen that in the programme all his relationships with Black women were dysfunctional while his relationship with a White woman had a much better story line. Television also runs special programmes on these issues including *An American Love Story*, a 10-hour PBS series broadcast in September 1999 (it aired in Britain in October 1999). Television adverts deploy similar imagery to that of the movies; with portrayals of multi-cultural schools and colleges, work forces, sports teams and politicians, mixing and matching, embracing and kissing, and more. To this can be added the numerous celebrities whose photographs adorn the front pages of television magazines. Most notable are David Bowie and Iman, Wesley Snipes and his Asian girlfriend, Donna Wong, Robert De Niro, and Black spouse, Grace Hightower; along with their predecessor, Sidney Poitier, his White wife, Joanna Poitier, and their daughter Sydney Tamiia. Hip Hop videos are replete with light-skinned, scantily clad women – could be Black, could be mixed, could be White, could be Asian or Chicana – decorating the sets of ghetto gangsters. From Janet Jackson and Michael Jackson, to Mariah Carey and Sean 'Puff Daddy' Combs, from Jennifer Lopez to Sole, video after video is suggestive of the increasing patterns of transgressive racialised relationships, especially among the nation's youth.

Carnal Delight

In the fourth discourse, the discourse of carnal delight, the articulation is one of innate heterosexual hypersexuality and natural lasciviousness; the motivation is personal sexual desire and tasting the forbidden fruit. Pleasure can be obtained without guilt (women of colour do it because it's in their nature to please, to serve, to deprave) and because privacy means one's peers never know about the transgression. The constituency is all men, especially White men; and the designated methods are private consumption and value for money. The most common method through which this discourse is articulated is magazines and pornography; but also common is prostitution and sex workers. The primary audience of producers are after profits; the consumers are after value for money. At one end of this continuum are romance novels in which true love battles with hypocrisy and bigotry. Further along are factual and fictional accounts of sexual fantasies, as in the best-selling collection, *My Secret Garden*, in which one White woman relates: 'If I see a picture, for example, of a Black man and a White woman, I'm ready for sex almost immediately.'[18] Close by are adverts in newspapers for sex partners from different racialised groups. At the other end of the continuum are requests by White men for sex workers of colour in San Francisco, New York; or alternatively Bangkok, and other 'exotic' destinations, for those with a more heavily endowed exchequer.[19] Somewhere in the midst of all this – unfortunately for him – was the Hugh Grant manoeuvre in Los Angeles, which pandered to all the stereotypes; rich, White, desirable male, with beautiful, intelligent, White girlfriend, just had to get the forbidden fruit attributed to Black carnality.[20]

Individualism and Personal Rights

The discourse of individualism and personal rights is prevalent in the 'Mixed Race Movement'. Central to this domain are articulations of the inveterate American principles of individualism, free choice, the rule of law, avoidance of persecution, and the rights of representation for those that pay taxation. The motivations underlying this discourse are acknowledgement, respect, identity, inclusion and participation in the body politic. The primary constituency is people of mixed origins themselves, especially middle-class, college-educated ones, and their families. The goals are inclusion of people of mixed heritage in all government agencies, especially the census, so that a far more nuanced appreciation of racialised diversity can be acknowledged, and the implications of such nuances for the health and welfare of these people can be addressed. The designated methods are research and evidence, lectures and publications, especially biographies, lobbying of governments, dissemination of information about the range of problems faced by people of mixed origins. The designated audience is primarily the government, educators and policy makers.

Motivated by the potentially painful contradictions of mixed heritage, the rigidity of racialised classifications and the rule of hypodescent, the movement comprises a set of organisations, institutions, marches and demonstrations, support groups, families and individuals who have produced books, articles, journals and newsletters. While people of mixed heritage are prominent here, as Chapter 5 illustrates, it is their parents who were the primary force behind the establishment of the movement. Groups include the Association of Multi-Ethnic Americans, RACE (Reclassify All Children Equally), HAPA Issues Forum, I-Pride, Interracial Network, and the Interracial Family Alliance. The movement is heavily shaped by class, most of those involved possessing élite educational qualifications and professional jobs, and an inordinate number originate in élite universities, including Harvard, Yale, Wesleyan, Brown and UC, Berkeley. Cynthia Nakashima identifies three goals for the 'Mixed Race Movement': to seek inclusion and legitimacy in existing 'racial/ethnic communities'; to shape a common identity and agenda in 'new multiracial community', or to dismantle the dominant racial identity in a 'community of humanity".[21] She prefers to see these as different approaches and dimensions of the movement, rather than as divisions.

The 'Mixed Race Movement' is far from homogeneous in its goals and methods, but there is a widespread belief that the introduction of a category in the census 2000 will highlight their concerns, and facilitate discussions. The movement claims that the census will reveal the inadequacies of current racial identifications, provide more accurate numbers of people of multiple heritage, affirm an identity of multiple heritage, and provide access to resources. A 'check all identities' option was used in the US census 2000, (in April 2000) largely as a result of the movement's activities. This option allowed respondents to specify the 'race' to which they belonged, with choices from a list of 14 categories, plus space to write in any other categories. While some might claim this was a success, the Movement has made explicit many antipathies and antagonisms which have generally remained implicit (about skin colour, derogatory images of Black women, stereotypical images of women of colour, the impetus behind White men who date women of colour, and questions of political cooperation and commitment). A number of organisations like the National Association for the Advancement of Colored People oppose the census procedure and see it as both a distraction and a dilution of the collective power of people of colour. The next section will explore some of these tensions in greater depth.

'Race Mixture' and the Social Fabric of the USA

Individuals in the 'Mixed Race Movement' have made bold claims about the range and scope of their influence on American society. The movement highlights the manipulations and idiocy of the 'one drop rule', its introduction by Whites for exploitation and control, and the *de facto* acceptance of this rule by people of colour. It also highlights the inconsistencies and contradictions of systems of racialised classification in the USA today, the changing social and political climate, and the need to respect individual decisions over racialised identities. It portrays the many obstacles and problems experienced by people of mixed origins, and the many tragic consequences for individuals and families. Specifically, a Bill of Rights has been proposed, including the right 'to identify myself differently than how my parents identify me'; 'to change my identity over my lifetime and more than once'; and the right 'to freely choose whom I befriend and love'.[22]

But the movement has its problems.[23] It is dominated by middle-class Americans, largely unreflective about the class basis of their own demands, and one searches in vain to hear what people from working class and poor communities might have to say. Much of the focus of the movement is on the psychological issues involved in identity formation, and is frequently indifferent to the social consequences of the demands. These are often articulated through an excessive reliance on notions of individualism and 'free choice' while neglecting the continued pressures – stereotypes, patterns of demography, racialised discrimination and segregation – which ensure that patterns of sexual relationships and marriage largely remain within racialised boundaries. Many herald the rising patterns of dating and marriage as an end to the racialised classifications that have historically dominated this nation. But it is clear that 'race' remains central to their enterprise. Adverts for sexual partners from different racialised groups display a fetishism of racialised sexuality. Finally, even as they communicate many of the genuine problems they have experienced – stereotyping, exclusion, victimisation, family disintegration – they fail to acknowledge that significant benefits have sometimes also accrued to them. Today, it is clear that this society places a value on lighter skin color, and there is a certain vogue in media for people of mixed origins.

For these reasons, the bold claims of the 'Mixed Race Movement' cannot be sustained. Context is crucial. In the USA at the present time, the movement is gaining ground in a climate defined by a relentless move to abolish all talk of 'race', and to pursue the fleeting illusion of 'color blindness' (as with the abolition of Affirmative Action at the University of California).[24] Marriage across racialised groups, and people of mixed origins, is deployed thematically to insist on the declining significance of 'race', and to demand that colour is never mentioned. In 1997 the Speaker of the House of Representatives, Newt Gingrich, asked: 'What does race mean when many Americans cannot fill out their census forms because they're an amalgam of races?'[25] Besides, as I've demonstrated, the 'Mixed Race Movement' is simply one discursive terrain among several social domains in which these issues are articulated. Nor is it the most significant domain.

The discourses of 'race mixture' identified above involve far greater numbers of proponents, reach far more people, and in a far more sustained way. Their proponents also have far greater resources at their command. These discourses reproduce long-established notions, and display a flexibility and adaptability that offers far more options to the American public than does the 'Mixed Race Movement' (which seeks to challenge and overthrow hegemonic notions). The roots of these discursive terrains sink more deeply, more ubiquitously, into the soil of the American social formation and psyche than do the initiatives associated with the 'Mixed Race Movement'. This suggests that, overall, ideas about 'race mixture' will require far more than the exercise of personal choice to be dislodged.

A Way Forward

The problem that confronts analysts is how to engage with the range and diversity of discourses articulated around 'race mixture' and how to begin to challenge the assumptions and language deployed. The prevalent language reifies 'race' and 'race mixture' and treats such relationships as anomalous. This is one of the fundamental challenges to those of us who try to swim in these murky waters: we find ourselves tossed about by the tremendous forces of a historical and linguistic legacy which we do not control, just as the tide sways the helpless weed. In this respect, the most important point of departure is to recognise that we don't have to use the language we have inherited, or the analytical framework which its usage implies, or, in fact, requires. We have a decision to make. When I was young I used to struggle to find a perfect analytical language, and now I just struggle to find a language that does not lock me into an inescapable cage. In any analysis of 'race mixture', that is always difficult. Some people want to embrace and resuscitate the language of 'race', and seek to build a new de-stigmatised discourse; others, like me, want to grab and strangle the language of 'race', choking the last breath from its moribund body, and find an entirely new vocabulary, predicated on an entirely new framework.[26] This will take some doing, but I believe that we can, and must, reject the existing framework, the existing language, and most of its assumptions. The analyses presented in a book like this may be an important first step.

In her recent book, *Scattered Belongings*, Jayne Ifekwunigwe offers a promising critical approach, one which challenges the entire conceptual apparatus, calls for an archaeological excavation, and makes concrete suggestions for alternative sources of conceptual clarity and rigour.[27] Class analysis is central to her analytical enterprise, and she demonstrates that some concepts in vogue – like hybridity – are not as unsullied as their proponents suggest. Ifekwunigwe herself is in favour of 'metissage', and she makes a strong case for it. Yet in her contribution to this book she expresses some of my doubts about the term. I'm yet to be convinced that French concepts are free from the kind of problems associated with their counterparts in English, especially given their incubus in the civilising world of colonisation and conquest.[28] However, I suspect we might find more promising concepts and theories outside the civilising hemispheres that remain hegemonic. This will provide a corrective to the tendency to discuss such patterns as anomalous and aberrant. In fact, no society in the world has been constituted without a comprehensive mixing of human populations and cultures. We put the cart before the horse when we work, even implicitly, from a model that implies original pure societies, that later became 'miscegenated'.[29]

Relatedly, I think it is indispensable here to conceptualise ideas about 'race' and 'race mixture' as always and only one issue among many (albeit frequently the most important issue), including class (marriage rates reflect class standing); gender (conflict between men over access to women); family (parents over control of daughters); demography (distribution of racialised groups, by gender and age); nationality and citizenship (opposition to immigration predicated on alleged links between marriage and economics); and other apparently less racialised issues. This is frequently apparent in films about these issues. For example, in *Jungle Fever* as the micro-drama of the relationship unfolds it is juxtaposed against the destruction and decimation of the Black community through poverty, inequality and drugs. Flipper's brother, Gator, a long-time drug addict, lounges in a drug-induced stupor in the 'Taj Mahal', a massive drug den. In pursuing his brother, Flipper is introduced to the breadth and depth of these problems, and his own anxieties seem less salient. A preoccupation with racialised identity and family on their own, cannot resolve these larger problems, and until these larger problems are addressed, the resolution of identity and family issues will remain fleeting.

I don't want to contribute to the tendency of North American analysts to universalise this nation's experiences. The USA has its distinctive features and the patterns of sexual interaction and marriage across racialised groups in other nations, as with the experiences of people of mixed origins, are strikingly different. The institutional domains and discursive terrains that reproduce ideas and images of 'race mixture' are also different. In this respect we must analyse these nations on their own terms. South Africa cannot be understood outside the particular history of apartheid, nor Brazil outside its unique demographic and cultural ensemble. Japan, Korea and Vietnam can't be understood outside of their recent experiences of war, and the presence of large numbers of American male military personnel. However, we would be wrong if we conclude that there is little in common across these nations. The multiple factors might crystallise in different ways, but none of them exceeds the institutional and discursive dynamics identified across the chapters of this book. In this respect, the analytical enterprise in which we are involved must continue to focus on structural contexts, institutional patterns, and ideological articulations, as they are expressed in the light of local histories.

Conclusion

My goal in this chapter has been to describe and discuss the various discursive terrains and institutional domains through which issues of 'race mixture' are articulated in the contemporary USA. I have offered this social structural analysis as a context for interpreting the claims of the 'Mixed Race Movement', and as an opportunity for analytical interrogation. Along with other chapters in this book my goal has been to demonstrate some of the ways in which these issues remain central to theoretical discussions of race and racialisation. I have tried to show how historically endemic ideas and images of 'race mixture' reiterate themselves in the social fabric of the contemporary USA. I have demonstrated how old-fashioned, antiquated and scientifically discredited notions of race purity, allegations of degeneration or assertions of invigoration that accrue from 'race mixture', which were pervasive in the nineteenth century, have found their way into the heart of the discourses at the start of the twenty-first century. In this way I have tried to demonstrate that structural contexts, institutional patterns, and ideological articulations that are routine and recurrent continue to have decisive impacts on these issues. This I hope will act as a salutary rejoinder to the hyperbole about private issues, personal decisions and free choice.

The changing patterns of racialised dating and marriage, and the growth of a population of diverse origins, offer us an opportunity through which to contemplate larger issues theoretically, politically and in policy terms. The increase in marriages across racialised groups – especially among middle-class people – and dramatic growth in the numbers of people of mixed origins have heralded many claims about the end of 'race' and racism. These patterns have been accompanied by, and are inextricably linked to, other institutional domains and discursive terrains that reproduce images of 'race mixture' and hybridity in the social formation of the contemporary USA. Discourses that utilise notions and ideas about 'race mixture' remain socially endemic, continue to form a central constitutive component of the social imaginary, and will continue to be reproduced throughout several institutional domains. These domains are comprised of agencies and agents who appropriate ideas and images of 'race mixture' to meet their own goals and priorities. These dynamics follow vectors intrinsic to these institutions, but are also shaped by, and refract, dynamics associated with broader patterns of racialisation and globalisation.

While some of these developments offer the potential for a critical interrogation of racialisation and 'race mixture', of gender and class relations, and of nationality and identity, it is more likely that they will contribute to the reaffirmation of an uncritical individualism, the denial of class advantage, the subordination of group identity and collective action to the pretext of individualism and romantic love, to increased demands for colour blindness and to an untenable heralding of the end of racism. In this respect, the roots of racialisation remain deeply embedded in contemporary life.

Acknowledgements

I would like to thank two colleagues, with whom recent conversations and dialogues have provided paradigm shifts of profound proportions to my thinking on miscegenation and hybridity. I am sincerely appreciative of the insights provided by Professor Michel Laguerre, whose innovative articulation of multicultural constituencies in the USA in his forthcoming book, *The Global Ethnopolis*, has been invaluable. I would also like to thank Dr Barnor Hesse, whose questions, insights and suggestions have been equally profound. I expect the reverberations of their suggestions to insinuate themselves in my work for years to come, and for that I am extremely grateful. I would also like to offer my sincere appreciation to Kimberly Cooper for her diligent and meticulous research on White supremacist groups.

Notes

1. This is not a social movement in the usual sociological sense, and I use the term 'movement' only with caution.
2. All sexual relations are racialised, including those within the same racialised group. Relationships usually called 'inter-racial' are simply another variant, rather than being analytically different. I undertake the analysis through the lens of the racialisation problematic. See Stephen Small, *Racialised Barriers: The Black Experience in the USA and England in the 1980s* (London and New York: Routledge, 1994); Stephen Small 'The Contours of Racialisation: Structures, Representations and Resistance in the USA', in Rodolfo D. Torres, Louis F. Miron and Jonathan Xavier Inda, *Race, Identity and Citizenship: A Reader* (Malden, Massachusetts; Oxford, England: Blackwell, 1999).
3. Racialisation refers to the ideological process, and the institutions that accompanied this process, through which racial identities were attributed to people of diverse physical and cultural backgrounds during the conquest and colonisation of Africa and what became the Americas, by people from Europe. See Small, *Racialised Barriers*.
4. The data for these patterns are far from consistent, or complete. Data on attitudes come from social surveys, data on marriage from either the

census or from individual studies. Also patterns are dramatically changing, so it is necessary to exercise caution. A language for describing these populations still eludes us. Unless otherwise mentioned, the data in this section are taken from the following source: Joel Perlmann, *Reflecting the Changing Face of America: Multiracials, Racial Classification, and American Intermarriage* (The Jerome Levy Economics Institute of Bard College: Public Policy Brief, No. 35, 1997).

5. US Bureau of the census. *Current Population Reports, Marriage, Divorce, and Remarriage in the 1990s* (Washington DC: US Government Printing Office, 1992), pp.23–180.
6. Black women earn more compared to Black men, than do White women compared to White men, and therefore have less to gain economically from marriage to Black men than do White women from marriage to White men. See M. Belinda Tucker and Claudia Mitchell-Kiernan, *The Decline of Marriage Among African Americans* (New York: Russell Sage Foundation, 1995).
7. In the past it was argued that White women of lower class standing married Black men of higher class standing. If it was true then, it is no longer true now. For an overview, see Paul Spickard, *Mixed Blood: Intermarriage and Ethnic Identity in Twentieth-Century America* (Madison, Wisconsin: The University of Wisconsin Press, 1989). For future population estimates see Dale Maharidge, *The Coming White Minority: California, Multiculturalism, and America's Future* (New York: Vintage Books, 1999).
8. Spickard, *Mixed Blood*, 1989.
9. *Ibid.*
10. Joel Perlmann, *Reflecting the Changing Face of America: Multiracials, Racial Classification, and American Intermarriage* (The Jerome Levy Economics Institute of Bard College: Public Policy Brief, No. 35, 1997).
11. 'Interracial Dating', *USA Today*, 3 November 1997, p.1.
12. The rule of hypodescent, or the 'single drop of blood' forces people of mixed heritage to choose one identity, almost invariably the subordinate identity of color. See Maria P.P. Root, *The Multiracial Experience: Racial Borders as the New Frontier* (Thousand Oaks: Sage Publications, 1996).
13. Robert Schoen, p.107 in M. Belinda Tucker and Claudia Mitchell-Kiernan, *The Decline of Marriage Among African Americans* (New York: Russell Sage Foundation, 1995).
14. Martha Hodes (ed.), *Sex, Race, Love. Crossing Boundaries in North American History* (New York and London: New York University Press, 1999); Werner Sollors, *Neither Black Nor White Yet Both: Thematic Explorations of Interracial Literature* (New York; Oxford: Oxford University Press, 1997).
15. Of course, this purview does not exhaust the discursive terrains. There are others including a 'discourse of liberalism' (articulated through the idea of 'colour blindness') which proclaims the irrelevance of 'race' to decisions about dating and matrimony, as well as the large and growing discursive

terrain of the academy. This means that all discourses manifest a more general social currency.

16. For other examples, see Abby Ferber, *White Man Falling* (Lanham: Rowman and Littlefield, 1998).
17. *Ibid.*
18. Nancy Friday, *My Secret Garden* (New York: Women's Sexual Fantasies, Pocket Books, 1998), p.128.
19. Julia O'Connell-Davidson, *Prostitution, Power and Freedom* (Ann Arbor: The University of Michigan Press, 1998).
20. Hugh Grant, a White British actor famous for his portrayal of diffident, upper-class Brits, was charged with soliciting sex from an African American street sex worker in Los Angeles in the early 1990s.
21. Cynthia L. Nakashima, 'Voices From the Movement: Approaches to Multiraciality', in Maria P.P. Root, *The Multiracial Experience: Racial Borders as the New Frontier* (Thousand Oaks: Sage Publications, 1996), p.81.
22. Root, *The Multiracial Experience*, p.7.
23. For a critique of the movement see Jon Michael Spencer, *The New Colored People: The Mixed Race Movement in America* (New York: New York University Press, 1997).
24. John Gabriel, *Whitewash: Racialised Politics and the Media* (London and New York: Routledge, 1998).
25. Website for RACE (Reclassify All Children Equally) http://www.projec-trace.com/
26. For the former view, see Maria P.P. Root, *The Multiracial Experience: Racial Borders as the New Frontier* (Thousand Oaks: Sage Publications, 1996). For the latter, see Stephen Small, 'Concepts and Terminology in Representations of the Atlantic Slave Trade', *Museum Ethnographers Journal*, 6 (December, 1994), pp.7–21.
27. Jayne O. Ifekwunigwe, *Scattered Belongings: Cultural Paradoxes of 'Race', Nation and Gender* (London and New York: Routledge, 1999). Also, see Chapter 2, this volume.
28. See Stephen Small, 'Concepts and Terminology in Representations of the Atlantic Slave Trade', *Museum Ethnographers Journal*, 6 (December, 1994), pp.7–21.
29. Joel Williamson, *New People: Miscegenation and Mulattoes in the USA* (Baton Rouge and London: Louisiana State University Press, 1995).

7

'Mixed Race' in Official Statistics

Charlie Owen

Statistics are not neutral. They both reflect and contribute to important dimensions of difference and power in society, and they are firmly located in the aims and tensions of the society that produces them.[1] This is very clear when we talk about statistics of race and of ethnicity. The very language we use is highly charged: terms which some people see as natural may be seen as arbitrary or offensive by others. Furthermore, no terms can remain permanently 'right'. This is because groups define and redefine themselves, and their sense of who they are culturally and politically, and the preferred terms groups use to describe themselves, are bound to change. Also, within a group, one person may like a term which another may not.[2]

This chapter looks at the way official statistics have treated notions of mixed race in Britain. As with all racialised terms, there has been significant dynamism and contestation around the terms used to refer to mixed relationships and people of mixed parentage.[3] Statisticians in Britain had difficulty developing a question on ethnic origin for the 1991 census. Part of the difficulty in designing an acceptable question was the notion, implicit in a set of mutually exclusive tick boxes, that there is a set of 'real' ethnic categories and that everyone belongs to just one. This assumption is particularly difficult to apply to people whose parents are manifestly from different ethnic groups. This chapter considers the meagre data from the 1991 census on mixed parentage and looks ahead to the new question in the 2001 British census.

People of colour in Britain have long been established in the UK, and there have always been some who have married and had children with the white population (and to a lesser extent, intermarried with other ethnic minority groups other than their own). Sometimes this has been to the great consternation of sections of the white population.[4] Those children, over many generations, have blended into

British society, so that many 'white' people in Britain will have black or other ethnic minority group ancestors. In the same way, many black people or people from other ethnic minorities, will have white ancestors, many, in the past, as a result of the exploitations of imperialism and slavery, but increasingly, as the result of loving, consensual relationships. Many people will therefore have mixed heritage without being aware of it.

Data from official statistics in Britain seem to show that mixed relationships are occurring in increasing numbers. Ann Berrington analysed data on mixed relationships from the 1991 census, and she found that among ethnic minority respondents living with a partner at the time of the census, either married or cohabiting, 16 per cent of the men and 13 per cent of the women were living with a white partner.[5] She also found that mixed relationships were more common among the black, Chinese and so-called 'Other Asian' (people with ethnic origins from countries such as Sri Lanka, Japan, the Philippines, Malaysia and Vietnam, to name a few) groups than among the South Asian groups (Indian, Pakistani and Bangladeshi). They were also more common for younger people (aged under 35) and for those born in the UK. There were other forms of mixed relationships, but these were numerically too small to estimate accurately. In fact, some other recent figures suggest that almost 50 per cent of African Caribbean men and 30 per cent of African Caribbean women under age 30 (who are partnered) have white partners.[6]

Nevertheless, while opinion polls and attitude surveys going back to the 1950s show an increasing acceptance of mixed marriages in Britain, there is still continuing hostility. Sometimes this hostility can show itself in a very violent form. To give just *one* recent example, Ashia Hansen, a Black British athlete, had to go into hiding after her white boyfriend at the time was initially alleged to have been stabbed by white men who had threatened him about his relationship with Hansen.

The Fourth National Survey of Ethnic Minorities, conducted by the Policy Studies Institute, and published in 1997, asked white and ethnic minority respondents for their views on mixed marriages.[7] When asked their opinion on: 'If a close relative were to marry a person of ethnic minority origin', 71 per cent of white respondents said they would not mind, but 14 per cent said they would mind very much. Opposition to mixed marriage, however, does not come just from the white population. Ethnic minority respondents were also asked how they would feel if a close relative married a white person. Of the black Caribbean respondents, 84 per cent said they would not mind while 7 per cent said they would mind very much (responses which are very similar to those of Chinese respondents); by contrast, 41 per cent of Pakistani respondents said they would not mind but 40 per cent said they would mind very much. Responses from other ethnic minority groups fell between those of the black Caribbeans and the Pakistanis.

Official Statistics

There are very few official statistics on the mixed race population in Britain. The main source of such statistics has long been the Labour Force Survey (LFS). The LFS is a sample survey of about 60,000 households per quarter, from across the UK, conducted by the Office for National Statistics (ONS). It includes a question on ethnic group. Jeremy Schuman, from ONS, has used data from the LFS for 1995 to 1997 to look at the age structure of the population of Great Britain by ethnic group.[8] In the analysis he included two categories of 'mixed': 'Black-Mixed' and 'Other-Mixed'. The analysis showed that the mixed population is a very young group (see Figure 1). While 7 per cent of the total population were children aged 0–4 years, as were 11 per cent of all minority ethnic groups combined, 24 per cent of the 'Black-Mixed' group and 20 per cent of the 'Other-Mixed' group were of this age. Taking the first three age groups together, 59 per cent of the 'Black-Mixed' group were children aged under 15, as were 51 per cent of the 'Other-Mixed' group. This compares to 31 per cent of all minority ethnic groups and only 20 per cent of the whole population. Schuman also estimated that 0.7 per cent of all children under 15 were of mixed parentage. Although this is still small, it also means that 10 per cent of all ethnic minority children were of mixed parentage. Taking just pre-school children, Schuman estimates that 2 per cent of all children under five were of mixed parentage, and 20 per cent of all minority ethnic children under five were of mixed parentage.

A question arises, though, as to whether this observed trend reflects a real growth in the mixed race population or whether it is simply a result of who actually answers the question. For children, parents will fill in the census form or answer the LFS interviewer's questions. Many of these children will be living with a white parent, often a lone white mother.[9] Under these circumstances the parent – especially the white parent – might want to emphasise the child's mixed ancestry. Later, when those children grow up and can choose an ethnic descriptor for themselves, they may, among various options, choose to identify with just one part of their ancestry – for instance the minority ethnic part. This could account for why there are fewer people of mixed parentage at older than at younger ages.

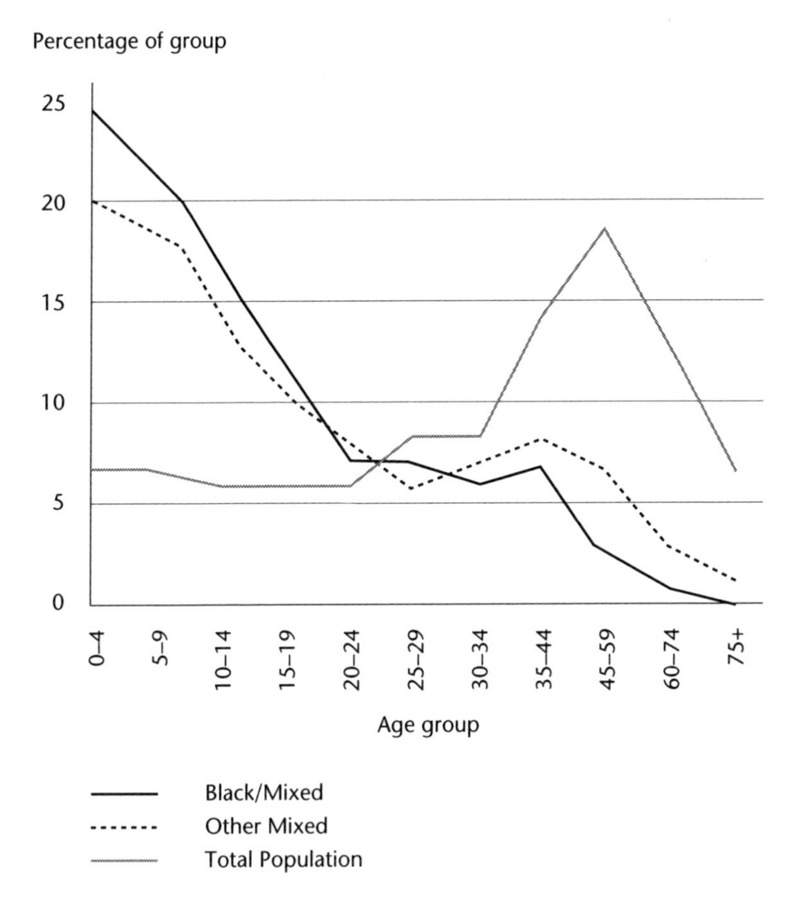

Figure 1 Percentages of population by age group

Source: J.Schuman, 'The ethnic minority populations of Great Britain – latest estimates', *Population Trends*, 96 (1999).

However, this account is unlikely to be correct for two reasons. Firstly, if the reason there were more children than adults in the mixed groups is because parents were more likely to describe their children as mixed than the children would themselves, there should be a sharp change in the graph after age 18. Instead there is a slow decline, with the highest percentages at the youngest ages. This makes the increasing numbers at younger ages look like a real phenomenon rather than an artefact determined by who completes the form. Secondly, if the fall in numbers reflected a change from parents describing their children to adults describing themselves, then the official statistics must be missing those adults of mixed parentage who do not classify themselves as such. If this were the case, then the real size of the mixed parentage population is much larger than has been estimated, because even more adults should really be classified as mixed. This seems unlikely.

Given this very young age profile, the mixed race population must be growing very rapidly, and is therefore demographically significant. Why, then, are there so few statistics? The main reason involves the difficulties government statisticians have had in developing questions and classifications that capture important dimensions of difference in society *and* which are acceptable to those who have to answer the question. This is best illustrated by a consideration of the ethnic question for the 1991 census.

The 1991 Census Question

The 1991 census in Great Britain was the first to include a question on ethnic group. The question is shown in Figure 2. The Office for Population Censuses and Surveys (OPCS, now the ONS) conducted a long series of field trials to develop an acceptable question. In a summary of these trials, Ken Sillitoe stated that, 'the purpose of these tests has been to try to devise a question and a system of classification which will not only furnish reliable data, but also to do so in a manner which is acceptable to all sections of the public.'[10]

However, this simply begs the question of whether there is a single classification of ethnic groups that is generally acceptable across British society. Acceptable classifications certainly shift over time, and what is acceptable to one person may not be to another. For example, Martin Bulmer traced the changes in terminology used by researchers in 17 major empirical studies published between 1948 and 1983.[11] He found a shift from 'negro' to 'coloured', 'immigrant', 'Commonwealth coloured immigrant', 'Indians, Pakistanis and West Indians' and 'racial minorities'. For a long time official statistics referred to the 'New Commonwealth and Pakistan (NCWP) population'. This shift over time belies the existence of some objective classification that can be applied to the ethnic minority population in a value-free manner. In the recent US 2000 census, the majority of the complaints received by the US Census Bureau concern the probing nature of the questions on 'race'. This is because many ethnic minorities in the USA are suspicious of government attempts to monitor or categorise them along racial and ethnic lines.[12]

Ethnic Group

11

White	☐	0
Black-Caribbean	☐	1
Black-African	☐	2
Black-Other	☐	

please describe:

Indian	☐	3
Pakistani	☐	4
Bangladeshi	☐	5
Chinese	☐	6
Any other ethnic group	☐	

please describe:

If the person is descended from more than one ethnic or racial group, please tick the group to which the person considers he/she belongs, or tick the 'Any other ethnic group' box and describe the person's ancestry in the space provided.

Figure 2 Question on ethnic group in the 1991 census

Throughout the reports of the field trials for the 1991 British census, mention was made of the difficulties the questions on ethnicity posed for people of mixed ancestry. However, in the 1991 census, the inclusion of a 'Mixed' category, or the possibility of ticking more than one box, were, at that time, explicitly rejected.

How The 1991 Census Handled Mixed Parentage

The ethnic group question on the 1991 census encouraged people of mixed parentage to assign themselves to one of the main categories: 'If the person is descended from more than one ethnic or racial group, please tick the group to which the person considers he/she belongs, or tick the "Any other ethnic group" box and describe the person's ancestry in the space provided.' People were also asked to 'please describe' if they ticked the 'Black-Other' box. The written answers for these two responses were assigned to one of 35 categories (0–34), including one of the original seven codes (see Table 1).

Coders working on the census forms had two documents to work from: a set of detailed instructions (*Classification of Ethnic Group*) and a *Flowchart and Index*, which together instructed them how to classify any particular written answer.[13] The Flowchart gave step-by-step instructions on how to deal with each kind of answer, including multiple and written answers.[14] The Classification included examples of answers and how they were to be coded. Answers which the coders could not assign to a category were passed to a supervisor for closer attention.

The document called Supervisor Instructions included more detail on coding answers into 'Mixed' and 'Non-mixed' categories. Where someone had written more than one word, there was the possibility that they were indicating that they were of mixed parentage; however, this may not always be the case. For example, does 'Black English' imply mixed descent or not? Such a response is ambiguous. In order for answers to be treated consistently by different coders, there had to be detailed instructions, since different coders might have made different decisions on the same answer. The instructions therefore had to be very clear as to when an answer was to be coded as 'Mixed' and when not. Some examples are shown in Figure 3.

The Supervisor Instructions stated that where two words or phrases are used, if one of them seems to be a 'descriptive adjective' for the other then the answer should be coded as Non-mixed: e.g. 'Indian Chinese would be regarded as someone of Chinese origin born in India, or vice versa.' Similarly, if the words were not linked in a way that implied mixed descent, then the answer should be coded as 'non-mixed'. However, if the words are linked by 'and', dashes or a slash then the answer was to be coded as 'Mixed'. The following example is given to illustrate this distinction: 'English West Indian would imply Non-mixed, but English and West Indian would imply mixed origin.' The instructions state that mixed origin is also indicated by prefixes

Table 1 Complete list of ethnic categories used in the 1991 census

0	White
1	Black Caribbean
2	Black African
3	Indian
4	Pakistani
5	Bangladeshi
6	Chinese
Black non-mixed origin	
7	British
8	Caribbean Island, West Indies, Guyana
9	North African, Arab, Iranian
10	Other African Countries
11	East African Asian, Indo-Caribbean
12	Indian Sub-Continent
13	Other Asian
14	Other Non-Mixed
Black mixed origin	
15	Black/White
16	Asian/White
17	Other Mixed
Other ethnic group: non-mixed origin	
18	British – ethnic minority indicated
19	British – no ethnic minority indicated
20	Caribbean Island, West Indies, Guyana
21	North African, Arab, Iranian
22	Other African Countries
23	East African Asian, Indo-Caribbean
24	Indian Sub-Continent
25	Other Asian
26	Irish
27	Greek (including Cypriot)
28	Turkish (including Cypriot)
29	Other European
30	Other Non-Mixed
Other ethnic group: mixed origin	
31	Black/White
32	Asian/White
33	Mixed White
34	Other Mixed

5.6.3 Non-mixed is indicated by the writing of

a) one ethnic group, country or continent

b) two words (ethnic groups, countries or continents) where one of the words seems to be a descriptive adjective implying nationality or religion
e.g. Indian Chinese would be regarded as someone of Chinese origin born in India, or vice versa

c) two words (ethnic groups, countries or continents) not linked in any way to suggest that the person is descended from more than one ethnic group
e.g. English West Indian would imply non-mixed, but English and West Indian would imply mixed origin.

5.6.6 Mixed Origin is indicated by the writing of

a) Anglo, Euro or Half with one or more ethnic groups e.g. Anglo Asian, Half Pakistani

b) two ethnic groups (written as countries, continents, nationalities or religions) linked by 'and', dashes, or a slash, or more likely by reference to ancestors. However, there are some nationalities to be wary of:
e.g. English mother, West Indian father implies mixed whereas English West Indian implies non-mixed.

Figure 3 Extracts from OPCS internal document 'Supervisor Coding Instructions for Ethnic Group'

such as 'Anglo', 'Euro' or 'Half'; e.g. 'Anglo Asian' is taken to be mixed. Some of the examples given are very specific: 'English mother, West Indian father implies mixed whereas English West Indian implies non-mixed.'

Anyone who wrote 'Half caste' was assigned to an 'Other Mixed' category, as was anyone who wrote 'Mixed parentage' or 'Mixed race'. Those who wrote 'Cape coloured' or 'South African coloured' were assigned to 'Black-African', and not to a mixed category. People who ticked two of the main boxes were assumed to be a mixture of the two categories they had indicated.

While these coding rules are clear, and provide consistent coding rules for different coders, it is obvious that they are arbitrary and in no way objective. Of course, the rules were not known to people when they completed their census forms. So someone with a White English mother and a Black Caribbean father, for example, would not have known that if they had written, 'English mother, West Indian father' or 'English-West Indian' they would have been classified as 'mixed', but writing 'English West Indian' would have got them coded as 'Non-mixed. If the question had included a category for mixed parentage, much of this ambiguity could have been avoided.

What We Know about Mixed Parentage from the 1991 Census

Using the coding rules discussed above, all answers were assigned to one of the 35 ethnic classification codes (Table 1). Seven of these were mixed categories: each of the 'Black mixed origin' and 'Other ethnic group: mixed origin' answers had sub-codes of 'Black/White', 'Asian/White' and 'Other Mixed'. In addition, the 'any other ethnic group' answer had a category of 'Mixed White'. Only one table showing the full 35-way ethnic classification has been published. That is Table A in the Ethnic Group and Country of Birth volume.[15] This table gives the population count, down to district level. However, no further information is given. In particular, there is no breakdown by age. The total numbers in the seven mixed categories are shown in Table 2; they are also shown as rates per million of the population.

Table 2 OPCS/GRO(S) Classification of Ethnic Group

Code	Category	Example of answer	N	per million
	Black Other			
78	Black/White	African/White	24,687	450
79	Asian/White	Anglo Asian	69	1
80	Other Mixed	Euro Afro Asian	50,668	923
	Any Other Ethnic Group			
94	Black/White	Black Caribbean/Irish	29,882	544
95	Asian/White	English/Pakistani	61,805	1,126
96	Mixed White	Anglo Germanic	3,776	69
97	Other Mixed	African/Lebanese	61,393	1,118
	All People		54,888,844	1,000,000

The first thing to note is that the numbers are quite small: ignoring the 'Mixed White' category, the total mixed parentage population counted in the 1991 census was 228,504. This amounts to less than 0.5 per cent of the population. However, the 'Mixed' groups formed a more significant part of the minority ethnic population – almost 8 per cent. Prior to the census, the LFS had for many years included a question on ethnic group. This question was different to the census question, and included a specific 'Mixed' category. From 1992 onwards the LFS has adopted the census question. However, it is possible to use LFS data for the years up to and including 1991, the same year as the census, as a check on whether including a specific 'Mixed' category made any difference to the response. Table 3 shows a comparison of census and LFS rates for three 'Mixed' categories. (For the census, answers derived from the 'Black Other' and 'Any other' boxes have been combined; for the LFS, data for the three years 1989–91 have been combined, since one year gives only small sample sizes.)

Table 3 Numbers identified as of mixed-parentage in the Census and the Labour Force Survey

	Census		LFS	
	N	%	N	%
Black/White	54,569	0.099	570	0.126
Asian/White	61,874	0.113	591	0.131
Other Mixed	112,061	0.204	1,192	0.264
All Mixed	*228,504*	*0.416*	*2,353*	*0.521*
TOTAL	54,888,844	100	451,648	100

Sources: Census 1991, Great Britain; LFS, 1989–91.

Combining all the 'Mixed' categories for the census gives an estimate of 0.416 per cent of the population being of mixed race. This compares to an estimate of 0.521 per cent from the LFS. While these percentages are very small, including a specific 'Mixed' category that people could choose does make a difference: in actual numbers, the LFS estimate for the mixed parentage population (0.521 per cent) is significantly higher than the census estimate (0.416 per cent).

The second thing to note is that the 'Black/White' group is the smallest of the three 'Mixed' groups, amounting to only 54,569 in total. The 'Asian/White' group is slightly larger than that: 61,874. Most people find this surprising, as it is the 'Black/White' mixed parentage group that gets more attention (and in light of the high rates of black people partnering with white people in Britain). However, the 'Other Mixed' group is almost as large as these two groups combined: 112,061. Many people classified as 'Other Mixed' could have been put into one of the other two groups if more information had been made available. As we saw above, people who wrote such things as 'mixed race' or 'half caste' were assigned to the 'Other Mixed' category, when a more detailed description might have allowed them to be assigned to one of the other two categories. Consequently, the relative sizes of the 'Black/White' and 'Asian/White' groups is uncertain.

Table 4 Correlations between percentages of the population in local authority districts by ethnic group (N = 411)

	Black/White	Asian/White	Other Mixed
White	–0.69	–0.71	–0.86
Black Caribbean	0.67	0.58	0.91
Black African	0.58	0.54	0.83
Black Other	0.85	0.58	0.91
Indian	0.43	0.57	0.48
Pakistani	0.34	0.29	0.37
Bangladeshi	0.24	0.16	0.32
Chinese	0.59	0.74	0.81
Other Asian	0.56	0.82	0.72
Other	0.71	0.80	0.86

Using the data from census Table A, it is possible to correlate the percentages of each ethnic group, including the 'Mixed' categories, across districts. This indicates which ethnic groups are relatively common in the areas where people of mixed parentage are living (see Table 4). Unsurprisingly, the 'Black/White' group occurs more frequently in areas with larger percentages in the three 'Black' groups: the correlation between the percentage of people in the 'Black/White' group with the percentage in the 'Black Caribbean' group is 0.67, which suggests that this mixed group is largely found where Black Caribbean people live. The correlation with 'Black African' is lower, at 0.58, suggesting that the 'Black/White' group is less strongly linked to this group. The correlation with the percentage of 'Black Other' is very high, at 0.85: this is hardly surprising since most of the 'Black/White' group had ticked 'Black Other' on the census form (see Table 2). The correlations with the 'Asian' groups are lower (0.24–0.59), indicating that the 'Black/White' group are less likely to live in areas with high percentages in these categories. The correlation with the 'Other' group is again high, but many of the 'Black/White' group would have ticked the 'Other' box on the census form.

The 'Asian/White' correlations with the Pakistani and Bangladeshi percentages are low (0.29 and 0.16 respectively), implying that these two groups play little part in this 'Mixed' group. The correlation with 'Indian' is higher (0.57), but the correlations with percentage 'Chinese' (0.74) and 'Other Asian' (0.82) are much higher. This suggests that many of the 'Asian/White' mixed parentage group are in fact 'Chinese/White' or 'Other-Asian/White' – a finding which corresponds to the relatively high rate of intermarriage by Asian Americans with white Americans.[16]

The correlations for the 'Other Mixed' group are like those for the 'Black/White' group, suggesting that many of the 'Other Mixed' are in fact 'Black/White' who could not be classified on the information given. These correlations demonstrate that conclusions about the numbers of particular 'Mixed' ethnic groups are necessarily tentative. These ambiguities lie behind the introduction of a 'Mixed' category in the forthcoming census explained in the next section.

The 2001 Census Question

The question on ethnicity for the 2001 census was published in the 1999 census White Paper and is shown in Figure 4. (This is the question for England and Wales: different questions are to be asked in Scotland and Northern Ireland.) The 'Mixed' category is one of five possible boxes respondents can tick (along with 'White', 'Asian or Asian British', 'Black or Black British', and 'Chinese or Other ethnic group').

Interestingly, for the question, 'What is your ethnic group?', Figure 4 shows that the box for 'White' is at the top, immediately followed by the 'Mixed' category, then by 'Asian or Asian British', then 'Black or Black British', and finally, 'Chinese or Other ethnic group'. Given the relatively small numbers of the mixed population in Britain, it seems significant, somehow, that the 'Mixed' category is the one that follows the category at the top – 'White'. The 'Mixed' category itself contains four subheadings ('White and Black Caribbean', 'White and Black African', 'White and Asian', and 'Any other mixed background – please describe'). Note that 'White and Chinese' is not an option – unlike the case for Black and Asian groups.

The introduction of the 'Mixed' category is bound to give more accurate information on the mixed race populations than did the 1991 census. The British census will, therefore, officially validate the notion of mixed race and the existence of mixed race people in British society. However, such orderings and omissions are not explained by the Office of National Statistics, and they raise questions about the rationale behind the design of the question on ethnic origin.

The preparations for the 1991 census explicitly rejected a Mixed category, yet just 10 years later such a category appears on the census form. How did this reversal come about? As can be seen from the discussion above, very little information on the mixed parentage population could be obtained from the 1991 census. Furthermore, what data could be obtained were only arrived at by the ONS second-guessing what people had meant when they gave a written description. This was clearly unsatisfactory. Given the significance of this group – sociologi-

What is your ethnic group?

Choose one section from (a) to (e) then tick the appropriate box to indicate your cultural background.

(a) **White**
- ☐ British
- ☐ Irish
- ☐ Any other White background. Please describe:

  ....

(b) **Mixed**
- ☐ White and Black Caribbean
- ☐ White and Black African
- ☐ White and Asian
- ☐ Any other mixed background. Please describe:

  ....

(c) **Asian or Asian British**
- ☐ Indian
- ☐ Pakistani
- ☐ Bangladeshi
- ☐ Any other Asian background. Please describe:

  ....

(d) **Black or Black British**
- ☐ Caribbean
- ☐ African
- ☐ Any other Black background. Please describe:

  ....

(e) **Chinese or Other ethnic group**
- ☐ Chinese
- ☐ Any other. Please describe:

  ....

Figure 4 Ethnic question for 2001 census for England and Wales

Source: The 2001 Census of Population (1999), Cmnd 4253.

cally, psychologically and demographically – it was concluded that better information was needed from the 2001 census.

In an ONS report of a consultation on the ethnic group question, a number of factors were identified as indicating the need for an explicit 'Mixed' category. These included demand from the mixed race population, the growing size of the group, and users' needs. According to this report:

> The 'mixed group', known from the full census classification and the Labour Force Survey to be one of the largest ethnic groups, is regarded as a strong candidate for inclusion, based on the group's happiness to describe themselves as such and the increasing numbers in the group. Also, users' needs for a reliable count of the numbers in this group are not currently met by identification through free-text responses.[17]

The consultation found that people of mixed parentage wanted to be able to identify themselves as such. This positive identification with being mixed had already been found in a study of (black and white) mixed race adolescents in London schools,[18] and had contrasted with earlier studies, particularly from the USA, which had suggested that people of mixed parentage would necessarily experience problematic and painful identities (see Chapter 1).[19]

An issue discussed in the ONS consultation report was how many categories to include. Would it be sufficient to have a single category of 'Mixed', or was more detail required?:

> Discussion took place on the issue of whether the needs of the population of Mixed Black and Mixed Asian parentage were significantly different from other groups to justify identification. In addition to differences in age structure, the different geographical distribution of the group was commented on (mainly outside metropolitan areas in contrast to the Black and South Asian groups).[20]

As has been noted above, the mixed race groups form over 10 per cent of the ethnic minority population in Britain. In addition, their very young age profile and the growth in mixed relationships mean that the group will form an increasingly large part of the population in the future, making them demographically even more significant.

One problem identified by users of the data involved the elaborate processing applied to the written answers in the census. This was not feasible for other agencies using the census categories, such as local authorities. Consequently it was difficult to compare local data with census figures. Among those supporting an explicit 'Mixed' category was the Commission for Racial Equality (CRE). In their submission to the ONS consultation, the CRE highlighted two issues: one was that, in their view, ethnic monitoring must be based on self-identification, so that official categories need, as far as possible, to reflect the way people see themselves. In the CRE's view, a significant number of people want to identify themselves as mixed race. Their second argument was that particular problems experienced by children of mixed parentage (such as their over representation in the care system)[21] indicated the possibility of failures in social services, which was an important issue for the CRE.[22]

Other organisations, such as People in Harmony, a British organisation which supports mixed couples and people of mixed race, also supported a mixed option on the census. Some voices, though, were raised against. Perhaps the best known was that of the late Bernie Grant, the black Labour MP, who argued that people of mixed race are subject to racism in the same ways as other minority ethnic groups. For that reason, Grant claimed, mixed race people (with black heritage) should be counted together with other black people. Furthermore, in the *Guardian* newspaper, Grant argued, 'Society sees mixed-race people as black, and they are treated as black. They are never accepted as white, so they have no choice' (see Chapters 4 and 5 on opposition to a mixed category and the question of choice).[23]

Unfortunately the ONS has no plans to publish the reasons for its final question choice before the 2001 census. This contrasts with the very full publication of details of field trials prior to the 1981 and 1991 censuses. The US 2000 census has decided not to include a 'Mixed' category, but to allow people to tick more than one category, even though this was fiercely opposed by some mixed race groups and organisations such as Interracial Voice (the Internet journal), who advocated a 'mixed race' box. It is not known whether this option was considered by the ONS, and, if it was, why it was rejected.

Conclusions

We know very little from official statistics about the mixed race populations of Britain. This is partly due to the fact that the 1991 census ethnic question had no explicit 'Mixed' category. The census question on ethnic group is very important because it was adopted as the standard ethnic classification in all official statistics and was widely adopted by other organisations conducting research or monitoring. In this way the question and its classification came to be seen as an objective description of British society. Yet the question itself was a compromise, arrived at by trying to steer between competing priorities. Importantly, by not including a 'Mixed' category, either in the question or in the outputs from the census (except for one table), the census has not only hidden information about the mixed parentage populations, but it may even have reduced the information we have, by displacing questions from other surveys which had previously included a 'Mixed' category, such as the Labour Force Survey.

The 2001 census question, which includes a 'Mixed' category (with four sub-groups), will, in turn, become the new mode of standardised classification. This means that far more data on mixed race people in Britain will become available following the 2001 census, not just from the census itself, but from other sources which will use the census question.

The statistical information we have can be summarised as follows:

- The 1991 census estimated that there were 230,000 people of mixed race in Britain. According to the Labour Force Survey, this is almost certainly an underestimate, with the correct figure being at least 290,000.
- The mixed populations constitute 0.6 per cent of the total population of Britain, but 11 per cent of the minority ethnic population.
- The mixed population is younger than the population in general, with 54 per cent being children under 15 (compared to 20 per cent of the total population). Two per cent of children under 5 are of mixed race.
- In the 1991 census, of ethnic minority respondents living with a partner, 16 per cent of the men and 13 per cent of the women were living with a white partner. Mixed relationships were more common among the black and Chinese populations than among South Asian groups; they were also more common for younger people (aged under 35) and for those born in the UK.
- Reported attitudes towards mixed relationships are generally accepting, and have become more so over time, although South Asian groups generally report themselves to be more opposed to such relationships than do other ethnic minority groups.

These statistics, however, cannot be taken to imply that Britain is moving inexorably towards a society where everyone is so mixed that ethnicity or the recognition of racial distinctions cease to be an issue. There is still opposition to mixed relationships by some white Britons, and this opposition can take violent forms. Furthermore, the racial and ethnic terms in usage at any one time in society (and which are acceptable to ethnic minority groups) are not neutral but carry social and political distinctions and values. If the terms which people use are constantly in flux, this can pose some major problems for demographic analysis.

This is why some analysts such as Richard Berthoud have argued that the British census needs to obtain a more accurate picture about people's ethnic origins. Berthoud suggests that the census question should ask for the ethnic origin of each parent, with separate columns for 'your mother' and 'your father'.[24] By phrasing the question on ethnic origin in this way, we can, according to Berthoud, avoid the real possibility that people conflate their ethnic origins with their ethnic identities. We must remember that people's ethnic identities may differ from their actual ethnic origins; there is no automatic correspondence between the two, and avoiding such confusion between the two is crucial in getting an accurate picture of multiethnic societies such as Britain today.

Although the introduction of a 'Mixed' category has not conclusively resolved these thorny issues, by revising the question to include a 'Mixed' category, the census has adapted to an important social trend in Britain's racialised demography. The significance of the change goes far beyond the census itself: the change signifies that mixed race is – officially – part of social reality.

Acknowledgements

Material from the Labour Force Survey is Crown Copyright; has been made available by the Office for National Statistics through the Data Archive and has been used with permission. The census data analysed in this chapter were made available by ONS, also Crown Copyright and used with permission. Neither the ONS nor the Data Archive bear any responsibility for the analysis or interpretation of the data reported here.

Notes

1. D. MacKenzie, *Statistics in Britain, 1865–1930: The social construction of scientific knowledge* (Edinburgh: Edinburgh University Press, 1981); D. Dorling and S. Simpson (eds), *Statistics in Society* (London: Arnold, 1999).
2. Early Years Trainers Anti-Racist Network, *The Best of Both Worlds ... Celebrating Mixed Parentage* (London: EYTARN, 1995).
3. A. Phoenix and C. Owen, 'From miscegenation to hybridity: mixed relationships and mixed parentage in profile', in B. Bernstein and J. Brannen

(eds), *Children, Research and Policy* (London: Taylor & Francis, 1997), pp.111–35.

4. P. Fryer, *Staying Power: The History of Black People in Britain* (London: Pluto Press, 1984); R. Visram, *Ayahs, Lascars and Princes: Indians in Britain 1700–1947* (London: Pluto Press, 1986).
5. A. Berrington, 'Marriage patterns and inter-ethnic unions', in D. Coleman and J. Salt (eds), *Ethnicity in the 1991 Census. Volume 1: Demographic characteristics of the ethnic minority populations* (London: HMSO, 1996), pp.178–212.
6. G. Younge, 'Beige Britain', G2 section, p.2, *Guardian*, 22 May 1997.
7. T. Modood, 'Culture and identity', in T. Modood, R. Berthoud, J. Lakey, J. Nazroo, P. Smith, S. Virdee and S. Beishon (eds), *Ethnic Minorities in Britain* (London: Policy Studies Institute, 1997), pp.290–338.
8. J. Schuman, 'The ethnic minority populations of Great Britain – latest estimates', *Population Trends*, 96 (1999), pp.33–43.
9. A. Phoenix and C. Owen, 'From miscegenation to hybridity: mixed relationships and mixed parentage in profile', in B. Bernstein and J. Brannen (eds), *Children, Research and Policy* (London: Taylor & Francis, 1997), pp.111–35.
10. K. Sillitoe, 'Developing questions on ethnicity and related topics for the census', Occasional Paper 36 (OPCS, 1987), p.83.
11. M. Bulmer, 'Race and ethnicity' in R.G. Burgess (ed.), *Key Variables in Social Investigation* (London: Routledge & Kegan Paul, 1986), pp.54–75.
12. M. Dejevsky, 'America objects as the census gets too personal', *Independent*, 17 March 2000, p.14.
13. I am most grateful to Andy Teague of ONS for sending me copies of these documents.
14. The Flowchart is reproduced in M. Bulmer, 'The ethnic group question in the 1991 census of Population', in D. Coleman and J. Salt (eds), *Ethnicity in the 1991 census. Volume 1: Demographic characteristics of the ethnic minority populations* (London: HMSO, 1996), pp.33–62.
15. OPCS/GRO(S), *1991 Census: Ethnic Group and Country of Birth, Great Britain* (London: HMSO, 1993).
16. C.M. Snipp, 1997, 'Some observations about racial boundaries and the experiences of American Indians', *Ethnic and Racial Studies*, 20, 4, pp.667–89.
17. P.J. Aspinall, 'The Development of an Ethnic Question for the 2001 Census: The findings of a consultation exercise of the 2001 Census Working Subgroup on the Ethnic Group Question' (Office for National Statistics, 1996), p.50.
18. B. Tizard and A. Phoenix, *Black, White or Mixed Race?* (London: Routledge, 1993).
19. See, for example, E.V. Stonequist, *The Marginal Man: A study in personality and culture conflict* (New York: Russell & Russell, 1937).

20. P.J. Aspinall, 'The Development of an Ethnic Question for the 2001 Census: The findings of a consultation exercise of the 2001 Census Working Subgroup on the Ethnic Group Question' (Office for National Statistics, 1996), p. 60.
21. R. Barn, *Black Children in the Public Care System* (London: Batsford, 1993); M. Boushel, 'Vulnerable Multiracial Families and Early Years Services', *Children & Society*, 10 (1996), pp.305–16.
22. D. Owen, *Towards 2001: Ethnic Minorities and the Census* (Coventry: University of Warwick, 1996).
23. G. Younge, 'Beige Britain', G2 section, p.2, *Guardian*, 22 May 1997.
24. R. Berthoud, 'Defining Ethnic Groups: Origin or Identity:', *Patterns of Prejudice*, 32, 2 (1998).

8
Learning to Do Ethnic Identity: The Transracial/Transethnic Adoptive Family as Site and Context

Barbara Ballis Lal

Debate about transracial and intercountry adoption is both emotive and controversial because it reveals divergent views about the crucial matters of what constitutes a 'proper' family and what is in the best interests of children. Such discussion also raises questions about the appropriate roles of professionals, such as social workers and lawyers, and the state, in regulating family life. In addition, recent efforts in both Britain and the USA to facilitate transracial/transethnic adoption have raised concerns about ethnic identity and the adequacy of adoptive mixed-race/mixed-ethnicity families as venues for raising children in predominantly white societies.

Outcome data on both domestic and intercountry transracial/transethnic adoptees in Britain and the USA substantiates the benefits of family life. Same-race/same-ethnicity placements are no more successful than transracial/transethnic adoptions. Both sets of adoptees have dramatically improved life chances compared to either children in foster placements or in residential care. What is also demonstrated by the outcome data is that age at time of adoption is the most significant determinant of success or failure of the adoption.[1]

Yet, despite the above data, many child welfare professionals, lawyers, community leaders and politicians in Britain and the USA continue to contest domestic and intercountry transracial/transethnic adoptions by invoking a flawed, 'essentialist' concept of ethnic identity. I begin this chapter by pointing out the problematic aspects of an essentialist approach to identity whose central tenet is that biological origins inevitably tie children to a culture of descent and membership in a nominal community of descent. I then go on to present an alternative perspective, namely 'learning to do ethnic identity' which escapes the pitfalls of essentialism and which I argue should inform public policy decisions relating to adoption.

This chapter is based on outcome data and other research findings on transethnic/transracial adoptions in Britain and the USA over a period of about thirty years. It includes references to autobiographical accounts of children and parents living in biological and adoptive mixed-race/mixed-ethnicity families. I also refer to public policy documents, such as government legislation and the evidence used to formulate policy, such as hearings and specially commissioned government reports, and the statements of child welfare professionals.

The Essentialist Concept of Ethnic Identity

An essentialist model of identity argues that one facet of a person, such as race, ethnicity, gender or sexual orientation, 'trumps' all other aspects of selfhood. In assuming that one feature of a person such as race or ethnicity determines experience and life chances and ties individual destiny to that of the group, identity essentialism overlooks variations among members of a putative group. For example, ethnic identity essentialism overlooks the importance of social class, gender and generation in effecting differences between African-Americans.[2] It also overlooks factors such as religion in discussions of a deceptively undifferentiated population of non-white Britons.[3] Identity essentialism also disregards the similarities between ethnic minorities and a dominant white group.[4]

Identity essentialism rules out a concept of the self based on a combination of identities representing a variety of social bonds, some of which are based on descent and kinship but others that are based on consent and voluntary affiliation. This range of identities may be of varying degrees of generality and intensity. The question of how ethnic identity relates to other kinds of identities, such as those of gender, sexual orientation, religion and social class, and identity based on individual, for example educational, achievement, is not adequately addressed by identity essentialism. Moreover, as I argue below, what ethnic identity is and how ethnic identity relates to culture, are misconstrued.

The essentialist concept of ethnic identity suggests that ethnic culture inheres 'naturally' to those persons possessing a common descent and that those so designated are bound together as a 'natural', affect-laden and objective social group.[5]

Identity essentialism constructs deficits which allegedly stem from a lack of knowledge of a culture of biological descent and insufficient commitment to a nominal community of descent. These deficits include confusion about who one is and where one 'belongs', anger, low self-esteem, self-hatred, inability to deal with racism, inability to make friends, emotional instability, lack of achievement in school and career, delinquency and deviance.[6] Yet, as already pointed out, these gloomy prognostications are not borne out by the outcome data to hand.

Advocates of same-race placements who employ an essentialist concept of ethnic identity see descent as naturally implying not only inherited physical characteristics but an inherited culture. Transracial/transnational adoptees are cast as the purveyors of a primordial culture of descent which conflicts with the identities and learned culture acquired in their white adoptive family in a process of socialisation that extends from childhood through adolescence and adulthood.

Thus, an oft quoted statement issued in 1972 by the National Association of Black Social Workers in the USA declared that: 'Black children must not lose their cultural identity by being reared in a white home.' There is a logical flaw in the representation of culture and ethnic identity as an attribute that will be lost even if it was never developed in the first place. A more accurate statement would read 'Black children must not lose their opportunity to develop an appropriate cultural identity by being reared in a white home.' In this rendering, the prescriptive character of the statement is more fully revealed: that black and mixed-race children ought to develop a black cultural identity.[7]

The same hidden prescription is encountered in the recent report by June Thorburn, Liz Norford and Stephen Parvez Rashid on permanent family placement of children of minority ethnic origin in Britain. Although their research found no statistical difference in outcome between racially matched and non-matched placements, the researchers recommend that transracial placements remain a policy of last resort in line with the earlier guidelines of the 1989 Children's Act.[8] Defending this earlier prohibition against transracial placements in light of a directive intended to reverse this policy by Paul Boateng (the Labour Minister for Health and Welfare in 1998), the Department of Health (DOH) concluded in 1999 that 'transracially placed children suffered additional stress as a result of losing contact with their racial and cultural origins as well as their birth parents'.[9]

In addition to ignoring the major research finding that age at time of placement *rather than* racial matching is the most important determinant of placement outcome, the policy recommendations of Thorburn, Norford and Rashid and the DOH conclusion concerning additional stress are made on the basis of a survey in which about 40 per cent of the children had a white-European mother and either an African-Caribbean, African or Asian father.[10] This further calls attention to the wholly problematic characterisation of ethnicity, culture and identity in these debates. That such children should be given the opportunity to develop the cultural identity of their mother as well as their father, or of developing a new, syncretic hybrid mixed-ethnicity identity is not envisaged by either the research team or by the Department of Health.[11]

Moreover, given that, overall, 80 per cent of biological fathers surveyed by Thorburn, Norford and Rashid were either unaware of or indifferent to their child's birth, it is likely that had the children not been placed for adoption or permanent foster care, many of them would in any case have grown up in white homes, namely, the white homes of their biological European mothers. Should we conclude that leaving these mixed-ethnicity children in the care of their white-European biological mothers results in their being robbed of their roots and cultural heritages?

A more recent British Agencies for Adoption and Fostering (BAAF) circular on intercountry adoptions continues to reflect an essentialised concept of ethnic identity and an oversimplified view of culture. The BAAF circular points out that:

> For a child of a different ethnicity adopted from overseas, it may be that he or she has lost touch with many aspects of their culture, such as language, religion, diet, customs, etc. So later difficulties around knowing 'who they are' can result in a feeling of alienation from their community of origin. Even if a child has not had direct experience of their culture i.e. if he or she has been adopted as a very young baby, the importance of a sense of roots must never be underestimated.[12]

In this statement BAAF supposes that an infant adopted at an early age is in some primordial way attached to a community and culture of biological descent whose significance is as great as the culture of the family within which it has been nurtured and grown up. Furthermore, this statement, like other admonishments regarding the necessity for acquiring or retaining a cultural heritage based on biological descent, is without specific content as to what exactly is required here.

First, are we talking about intercountry adoptees learning only the language, religion, diet and customs of birth parents? Should we include information about how children born out of wedlock or with disabilities fare in many lately developed countries? What about the life-chances of abandoned children living in orphanages and on the streets? This too is part of a culture.[13]

Second, how should we handle those instances in which adoptees are not eager to learn about cultures of descent? Should we treat this as an expression of a parenting deficiency? Do we ask biological mixed-race children or second-generation immigrant children to commit themselves to these same undertakings and should we condemn their parents if these children refuse to do so? Is learning an ethnic culture of descent optional or required?

Third, the excessive costs of transnational (and in many instances domestic) adoptions, which discriminates against working-class families being able to adopt children, especially children from abroad, also results in most adoptees being brought up in middle-class families. Should we assume that if there is no affinity between these essentially middle-class children, for example, those who are not white, and all people of colour, regardless of social class, that these children are damaged and that their parents have been negligent with respect to bringing them up?

Fourth, should we standardise socialisation procedures so that transracial/transnational adoptees from Guatemala or India who wish to learn ancient Greek and become classics scholars are advised to make this a second-order activity and learn Spanish or Hindi in order to become community activists instead? The essentialist concept of ethnic identity that suggests that culture has more to do with biology than the complexities of lived experience is an expression of what the British sociologist Paul Gilroy calls an 'absolutist view of black and white cultures'. Commenting on the insistence by the Association of Black Social Workers and Allied Professionals in Britain in 1983 that black children remain in local authority institutions 'where they can be nurtured to a "positive black identity" by black staff' rather than being adopted into white families, he goes on to point out: 'This reductionist perspective eclipses commonalities and differences based upon age, gender, class or neighbourhood considerations and denies the multidimensionality and variability in the process of identity formation.'[14]

Ambiguities with respect to matching requirements in adoption further reveal the problematic aspects of efforts to uphold such an 'absolutist view of black and white cultures'. What exactly are the 'shared ways of behaving' that 'add up to the social life of the race or ethnicity' which child welfare professionals are asked to honour in domestic placements? How important are 'the distinctive ways of talking, dressing, interacting, eating and so on' when compared to the benefits of a stable family life?[15] Another way of considering these requirements is to ask what exactly do child welfare professionals object to when they assert that some black and mixed-race transracial adoptees 'have been socialised into thinking of themselves as white ... '[16]

An insistence on same-race placement is driven by the belief that pride in a heritage of descent 'empowers' ethnic minorities. It does this by relinquishing minority group members from the burden of assimilation to a mainstream culture which invokes criteria of difference, such as those of race and ethnicity, as justifications for exclusion or subordination. For example, naming and self-referencing is intended to construct new ways of organising difference and of contesting old ways of connecting to others.[17]

The point is, however, that identities, cultures and heritages are neither static nor uniform among a population. Children and parents in mixed-race/mixed-ethnicity families, whether adoptive or biological, are themselves creating a range of identities that capture their particular experience of living in multicultural families. In this respect it is useful to note that in Britain and the USA a greater number of mixed-race/mixed-ethnicity partnerships/marriages suggests that transracial/transethnic families will become more conventional. For example, the 1997 Policy Studies Institute survey of ethnic minorities in Britain notes: 'As many as half of British-born Caribbean men, and a third of women, had chosen a white partner ... and this may be an indication of the likely pattern for future generations'; and 'for two out of five children (39 per cent) with a Caribbean mother or father, their other parent was white'.[18] In the USA, while multiracial births still represent a small portion of all births, demographic projections suggest that current increases will continue in even greater magnitude.[19]

Despite its flaws, an essentialised concept of ethnic identity and an oversimplified 'absolutist' culture of descent remain fulcrums around which same-race matching policies are constructed. Child welfare professionals and other 'ethnic identity entrepreneurs' by virtue of their office and their expertise, use their very extensive power to enforce policies and programmes which conform to their specific conception of what ethnic identity is and the cultural requirements this fictive, essentialised identity entails.[20]

Ethnic Identity as Learned Culture

While it is often understood in terms of descent, ethnic identity is primarily a matter of learned culture.[21] Culture is not inherited; rather, it consists of learned 'symbols, stories, rituals and world-views which people may use in varying configurations to solve different kinds of problems' and which are the 'components that are used to construct strategies of action', that is to say 'persistent ways of ordering action through time'.[22] Culture enables 'the members of a collectivity to grasp their worlds'.[23]

The acquisition of ethnic identities such as that of being a Muslim, second-generation, Pakistani-British Londoner, or a Jewish, mixed-race African-American New Yorker, is learned through experience in a variety of situations along with the acquisition of other identities such as those based on gender, sexual orientation, social class, neighbourhood, school, occupation and hobbies. Learning and enacting identities takes place with respect to particular sites and contexts; like 'vocabularies of motive', identities are a type of 'situated action'.[24] In other words, the way in which we see ourselves on any particular occasion is influenced by the presence of real or imaginary significant others and the positive or negative value that we assume that a particular identity will confer in a particular situation and context.

For example, students entering university might invoke a common ethnicity as an expedient way of negotiating friendships. Ralph Turner observes:

> ... Japanese-Americans who had grown up in integrated neighbourhoods and schools with no special sense of favouring Japanese-Americans for friends often felt lost and alone upon entering a large state university. Desperate for companionship, they struck up acquaintances with other Japanese-Americans, joined ethnic student organisations, and soon found themselves caught up in movements to advance the ethnic group's interests.[25]

In this instance, as Herbert Gans and William Yancey, among others, point out, ethnicity is an 'emergent' response to 'current needs' and opportunities rather than a reflection of tradition.[26]

Like any other facet of socialisation, learning to do ethnic identity involves a process of interpretation that includes 'taking the role of the other' as well as the 'self' concept.[27] The 'semiotic self' empowers the actor insofar as he/she routinely employs reason, exercises choice and understands experience in reflexive, individuated ways.[28] The internal processes of interpretation, reflection and decision-making go on even in circumstances in which significant constraints of various sorts limit the kinds of activities the actor can reasonably hope to undertake. For example, transracial/transethnic adoptees may be excluded from dating during adolescence on the basis of racial preferences. However, the importance and meaning attributed to this kind of exclusion, as well as other instances of being 'raced', is not automatic but an outcome of reflection.

Transracial/transnational adoptees, like biological mixed-race children and children of colour generally, are not passive victims whose ethnic identities are affixed to the negative designations of others. To some extent, children may accept or reject racialised messages. Moreover, it is also worth noting with respect to strategies for dealing with racism, that transracial/transethnic adoptees have first-hand knowledge of the positive ways in which ethnically diverse people may relate to one another.[29]

Building on the elements of volition, reason and creativity, the self contests a deterministic understanding of causality whether located in social structure, the unequal distribution of power, or culture. In line with this view, identity is never wholly a category imposed by an environment, unavailable to manipulation on the part of the actor. Thus, Sandra Wallman's essays on work and ethnicity and her ethnography of six south London households suggest that work, neighbourhood and family are sites and contexts in which there are a range of available 'identity options' and that from the point of view of her informants, ethnic identity is not necessarily most significant in the construction of action in all situations.[30]

Learning to do ethnic identity, then, is not necessarily a matter of conforming to dominant expectations but may challenge these expectations. Because the actor is creative, intelligent and reflective, he/she may attempt to alter, rather than adjust to stereotypes or to challenge or disregard a submissive identity embedded in particular institutional arrangements. For example, an Asian-American transracial adoptee observes: 'I stick out like a sore thumb ... But I like being different. I'm the total opposite of the Asian stereotype. I'm very outgoing, I'm not studious and I have a very loud voice.'[31] However, transracial adoptees, like people of colour generally, encounter greater constraints with regard to the voluntary, self-directed construction of identities than do white people.[32]

Other sites and contexts in which ethnic identity is learned and/or reinforced are the neighbourhood, school, church, and ethnic enclave. Studies of 'segmented assimilation' demonstrate how the spatial distribution of ethnic groups in neighbourhoods influences the way in which the children of immigrants rework their original parental identity of descent and learn to do an 'American' peer-oriented, gendered ethnic identity. These children become purveyors of ethnic identities, some of which have to do with growing up in a particular neighbourhood and/or attending a mixed-race/mixed-ethnicity school.[33]

While a particular identity or identities may affect behaviour across the dimension of time as well as sites and contexts, the enactment of identities is never determined by external factors alone and apart from the reflexive deliberations of the self. The crucial question is, as Ralph Turner points out: 'What makes ethnic identity particularly salient among the assortment of identities that every person has?'[34] Amartya Sen has also observed that, 'there are different maps and different procedures of partitioning people', and that the possibility of multiple identities is highly context-dependent.[35]

The Mixed-Race/Mixed-Ethnic Adoptive Family as Site and Context

The most important site for the social construction of identities is the family – in its various forms. In a succession of situations children learn to do a variety of identities, that is to say, they learn to see themselves in a variety of contexts or roles within the family, such as that of being children, boys/girls, teenagers, grandchildren, nieces and nephews, as well as school achievers or school failures.

Ethnic identity is only one of the many categories around which children growing up in families organise a sense of who they are and how they relate to others. Identities may also refer to voluntary membership in groups requiring consent, such as neighbourhood peer groups, athletic clubs, and later, occupational associations and political interest groups. The family is also a site in which children learn to see themselves with respect to a range of categories that differentiate their family from that of others. These categories include social class and religion as well as ethnicity. Whether referring to family, or to affiliations outside the family, identities are linked to learned culture insofar as membership requires socialisation to the symbols and world-views inherent in the processes of interpretation and the construction of collective action.

Existing research with respect to both biological and adoptive mixed-race/mixed-ethnic families suggests that the process of socialisation within a family most influences a child's sense of self. Whatever the nature of ethnic/racial stratification experienced outside the immediate family, it is within a family that children first form a sense of the range of identities, including ethnic identities and affiliations that constitute him/herself.[36] It is therefore of importance to evaluate the arguments of advocates of same-race placements who argue that the white family, consciously or not, is a venue for the reproduction of racist domination and ethnic hegemony. John Small notes:

> The one-way traffic of black children into white families begs fundamental questions of power and ideology. It raises questions as to the type of relationship which exists between blacks and whites and furthermore, the type of society those involved in the practice are creating.[37]

However, interviews with both transracial/transethnic adoptees and their white parents suggest that it is more common for these families to celebrate the heritage and culture of descent of the adopted child alongside the culture of the child's ethnically diverse adoptive family. For example, in both Britain and the USA there are a variety of family-oriented associations in which transracial/transnational adoptees and their parents and siblings meet to revisit countries of adoptee descent and to explore the adopted child's culture of descent. These associations include the Latin American Parent Association (LAPA), Harmony in Britain, Multi-Racial Americans (MASC), and the Association of Multiethnic Americans (AMEA) in the USA.[38] What is crucial is that the adoptee's race or ethnicity of descent does not eclipse his/her status of being a son, daughter or sibling.

In transracial/transethnic adoptive families, children must create a sense of self which includes identities relating to their being adopted as well as having a physical appearance that might be different from one or both parents and possibly siblings. Identities that emerge from within the family may be reinforced and/or contradicted on the basis of social interaction in different sites and contexts such as those of neighbourhood and school. Neighbours, teachers, social workers and school friends might not support the meaning and importance of ethnic identity learned within the family. Transracial/transethnic adoptees, like biological mixed-race children, have to deal with the surprise and sometimes derision of peers curious about the difference in colour between themselves and their adoptive parents and siblings. Responses to such dissonance are not uniform, and range from embarrassment and discomfort to matter-of-fact reporting. A nineteen-year-old black adoptee recalls: 'When I was eight or nine years old I did not want to show my parents to my friends'; and a seventeen-year-old who described herself as 'basically white inside' remarks that: 'Just being black in a white family is special – it draws a lot of attention to me.'[39]

However, the experience of 'dissonance' between ethnic identity, as conveyed within the family and in sites and contexts outside of it, can sometimes result in a confused sense of self.[40] For example, a transracially adopted woman reflecting on her childhood remarks: 'And I was in denial a lot. When people asked how it felt to be black, I would say

I'm as much white as black, why are you focusing on the black?' She goes on to note that she was required to rethink her ethnic identity in college in part as a result of travelling to Africa and Cuba where she felt 'welcomed' as opposed to feeling excluded by both blacks and whites.[41]

On the other hand, reflection and choice, which are central to the process of learning to 'do' ethnic identity, explains why most children are able to confront dissonance on the basis of colour, where this occurs between the family and other sites and contexts, and to resolve dissonance in self-enhancing ways. Thus, for example, some transracial adoptees point out that they get 'the best of both worlds' insofar as they can have both black and white friends.[42] Moreover, children are often able to construct new meanings to express their understanding of their novel family status. Thus, a black male adoptee observes: 'My parents have never been racist. They took shit for adopting two black kids. I'm proud of them for it. The Black Social Workers Association promotes a separatist ideology.'[43]

The evaluation of dissonance beween self and parents and siblings is variable and changes over the course of the family life-cycle. For example, adolescence is a period during which transracial adoptees are likely to experience white parents or white siblings as a special source of anxiety.[44]

Critics of transracial/intercountry adoption cite the inability of white parents to transmit strategies for coping with racism outside the family as reason enough to insist on same-race placements. However, evidence suggests that transracial/transethnic adoptees *and* their parents learn to deal with racism as a result of encountering this, especially in sites and contexts outside the nuclear family. Thus, Thorburn, Norford and Rashid note that adoptees interviewed in their sample 'commented favourably' that both white and black parents 'did battle with teachers, employers or neighbours who racially abused their children or failed to protect them from such abuse'.[45]

Dissonance between learning to do ethnic identity within the family and the designations of others outside the family also occurs with respect to a range of behaviours which, although frequently encoded as race, is a reflection of social class. For example, children of colour adopted by middle-class white parents may be accused of 'acting white'.[46] However, if transracial adoptees are judged to be not 'black enough', they share this insufficiency with many middle-class African-Americans in same-race biological families. Pejorative terms such as 'oreo' or the accusation of being 'white-washed', are intended to convey to African-American and mixed-race children, as well as transracial adoptees, 'that there are a limited number of valid ways to express blackness'.[47]

In this spirit, a child welfare professional in favour of same-race placements observes that: 'When you close your eyes and listen to African-American adults who were raised in white families … you would think they were white. Things like that make it hard for them to identify with the African-American community.' She cites this as illustrative of white families not being equipped 'to give kids the coping skills they will need.'[48] Is there, or should there be, a speech code requirement for all African-American children – biological or adopted? How crucial is this compared to other features of family life such as having stable caretakers who provide food, shelter, education and affection?

Some contemporary scholars point out that ethnic identity may not be based on distinctive world-views or cultural practices but instead with 'subjective identification' having to do with a sense of 'with whom one belongs' and of membership in a community.[49] For transracial/transethnic adoptees (as well as children in biological mixed-race/mixed-ethnicity families) learning to do ethnic identities within the family and in sites and contexts outside of it, may result in dissonance with respect to the entitlements and especially the obligations incurred as a result of subjective identification and membership in ethnic groups that are generally seen as being mutually exclusive.

On the one hand, membership 'entitles one to participate in the population's particular styles of support, nurture, family and politics. It gives one a claim to distinctive ways of talking, dressing, interacting, eating and so on.' On the other hand, membership involves obligations; it demands loyalty and solidarity to the group such that other members have 'a presumed right to expect a degree of conformity or similarity in social dimensions of ethnicity'. Moreover, the demonstration of commitment to 'the social life of the race or ethnicity at any given time' are not always matters of individual choice and 'agreement on issues about which there is a broad consensus within the group, is often not negotiable'.[50]

For the transracial/transethnic adoptee, personal experience, especially as this occurs within the family, will have to stand up to the expectations embedded in conventions supporting the maintenance of social boundaries and ethnic hierarchy. He/she might also have to deal with the essentialist, politically motivated views of child welfare professionals, politicians and community representatives for whom all ambiguities concerning choice with respect to subjective identification and membership are automatically resolved in favour of affiliation with a minority group.

The question of whether or not transracial/transethnic adoptees seek inclusion in ethnic associations based on their biological origin and honour the obligations such membership entails, or the question of how important membership in ethnically-oriented associations is compared to membership in other groups over the course of a lifetime, requires further research. Moreover, whether and how commitment to an ethnic group based on biological descent affects decisions to do with dating, partnerships, marriage and family formation, are all empirical questions.

For example, autobiographical accounts indicate that for at least some Korean-American adoptees, associating with other Korean-American adoptees and re-establishing links with their biological families and cultures of descent is very important. This tends to be characteristic of those adopted later in childhood and for whom there remain memories of life in Korea prior to joining their adoptive families in America.[51]

Transracially adopted Chinese-Americans as well as Korean-Americans now have associations in which to explore their particular life histories. There are increasing numbers of adoptee ethnic associations which offer information about cultures of descent and families of origin. Such associations also offer therapy to counteract ethnic dissonance and negative consequences of transracial/transethnic adoption.[52] Another possibility is to provide summer 'culture' camps in which transracial adoptees are given the opportunity to share experience with other adoptees of the same ethnicity.[53] Whether or not, or how important participation in racial/ethnic associations is for adoptees, in general, is difficult to ascertain because the percentage of transracial/transethnic adoptees participating in such organisations is unknown.

There are a number of studies that suggest strategies for mitigating the effects of the aforementioned sources of ethnic identity dissonance. Carl Kallgren and Pamela Caudill urge that white parents eschew colour-blindness and instead take on parenting in ways that directly address the issue of colour and racial difference between themselves and their transracially adopted children.[54] Others conclude that transracial adoptees, as well as biracial biological children, are less likely to experience dissonance as a crisis if they grow up in racially and ethnically diverse neighbourhoods and do not attend schools in which there are only white students.[55]

Conclusion

There are several important points to note about the perspective on ethnic identity/identities as learned culture. First of all, people's ethnic identities are labile and opportunist. Learning to do ethnic identity calls attention to the role of agency and choices about ethnic roles. It suggests that there are a range of ways in which ethnicity may be experienced.

Second, ethnic identities always exist alongside of a range of other identities based on membership in a variety of groups. The salience of ethnic identity is a variable. Within societies such as the USA and Britain, the significance of ethnic identity and culture, while not negligible, is not necessarily of greatest importance to children when compared to other identity-conferring facets of family life, such as social class or the absence of a male parent.[56]

Third, while a sense of ethnic identity has to do with how others see us, the ascriptions and treatment of others do not determine a sense of self. In liberal democratic societies, as opposed to totalitarian settings, an individual is able to decide whether or not to act in terms of the 'recognition' of particular (racist) others and to calculate the costs and benefits of accepting or rejecting the designations of others. The perspective on learning to do ethnic identity qualifies the ascriptive and structurally determined dimensions of ethnicity.

The perspective on ethnic identity as learned culture contradicts the essentialist model favoured by many child welfare professionals which sees adoptees as irrevocably tied to the ethnicity of their birth parents and to a nominal community of descent. For these child welfare professionals, psychological well-being is always measured by the degree to which adopted children organise their understanding of themselves around categories of descent and social constructions of race and ethnicity rather than in terms of membership in a range of different groups, including that of their adoptive family.

How representative the vociferous opposition to transracial and transethnic adoption is among all child welfare professionals, community leaders, academics and other official race relations spokespersons, is unknown. Moreover, the extent to which such opposition is an accurate reflection of the views of the wider population, is also unsubstantiated. For example, in both the 1971 and 1991 Gallop polls, 71 per cent of Americans said that they approved of transracial adoption while in a more recent 1999 study conducted by the Princeton Survey Research Association, 80 per cent of Americans approved of white couples adopting black children and 73 per cent approved of African-American couples adopting white children.[57]

During the 1990s, politicians and government in both Britain and the USA have initiated legislation and changes in public policy to facilitate transracial and intercountry adoption. For example, currently in Britain both the Labour Government and the opposition Conservative

Party have convened committees to investigate and remove obstacles to placing at least part of the estimated 50,000 children in care (of whom about 46,000 have been in care for over six months and an estimated 5,000 of whom are actually available and waiting for adoption) into permanent homes regardless of the race, ethnicity, religion, gender and marital status of parents.[58]

Mixed-race/mixed-ethnicity families, whether biological or adoptive, have the potential to undermine various forms of racism and ethnocentrism. To discourage the formation of these families is out of step in a globalising world in which people routinely move, intermarry and settle far from the places in which they were born. Moreover, to delay placing orphaned, abandoned or abused children in order to preserve an essentialised ethnic identity, which is itself a misguided construction of child welfare professionals, or in order to find ethnically matched parents, does not respect the child's best interest.

Acknowledgements

Ongoing support for this research was received from the Committee on Research, Academic Senate, UCLA. I would like to thank the members of this committee for this crucial input. Thanks are also due to Stanley Engerman, Nicky Hart, Jennifer Lee, Ivan Light, David Parker, Linda Levy Peck, Michael Petch, Miri Song and Allison Wolf for their helpful comments, and to my research assistant at UCLA, Mary Beth Kremmel.

Notes

1. For example, the SEARCH Institute's survey of 715 families in the USA concludes: 'We cannot overstate the power of early placement. It is likely a key ingredient in the successful attachment of child to parents (and vice versa).' Peter Benson, Anu Sharma and Eugene Roehlkepartain, *Growing Up Adopted* (Minneapolis, MN: Search Institute, 1994); Department of Health, *Adoption, Messages from Research* (Chicester: John Wiley & Sons, 1999, p.15; June Thorburn, Liz Norford and Stephen Parvez Rashid, *Permanent Family Placement for Children of Minority Ethnic Origin* (Norwich, East Anglia: Centre for Research on the Child and Family, University of East Anglia/Department of Health, 1998); Patricia Morgan, *Adoption and the Care of Children* (London: IEA Health and Welfare Unit, 1998); Rita Simon, Howard Alstein and Marygold Melli, *The Case for Transracial Adoption* (Washington DC: American University Press, 1994); Elizabeth Bartholet, *Family Bonds, Adoption and the Politics of Parenting* (New York: Houghton Mifflin, 1993); Centre For the Future of Children, *The Future of Children*, special issue on Adoption, Vol.3, No.1, (CA: Centre for the Future of

Children, Spring 1993), pp.104–18; Rita Simon and Howard Altstein, *Adoption, Race and Identity* (London: Praeger, 1992); William Feigelman and Arnold Silverman, *Chosen Children* (New York: Praeger, 1983); Owen Gill and Barbara Jackson, *Adoption and Race, Black, Asian and Mixed Race Children* (London: Bateson, 1983); Lucille Grow and Deborah Shapiro, *Black Children, White Parents: A Study of Transracial Adoption* (Lexington, MA.: Lexington Books, 1979).

2. See, for example, Julius W. Wilson, *The Declining Significance of Race, Blacks and Changing American Institutions* (Chicago: University of Chicago Press, 1978).
3. See, for example, Tariq Modood, Richard Berthoud, Jane Lakey, James Nazroo, Patten Smith, Satnam Virdee and Sharon Beishon, *Ethnic Minorities in Britain, Diversity and Disadvantage* (London: Policies Studies Institute, 1997).
4. See, for example, Russell Jacoby, 'The Myth of Multiculturalism', *New Left Review*, 208 (November 1994), pp.121–7. Steven Steinberg, *The Ethnic Myth* (Boston: Beacon Press, 1981).
5. Richard Handler, 'On Dialogue and Destructive Analysis: Problems in Narrating Nationalism and Ethnicity', *Journal of Anthropological Research*, 41, (1985), pp.171–82.
6. Among those whose research alleges damaging effects of transracial adoption see The National Association of Black Social Workers Conference, Nashville, TN., 'Position Paper' (9–12 April 1972). R. McRoy and L. Zurcher, *Transracial and Inracial Adoptees: The Adolescent Years* (Springfield, IL: Charles C. Thomas, 1983). John Small, 'New Black Families', *Adoption and Fostering*, 6, 3 (1982), pp.35–9. John Small, 'Transracial Placements: Conflicts and Contradictions', in A. Cheetham and J. Small (eds), *Social Work With Black Children and Their Families* (London: Batsford, 1986), pp.81–99. Hollingsworth, 'Promoting Same Race Adoption For Children of Color', *Social Work*, 4, 2 (1998), pp.97–116. British Agencies for Adoption and Fostering, 'Be my parent', Issue 42, October 1997.
7. 'Transracial Adoption', presented at the National Association of Black Social Workers Conference, Nashville Tennessee, 1972.
8. June Thorburn, Liz Norford and Stephen Parvez Rashid, 'Adoption', abstract, pp.ii, 24, 28.
9. Department of Health, 'Adoption', pp.155–9.
10. June Thorburn, Liz Norford and Stephen Parvez Rashid, 'Adoption', p.8.
11. For a discussion of hybridity see, for example, Pnina Werbner, 'The Dialectics of Cultural Hybridity', in Pnina Werbner & Tariq Modood (eds), *Debating Cultural Hybridity, Multi-Cultural Identities and the Politics of Anti-Racism* (London: Zed Books, 1997), pp.1–25.
12. British Agencies for Adoption and Fostering, Intercountry Adoption, Information and Guidance, (London: British Agencies for Adoption and Fostering, 1998), p.4.

13. See, for example, K. Johnson, H. Banghan and W. Liyao, 'Infant abandonment and adoption in China', *Population and Development Review*, 24, 3 (1998), pp.469–503; T. Scanlon, A. Tomkins, M. Lynch and F. Scanlon, 'Street Children in Latin America', *British Medical Journal*, 316, 7144, 23 May 1998.
14. Paul Gilroy, *There Ain't No Black In The Union Jack* (London: Hutchinson, 1987), p.66.
15. Naomi Zack, 'On Being and Not-Being Black and Jewish', in Maria Root (ed.), *The Multiracial Experience*, (London: Sage, 1996), p.143.
16. June Thorburn, Liz Norford and Stephen Parvez Rashid, 'Adoption,' p.27.
17. See, for example, Carlos Fernandez, 'Government Classification of Multiracial/Multiethnic People', in Maria Root (ed.), *The Multiracial Experience*, (London: Sage, 1996), pp.15–36.
18. Modood, Berthoud, Lakey, Nazoo, Smith, Virdee, Beishon, *Ethnic Minorities*, pp.18–59.
19. Maria Root, 'The Multiracial Experience,' in Maria Root (ed.), *The Multiracial Experience*, (London: Sage, 1996), pp.xiii–xxviii.
20. Barbara Ballis Lal, 'Ethnic Identity Entrepreneurs: Their Role in Transracial and Intercountry Adoptions', *Asian and Pacific Migration Journal*, 6, 3–4 (1997), pp.385–413.
21. The concept of ethnic identity as learned culture is generated from within the symbolic interactionist perspective. See Herbert Blumer, *Symbolic Interactionism, Perspective and Method* (Englewood Cliffs, NJ.: Prentice-Hall, 1969); Barbara Ballis Lal, 'Symbolic Interaction Theories' in John Stanfield (ed.), *American Behavioral Scientist*, 38, 3 (January 1995), special issue on Theories of Ethnicity, pp. 421–41.
22. Ann Swidler, 'Culture in Action', *American Sociological Review*, 51 (April 1986), pp.273–86.
23. John Higham, *Send These to Me: Jews and Other Immigrants in Urban America* (Baltimore: Johns Hopkins University Press, 1984), p.xi.
24. C. Wright Mills, 'Situated Actions and Vocabularies of Motive', in *Power, Politics and People* (New York: Ballantine Books, 1963), pp.439–52; Jonathan Okamura, 'Situational Ethnicity', *Ethnic and Racial Studies*, 4, 4 (1981), pp.452–65; Barbara Ballis Lal, 'Learning', in preparation.
25. Ralph Turner, unpublished paper (n.d.); F. Hosokawa, *The Sansei: Social Interaction and Ethnic Identification among the Third Generation Japanese*, (San Fransisco: R & E Research Inc., 1978).
26. William Yancey, Eugene Eriksen and Richard Juliani, 'Emergent Ethnicity: A Review and Reformulation', *American Sociological Review*, 41, 3 (June 1976), pp.391–403; Herbert Gans, 'Symbolic Ethnicity: the Future of Ethnic Groups and Cultures in America', *Ethnic and Racial Studies*, 2, 1 (1979), pp.1–20.
27. George Herbert Mead, 'The Self', in Charles Morris (ed.), *Mind, Self and Society* (Chicago: University of Chicago Press, 1934), pp.135–226.

28. Norbert Wiley, 'The Politics of Identity in American History', in Craig Calhoun (ed.), *Social Theory and the Politics of Identity*, (Oxford: Blackwells, 1994), pp. 131–49.
29. Rita Simon, 'Adoption Across Borders', in *Campaign For Intercountry Adoption, Conference-Issues of Identity*, (London: Campaign For Intercountry Adoption, 9 December 1999), p.14.
30. Sandra Wallman, *Eight London Households*, (London: Tavistock, 1984).
31. Tamar Lewin, 'New Families Redraw Racial Boundaries', *New York Times* (27 October 1998), p.A12.
32. Mary Waters, *Ethnic Options* (Los Angeles: University of California Press, 1990); Mary Waters, 'Ethnic and Racial Identities of Second generation Black Immigrants in New York City', *International Migration Review*, 28 (1994), pp.795–820.
33. Alejandro Portis and Min Zhou, 'The New Second Generation: Segmented Assimilation and its Variants', *The Annals of the American Academy of Political and Social Sciences*, 530 (November 1993), pp.74–96; see also Kathryn Neckerman, Prudence Carter and Jennifer Lee, 'Segmented Assimilation and Minority Cultures of Moblity, *Ethnic and Racial Studies*, 22, 6 (November 1999), pp.945–65; John Ogbu and Signithia Fordham, 'Black Students' School Success: Coping with the "Burden of Acting White"', *Urban Review*, 18 (1986), pp.176–206.
34. Ralph Turner, unpublished paper (n.d.).
35. Amartya Sen, 'Reason before Identity', *The Romanes Lecture for 1998* (Oxford: Oxford University Press, 1999), pp.14–15.
36. Anne Wilson, *Mixed Race Children, A Study of Identity* (London: Allen & Unwin, 1987).
37. John Small, 'The Crisis in Adoption', *The International Journal of Social Psychiatry*, 30 (1984), p. 129.
38. Rita Simon and Howard Altstein, *Adoption Across Borders* (Lanham: Rowman & Littlefield, 2000), pp.49–93.
39. Rita Simon and Howard Altstein, *Adoption, Race and Identity* (London: Praeger, 1992), p.148.
40. The concept of 'dissonance' originates and is discussed in Carl Kallgren and Pamela Caudill, 'Current Transracial Adoption Practices: Racial Dissonance or Racial Awareness?', *Psychological Reports*, 72 (1993), pp.551–8.
41. Tamar Lewin, 'Two Views of Growing up when the Faces don't Match', *New York Times*, (27 October 1998); Tamar Lewin, 'New Families Redraw Racial Boundaries', *New York Times* (27 October 1998).
42. For example, see Rita Simon, 'Conference – Issues of Identity', House of Commons, London, December 1999, p.19.
43. *Ibid.* p.18.
44. For example, see Rita Simon and Howard Altstein, *Adoption Across Borders* (Lanham: Rowman & Littlefield, 2000), pp.73, 101.

45. June Thorburn, Liz Norford and Stephen Parvez Rashid, 'Adoption', pp.14–15.
46. For example, see Rita Simon and Howard Altstein, *Adoption, Race and Identity* (London: Praeger, 1992), p.145.
47. Reginald McKnight, 'Confessions of a Wannabe Negro', in Gerald Early (ed.), *Lure and Loathing, Essays on Race, Identity and the Ambivalence of Assimilation* (New York: Allen Lane, The Penguin Press, 1993), p.103.
48. Tamar Lewin, 'New Families Redraw Racial Boundaries', *New York Times* (27 October 1998).
49. Modood, Berthoud, Lakey, Nazoo, Smith, Virdee, Beishon, *Ethnic Minorities*, pp.7–13, 335–7.
50. Naomi Zack, 'On Being and Not-Being Black and Jewish', in Maria Root (ed.), *The Multiracial Experience*, (London: Sage, 1996), p.143.
51. Tonya Bishoff and Jo Rankin, (eds), *Seeds From A Silent Tree* (Los Angeles: Pandal Press, 1998); Susan Cox (ed.), *Voice From a Distant Place* (San Diego: Pandal Press, 1998).
52. Ruth McRoy and Christine C. Injima Hall, 'Transracial Adoptions: In Whose Best Interest?', in Maria Root (ed.), *The Multiracial Experience*, (London: Sage, 1996), p.78; see also Audrey Mullender, 'The Ebony project: Bicultural Group Work with Transracial Foster Parents', in Kenneth Chau (ed.), *Ethnicity and Biculturalism: Emerging Perspectives of Social Group Work* (Birmingham, New York: Haworth Press, 1991), pp.3–41.
53. For a discussion of culture camps in the USA see Tamar Lewin, 'New Families Redraw Racial Boundaries', *New York Times* (27 October 1998), p.A12–13.
54. Carl Kallgren and Pamela Caudill, 'Current Transracial Adoption Practices: Racial Dissonance or Racial Awareness?', *Psychological Reports*, 72 (1993), *passim*.
55. John Small, 'Transracial Placements: Conflicts and Contradictions', in A. Cheetham and J. Small (eds), *Social Work With Black Children and Their Families* (London: Batsford, 1986), pp.94–99; Evan B. Donaldson Institute, 'Executive Summary', *Survey of Korean Adoptees* (New York: Donaldson Institute, 1999); Rita Simon and Howard Altstein, *Adoption Across Borders* (Lanham: Rowman & Littlefield, 2000), pp.77, 106.
56. Sara McLanahan and Gary Sandefur, *Growing Up With A Single Parent, What Hurts, What Helps*, (Cambridge; London: Harvard University Press, 1994).
57. Rita Simon and Howard Altstein, *Adoption Across Borders* (Lanham: Rowman & Littlefield, 2000), pp.78–9.
58. *The Adoption Forum*, 2, May–July 2000.

9

'I'm a Blonde-haired, Blue-eyed Black Girl': Mapping Mobile Paradoxical Spaces among Multi-ethnic Women in Toronto, Canada

Minelle Mahtani

In the last decade, we have witnessed an explosion in the employment of geographical metaphors, like inside/outside, and margin/centre, to describe the varied experiences of multiple, fluid and flexible identities within the social.[1] In this chapter, I explore the possibility of developing a more adequate symbolic language to describe the day-to-day experience of multiethnicity. Through an empirical study of multiethnic women in Toronto, Canada, and drawing from the work of feminist theorists Gillian Rose and Elspeth Probyn, I examine how multiethnic women inhabit what I call 'mobile paradoxical spaces'.

Before I begin, I would like to explain why I have used the word 'multiethnic' instead of the term 'mixed race'. The term 'race' is problematic and I employ the phrase somewhat suspiciously. Given that 'race' is a social construction, and that it is an 'arbitrary system of (dis)organisation',[2] I believe that the notion of 'race' can obscure, and sometimes even prevent, promising epistemological and pedagogical analyses of racialised experiences. I use the phrase multiethnic as opposed to multiracial because many of the women I interviewed expressed concern about the categories of 'race' and were more comfortable identifying as multiethnic. For example, one of the women identified as 'Armenian-French-Portuguese-Canadian' and wanted to acknowledge the complexity of that kind of identification – thus a focus on ethnicity as opposed to 'race'.

The women in this study see themselves as breaking outside of the confines of strict racial categories and thus the phrase 'mixed race' is only one of many identifications they choose. Many of them expressed deep ambivalence about this term. Indeed, on some days, they might see themselves as biracial, multiethnic, multiracial, *and* 'mixed race'. Inspired in part by the pioneering work of Jayne Ifekwunigwe (see

Chapter 2) who employs the term *métis(se)* to describe participants in her study, I emphasise here that the women I interviewed define their ethnic identities in a variety of ways, dependent upon many factors.[3]

I would also like to preface this chapter with a brief discussion about my own complex multiple positionings. I am a multiethnic woman myself – my mother Iranian, my father south-east Indian. My identity as a Toronto-born multiethnic woman both complicates and complements my exploration here. I also come from an academic background in geography, which provides a unique lens from which to view issues of multiethnicity. There are particular reasons why I have chosen to explore multiethnicity in this field. Friends have eyed me up oddly when I proudly describe myself as a geographer, protesting, 'But you're not studying soil erosion – or colouring in maps with brightly-coloured crayons!' Perhaps in a way, I am still that buck-toothed sixth-grader, intensely poring over the map of Canada, debating whether or not to use 'forest green' or 'shamrock'. But now I purposely colour outside the map-lines of discourse, using language instead of pencils. For, as Stuart Hall maintains, 'identities are constructed within, as opposed to outside, discourse.'[4] What better way to deconstruct identity than by colouring outside the rigid lines of racial categories? I hope to demonstrate the inadequacies of previous racialised identifications to describe people who live their lives 'outside the lines' of racial categories.

On a less flippant (not to mention personal) note, I believe human geography can provide the necessary tools to chart methods of daily living and surviving in the postmodern world, which calls for a drastic revision of previous models of identity. Geographers may be ideally suited to capturing the rapidly shifting registers and modalities of the forces that shape everyday life, in part due to their assertion that all social relations are spatial, and take place within particular physical contexts.[5] Therefore, it follows that racism creates particular spatial patterns and codes through which spatial and racial domination is maintained. This directly impacts on questions of identity. Liz Bondi, a feminist geographer, explores the potential of turning a politics of identity into a politics of location.[6] Like Bondi, I believe that a renewed emphasis upon where one is allows questions of identity to be thought through in new ways. Feminist geographers offer potential maps of routes towards understanding everyday lived experiences among women. I use this idea as a point of departure towards the exploration of a feminist geography which unravels the complexities of racialisation within particular places.

After a brief discussion of popular discourses surrounding the experience of multiethnicity, I introduce the methodology employed to interview multiethnic women in Toronto. This will set the scene for the empirical analysis which follows. I then explain why I have coined the term 'mobile paradoxical spaces' through a discussion of the work of Rose and Probyn. Finally, I turn to the voices from the interviews to unveil some of the ways participants occupy mobile paradoxical spaces by actively creating alliances with others, often transcending socially constructed lines of difference.

Discourses on the Multiethnic Experience

It would be impossible here to thoroughly explore the ways multiethnic people have been portrayed throughout history. I will leave this task to others in this volume, as well as refer the reader to the work of Maria Root for examples.[7] For my purposes, I will limit my discussion to simply a few of the existing myths which continue to be perpetuated about the experience of multiethnicity, based on research in the last three decades. Some clinical psychological evaluations of the experience of multiethnicity concluded that the multiethnic individual suffers from social maladjustment, anxiety and confusion related to identity development.[8] Several case studies have insisted that multiracial people are troubled by their status and that they experience more difficulties with family and peers than others. Some examinations went so far as to insist that it is impossible to create a positive multiethnic identity:

> It is not possible to develop a positive 'mixed-race' identity ... I do not think it is possible to have an identity on a psychosocial foundation that is at odds with itself.[9]

The public imaginary of the multiethnic individual often mirrors these notions. The popular discourse is made up of a series of myths which pronounce the multiethnic individual as 'out of place' or having 'no place to call home'.[10] The cultural geographer Tim Creswell has explored how the notion of being 'out of place' brings to mind images of isolation, fear, dread, terror, loneliness or despair.[11] These linear representations depend, or rely, on racial classification as a way of making sense of the multiethnic individual. Such research seems to insist that the individual chooses one particular identity rather than multiple identities, thereby implying that the monoracial individual by contrast relies upon only one kind of identification. This sort of premise dictates the (un)reality that it is impossible to identify with more than one racial category implicity.

More recent examinations of multiethnic identity as explored by multiethnic researchers accentuate the fluid and flexible nature of identity instead. There is a recognition that the multiethnic individual is not necessarily deviant, nor is he/she compared to those with supposedly 'stable' ethnic identities. Instead, researchers have explored how identities are multiple, fragmented and socially constructed. There is also an emphasis on the diversity of the multiethnic experience, often exploring the interconnectedness of 'race', gender, class and sexuality.[12] These works begin to explore how the history of racialised genders, maintained through sexuality, continue to influence current understandings of the co-construction of 'race' and gender as well as the role of heterosexuality in maintaining the separation of gender and purity of 'race'.

Maria Root claims that multiraciality poses no inherent types of stress that would result in psychological maladjustment; any distress related to being multiracial is likely to be a response to an environment that has internalised racist beliefs.[13] Multiethnic individuals protest against the confining nature of socially constructed racial categories. They have demanded to be recognised as descendants of more than one racial category. Recent theorising on multiethnicity emphasises the interaction of social, familial and individual variables within a context that interacts with history and moves away from models of adjustment and identity development. Much of the recent work considers the complex contexts in which identity formation takes place, focusing on the role society plays. Instead of concentrating on the absolute resolution of identity (as if identity is something that must be resolved), these studies of multiethnic identity conceive of identity as something which is continually shifting and changing. They allow for the possibility that the individual may have concurrent affiliations and multiple, fluid identities with different social groups.[14]

This kind of research suggests that the tendency to focus on multiethnic individuals' seemingly 'problematic' nature, through the use of phrases like 'marginal', 'groupless' or 'not fitting in', reflects a pervasive psychopathology which effectively fractionalises the multiethnic person's experience. I was inspired to embark on a research project about multiethnicity because I wanted to turn away from the model of inside/outside and exclusion as a guide for thinking about the experience of multiethnicity. I am much less interested in where informants feel out of place than where they feel *in* place. What are the productive spaces that are created out of the desire to create connections? I set off with a tape recorder to find out.

Methodology

In order to explore senses of belonging among multiethnic women, I interviewed thirty-five multiethnic women in Toronto, Canada.[15] Identifying participants for the study was challenging. It allowed me to see how I had been using the category of 'mixed race woman' as a self-evident category, and in the process creating all sorts of exclusionary effects. In order to further reconceptualise the category, I deliberately chose not to focus on a specific ethnic 'mix'. I interviewed women whose identities included the awareness, acknowledgement, and affirmation of multiple racial, cultural and ethnic ancestries – those women who defined themselves as 'mixed race' (or multiethnic, biracial, racially mixed, or mixed ethnic parentage). I preferred to give informants in this study the space to define themselves. I was curious about when and where they would choose these designations.

Previous research on multiethnicity has demonstrated that obtaining multiethnic participants for research is fraught with threats to validity.[16] The majority of participants were recruited largely through word of mouth – mostly through colleagues, friends and family mentioning my research to others. The women were between the ages of 20 and 35, and although the class categories within which these women defined themselves meant different things in different contexts, the majority of the women saw themselves as being part of the 'middle- to upper-class' segment of Canadian society because of their respective educational backgrounds. Although I did try to recruit women of varying class status, I discovered that low to lower-middle class multiethnic womens' experiences of racialisation were very much structured by the constrained financial nature of their lives.

The majority of women interviewed had access to a university education, where many women began to contemplate and craft a vocabulary to describe their experiences , and where they learned to identify themselves outside of constraining racial labels – something which they attributed to their access to higher education. This in turn affected how they 'read their race', reflecting the complex ways 'race' and class are co-constructed. Each interview lasted at least three hours and was conducted face-to-face. The interviews were based on open-ended questions. In large part, most of the interviews progressed smoothly, where the interviewee would simply chat about her own experiences of multiethnicity. All names that follow are pseudonyms to protect the participants' privacy. A last aside: I have prefaced each quote with a brief introduction of each woman – including her age at the time of the interview, her job, and how she defined her ethnic background in order to avoid defining her readings of her ethnic identity myself.

In this paper, I will only concern myself with one part of the interviews – in particular, with unveiling these women's varied and diverse senses of belonging. Instead of documenting my informants' hypothetical search for home, I examine 'their appreciation of many homes'.[17] Their stories suggested to me the need to develop a more reflexive, spatialised vocabulary to weave together these colourful tapestries of identity. It is important to explore the immensely complex context in which meanings about the experience of multiraciality were produced and contested continually by myself and participants during the interviews. The interview process is a loaded one, and might be envisioned as a site of performance. For example, I was aware that my own identification as a multiethnic woman caused a web of tensions, definitions and fields of insider/outsider positionings to emerge. I realised that it was critical to continually contemplate my own complex politics of positioning throughout the process of interviewing and evaluating the interview material.[18]

Gillian Rose: 'Paradoxical Space'

My concern in the rest of the paper is to explore a new spatial metaphor to map out the experience of multiethnicity as described to me by participants in this study. My metaphor of mobile paradoxical spaces is inspired by the work of two feminist theorists: Gillian Rose and Elspeth Probyn. In particular, I combine Rose's 'paradoxical space' and Probyn's exploration of 'outside belongings', which I examine in the next section.

Some non-geographical readers may object to the attempt to thread together an empirically based study with the use of a theoretical metaphor. I was initially reluctant to invent a new expression to describe the multi-textured belongings forged by my participants for fear of creating another vacuous identity category. However, in developing this metaphor, I hope to bridge the inevitable impasse between metaphoric and real space, or 'the comfort of the abstract and the relevance of the empirical, the seduction of the ivory tower and the romance of the street'.[19] The metaphors themselves are not meant to be pinned down – they are simply theoretical musings, and as such, they are flexible and amenable in themselves. No doubt the theorising of both Rose and Probyn are not 'exact fits' with the empirical material – nor should they be. Rather, I hope that their theoretical endeavours hint at the potential coalitions which can be forged between theory and practice. Thus, this exploration may give us pause for more productive reflection on the complex and contradictory relationships within the social.

In order to explore the dimensions of the term mobile paradoxical spaces, I now turn to examine each of the elements that make it up in turn. Firstly, I begin with 'paradoxical space' as developed by feminist geographer Gillian Rose. Rose has made a significant contribution in geography with her book *Feminism and Geography*.[20] In the final chapter of her book, Rose explores the possibility of a paradoxical space. This chapter resonated deeply with my own experiences as a multiethnic woman, and after reading through my informants' transcripts, I felt convinced that Rose's notion of 'paradoxical space' was also very useful to describe the spaces forged by multiethnic women in my study.

Firstly, a short synopsis of the book is useful to put Rose's argument about paradoxical space into context. Rose's aim is to question the enduring masculinism that has structured geographic inquiry. Her book demonstrates how masculinity has shaped geographical epistemology as well as the theoretical contributions of the discipline. It is the last half of the book which I find inspiring: namely, Rose's attempt to develop some possible feminist strategies to counter those sorts of powerful masculinisms inherent to the discipline.

Rose explores some descriptions of oppressive spaces as territories in which women are caught. She suggests that many women's difficulties in spaces might be understood through masculinist claims to knowing, reflected through claims to space and territory. Clearly, for many women, 'being in space is not easy' and Rose explains how women experience confinement in space – a recurring image in women's accounts of their lives.[21]

To challenge these oppressive spaces, Rose examines how feminist writers, such as bell hooks and Minnie Bruce Pratt, imagine a space beyond this masculinist territorial logic.[22] Although Rose does not provide concrete examples of paradoxical space herself, she draws on Pratt's way of seeing, which Rose claims moves beyond the exclusions of racial, sexist and classist exclusions toward a more complex prism through which we explore the world:

> I learn a way of looking at the world that is more accurate, complex, multi-layered, multi-dimensional, more truthful: to see the world of overlapping circles, like movement on a millpond after a fish has jumped, instead of the courthouse square with me at the middle, even if I am on the ground.[23]

Paradoxical space acknowledges multiple dimensions or ways of articulating 'a sense of elsewhere beyond the territories of the master subject'.[24] The key point is that women are envisioned as being located in several social spaces at the same time simultaneously. Rose examines the particular paradoxes of occupying these spaces at the same time, highlighting the subversive potential of this position:

> The simultaneous occupation of centre and margin can critique the authority of masculinism ... help[ing] some feminists to think about both recognising differences between women and continuing to struggle for change as women ... the spaces of separatism in these discussions ... is also a space of interrelations – another paradox.[25]

A politics of paradoxical space works towards an emancipatory geography that examines new relationships between power, knowledge, space and social action. Rose explores how the subject of feminism depends on a paradoxical geography in order to acknowledge both the power of hegemonic discourses while insisting on potential sites of resistance.

To summarise, paradoxical space is imagined as an intervention against masculinist claims of knowing. It evokes one possible geography that focuses upon women creating their own geographies of knowledge, where they are centred as subject and not marginalised as object. Rose explores a different kind of subjectivity, where women are neither victims nor perpetrators of the experiences of displacement. She imagines a reconceptualised territory where women are not positioned as 'out of place' but rather as constitutive of their own spatialities – spatialities which do not replicate ancient exclusions in geography.

Paradoxical space gets at the mobility and simultaneity of particular subject positions. I find the idea particularly appealing because it suggests a way to theoretically map a geography which goes beyond dominant and dualistic discourses of identity. Feminist geographers have long identified the importance of moving beyond singular mappings of dualistic social power relations onto territorial spaces, like masculine and feminine onto public and private, for example. Rose recognises the malady and comes up with a potential cure by suggesting the possibility of a space beyond dualisms.

Rose admits that her argument about paradoxical space remains partial because it surfaces largely from her own rooted experience of everyday places. She is therefore tentative in offering them as part of a new and improved feminist orthodoxy for thinking about space in geography. However, she ends *Feminism and Geography* by asking:

> for a geography that acknowledges that the grounds of its knowledge are unstable, shifting, uncertain, and above all, contested. Space itself [is] insecure, precarious, and fluctuating ... other possibilities, other sorts of geographies, with different compulsions, desires and effects, complement and contest each other. This chapter has tried to describe just one of them. There are many more.[26]

With that cliffhanger, Rose firmly sets a radical agenda for the future of feminist geography. I initially expected that such a bold call would set off a myriad of responses from feminist geographers. However, no one has yet attempted to map out the political terrain of Rose's paradoxical space.[27] Untouched in this manner, paradoxical space sadly sits gathering dust on the shelf of feminist geography scholarship, a concept which is only grounded through theoretical examples in feminist studies.

In this chapter, I want to take paradoxical space off the shelf in order to explore some potentially exciting readings of multiethnicity. Although Rose may read her ideas as partial, I see her discussion as rich and tantalising, pointing towards the possibilities of describing some new feminist geographies. I read many parallels between the interviews and Rose's idea of paradoxical space, where the women in this study explained to me that they see themselves located in a variety of spaces at the same time – spaces which are, all at once, multidimensional, shifting, and contingent. The metaphor of paradoxical space helps to illuminate some of these experiences. One participant, Marical, a 25-year-old television producer, who identified her mother as European from New Zealand and father as 'albino' from South Africa, explained how the experience of multiethnicity is rife with paradox:

> I'm a blonde-haired, blue-eyed black girl, you know? That's a strange positioning to be ... I exist against all odds. You know, in a lot of ways? Unfortunately, [laughter] my very existence stares all these basic theories about human existence right in their face. Like it challenges that. So your physicality, your whole body, totally, you know, challenges the idea that races shouldn't mix, that this is the way things are, that these facts exist, that the truth exists in this way. Because if all this were true, then I wouldn't exist. And I exist, therefore it cannot be true. You know it's like this total, it's ridiculous! It's like this existential nightmare! We are existential nightmares! [laughter]

Marical's mere existence trumpets a wake-up call to those who continue to mistakenly assume that racial categories exist as discrete entities. Living in this space is not easy – it is, as Rose reminds us, precarious and fluctuating. But it is not completely hard, either. Marical refuses to solely locate herself within a marginal space. Instead, she adopts a productive stance structured by the diversity of social relations.

Katya, a 30-year-old filmmaker who reads her father's ethnic identity as black from the West Indies and mother's ethnic identity as Irish, explores the construction of a different kind of space that articulates a troubled relation to the hegemonic discourse of the multiethnic individual:

> It wasn't until people started asking me [she says in a sad voice]: 'Oh you poor thing, how are you dealing with being mixed? You must be so confused!' And I would say, 'Oh really?!' [laughter] 'What am I supposed to be confused about?' And then, they would say, 'Oh you don't know who you are!' And I would say, 'Oh sure I do. My name is Katya L'Engle Atwood!' [laughter] As I got older, when I thought about what it meant to be biracial, or mixed, I had more articulate answers, like 'No, I'm not confused. I recognise that I occupy a space in both spheres. As well as something outside of that, that is unique to people like me.'

Katya resists the socially constructed myth about multiethnic individuals being 'out of place'. She articulates a self-conscious defiance against the limitations of the racialised language which imposes definitions upon her as a subject. She explains how she has moved through the use of various identifications over time, in order to more clearly explicate to others the variety of ways she reads her identity.

These interview segments provide only a brief description of the occupation of a paradoxical space. Like Rose says, there are many more. In order to respond to Rose's call, I will provide more examples among participants in order to work through the possibilities of grounding paradoxical space in the lived world. This is not an easy task. To take on this enterprise, I draw from the work of Elspeth Probyn, who complements the work of Rose.

Elspeth Probyn: 'Outside Belongings'

Themes of mobility and paradox thread through both Rose's and Probyn's explorations. In *Outside Belongings*, Probyn focuses upon notions of process and movement inherent in forging belongings.[28]

She asks how aspiration is played out among individuals, insisting upon the importance of mapping everyday manners of being. I find Probyn's work appealing for three reasons. First, she concerns herself with problematising the particularities of identity. Second, she expresses a desire to spatialise identifications. Finally, she provides a compelling critique of belonging.

Probyn longs for a term which captures more than the term 'identity' can express. In her critique of identity politics (where one is stuck within the fixities of an identity category: as a feminist I should do this, for example) Probyn proposes that we do not live out our lives as general categories. Instead, she hints that varied forms of existence offer alternative modes of belonging which spill over static identity boundaries. Insisting that identity classifications too often slide into modes of difference, where it becomes extremely difficult to talk of 'race', class and gender at the same time, she explains that she wishes to further 'ground' the particularities of identity instead:

> That identity is problematic is hardly news within theoretical circles, where identity is, of course, fragmented, decentred, and all the rest. However, it seems to me that the discourse of identity as fragmented continues to be abstracted from the local ground in which one lives one's presumably decentred life ... I wonder why there is so little discussion of how these factors are embodied and how they play out in Peoria (or Bloomington or Burlington or Regina).[29]

Probyn seems almost exasperated by the intellectual hegemony of American scholarship in cultural studies in particular, where the contemporary theoretical tone is one of 'nowhereness and everywhereness'.[30] Against this disembodied tenor, Probyn encourages us to develop expressions outside of the general to look at examples of specific local embodied practices in the everyday. She is concerned with how identity becomes altered and shaped along the rugged terrain of belonging. She insists that there is no fixed identity nor final destination. Instead, she is fascinated with how it is that people 'get along' and that leads her to ask how various forms of belonging are articulated. Probyn calls for new ways of intervening in the social by 'outsiding ourselves'.[31] She asks us to bring to the surface particular actions and feelings that are normally hidden even to ourselves. By doing so, Probyn imagines interconnectedness experienced between supposedly separate entities.

Lastly, I am inspired by Probyn's critique of the term 'belonging' in light of my own work. While I admit belonging can communicate ideas of home, security and stability, belonging is not always a warmly persuasive term. Probyn explains that belonging can convey notions of 'longing to be' somewhere, or the desire to be part of something. The implications of this idea for my own work struck me as invaluable. I have sketched out very briefly that the popular imaginary has made the multiethnic woman intelligible in often oppressive ways. In the analysis of my transcripts, I realised that participants did not dwell excessively upon passive or unfulfilled desires to belong. Instead, narratives were littered with stories about active connections forged through movement across social cleavages. Were there other theoretical ways, I mused, to talk about these processes of creating connections without using the phrase belonging? It was then that I turned to Probyn's reappropriation of the term.

Probyn asks us to contemplate notions of belonging as *movement* rather than as static positionings. She considers belonging not as fixed nor rooted in some deep authentic way, but rather as being in constant movement. Modes of belonging are envisioned as 'surface shifts' as she attempts to capture the range of desiring identities that are displayed 'all around'.[32] Her exploration is not divorced from that of paradoxical space. Fundamental to her argument about belonging is the paradox that 'any singularity of belonging must continually be freed and encouraged in its movement to constantly become other'.[33] Thus belonging can take on a myriad of forms. Probyn encourages the development of contradictory relations of belonging that may coexist, overlapping in paradoxical spheres.

Thus far, I have explained why I have borrowed largely from the work of Rose and Probyn to provide the theoretical underpinnings for the interviewees' narratives which follow. The phrase 'mobile paradoxical space' provides a flexible and rich metaphoric range, and I emphasise its ambivalent, fluid and contradictory nature. I believe the term conveys ideas about contradiction and movement, both of which were key themes emerging from the narratives of participants. The very experience of multiethnicity is one which often seems paradoxical. In my own life, I have been shocked and surprised to be located as 'white', 'black', or a 'woman of colour' in different contexts. These designations are continually changing. It is important to note, however, that this isn't the case for all multiethnic women, or people, more generally. Although many of the interviewees reported rapidly changing attributions by others regarding their 'place' in society, some women also explained that they were only seen as 'black' all the time – which made it impossible for them to identify as multiethnic among people who refused to see them as such. Thus not all multiethnic women have the freedom to identify as multiethnic. Strict racial rules about the politics of categorisation often makes this impossible.

Keeping this in mind, I ask how we might map mobile paradoxical spaces in relation to participants' daily lives. What struck me while reading the interviews were the multiple ways in which participants occupy mobile paradoxical spaces as they go about their daily living – dancing in crowded night clubs, shopping at the Quickie-Mart, and frantically finishing documentaries under tight time constraints. Participants actively moved away from thinking and living difference as a negative. Rather, they conveyed to me the importance of bridging dynamic tensions among groups. Narratives were sprinkled with stories about the day-to-day experience of making connections with individuals, exploring how it was that strangers became friends.[34]

Mapping Mobile Paradoxical Spaces

In this section, I argue that the creation of connections between individuals across traditional social cleavages, such as 'race', class and gender, are an everyday reality, and that the material engagements of those connections can be theorised more adequately. The discourse on difference acts as a vigilant gatekeeper which hinders the free-flow of dialogue about commonalities. In order to acknowledge and analyse the potential productivity and limitations of the contemporary discourse on difference, I consider how participants constructed alliances and affinities with others.

Many of the women in this study explained that their ability to cross over the demarcations of racial divides made it easier to transcend other social cleavages. Instead of envisioning herself as being 'out of place', Makeda, a 26-year-old graduate student who identified her mother as Japanese and father as 'English, white, born in England', explained how multiethnic individuals have a range of allegiances and homes:

> Being mixed defies any sort of absolute characterisation that you might have of community, or culture, because they can't really be applied to mixed race people? Because [we] have so many different allegiances, or affinities, or languages, or whatever ... being mixed is a kinda very interesting place to be. I think it's been very important to make sure that I do attach myself to collectives, in some ways? Because I don't feel that just one speaks to me?

Makeda insists that she forges several networks of connections. Women of multiethnicity in this study continually demonstrated the fluidity of discursive relations between and within a variety of communities. Given their multiethnic identities, they continually cross racialised boundaries, and these experiences lead them to question other sorts of boundaries. As Makeda suggests, having a wide range of cultural allegiances offers a way for her to transcend any essentialised generalisation of her identity. Makeda explains how she actively searches for meeting places in her desire to create connections. She recognises how her racialised position offers her an unusual vantage point by emphasising the particular spatiality of the multiethnic experience. Makeda revealed over the course of the interview that there are many collectives that she finds appealing. Some multiethnic writers have indicated how multiethnic individuals can occupy these mobile paradoxical spaces. The multiethnic writer Judy Scales-Trent has described what it is like to be 'both inside and outside the black community and the white community' by finding similarities between her life and the lives of others, 'thus finding a community I call home'.[35] Michael Thornton, a scholar of Japanese and African-American backgrounds, agrees, claiming that as a 'mixed race individual, I had to create my own community and sense of identity'.[36] Resonating with these writers, the women in my study also may be said to feel similarly. In my interview with Marical, I asked about the relationship between her own multiethnic identity and her perspective on 'race'. She responded:

> Oh yeah, I think I'm a genius! [laughter] I think it's great, definitely. Just because I always feel like I'm a fly on the wall, I feel kind of like I've been privy to certain ideas. I've always felt that I was different. And deciding not to hate myself forever! [laughter] I've decided that I'm special. And I think that gives you a lot of freedom. I don't feel like I have a lot of things that contain me. Because I've broken most of the rules already, just by existing. So I feel like I have unlimited potential, to a large degree? You know? And I think that that's a really good thing.

I do not want to dismiss the fact that at times, the multiethnic woman does in fact experience marginalisation or denigration a result of society's rigid rules about racialisation. However, alternate readings of the experience of marginalisation are in turn suggested by Marical. She deliberately decides that she is 'special' and although she recognises that she is seen as different in many ways, she also feels she has unlimited potential, thus turning her marginality into a productive site.

Women in this study suggested that the manner of occupying a space at the threshold of the margin can provide a perspective from which to view the complexities of difference. It suggests that individuals at the margins may read their marginality as a positive, or even superior, stance from which to forge new alliances. Some participants even likened their multiethnic status to an ability to understand marginality. Thus, they expressed to me that they often occupied spaces both at the centre and the margins. For these women, senses of identity were not described as rootless or homeless. Instead, they referred to notions of movement, of moving through categories, and developing scattered senses of belongings with a diverse range of collectives.

Katya specifically employed the metaphor of 'interpreter', 'ambassador' or 'translator' to describe how she feels about being multiethnic:

> [I think I can look] at things from both sides. In acting like an ambassador. Which is something I recognised, I think, for many years, but didn't realise what it was that I was doing. And trying to explain one side to the other. I act as a translator. Interpreter. And I think that I do that, I feel that is one of my roles. Not necessarily something that I asked to take. But I felt some sort of duty that I did not want black people to be misunderstood. And I didn't want white people to be misunderstood. Or I didn't want black people to misunderstand white people. And [I am able] to move between, move across a spectrum, being able to be the ambassador, to present different sides ... To come from an informed position on both sides ... And I don't necessarily think that someone that was 'here' or [points across] 'here' would be able to give that much information.

Katya sees herself as being able to interact with many groups, fostering communication and understanding. She contests the reading of the 'mixed race woman' as out of place. Instead, Katya explains that she is 'able to represent the other' in a variety of circumstances, for instance, by representing both the white and black perspectives at the same time – a position which might be seen as paradoxical.

Conclusion

> If racial and ethnic experience constitute a divide that cannot be spoken, an even greater paradox is the degree to which a sense of commonality may be simultaneously created as well as threatened by notions of ethnicity and race.[37]

I have begun to suggest some of the complex ways participants in this study inhabit mobile paradoxical spaces. By thinking about how people get along and get by in a racialised world, I have argued that not only can multiethnic people experience their mixedness in positive ways, but also that relations of proximity between individuals can be more adequately theorised than presently envisioned. Participants explored the necessity of considering multiethnic relations as co-constructed with other axes of domination and resistance, emphasising that to be multiethnic means to be internally and externally differentiated through intersections with other unfolding relationships.

Multiethnic women in this study are actively engaged in the process of developing new conceptions of belonging and identity which transcend old totalising categories. They relayed to me the variety of relationships they forge through apparent difference. In attempting to develop an alternative reading of the experience of multiethnicity, I have tried to tease out a more mobile and paradoxical voice which emerges in the narratives. This is only one of many potential mappings. As Rose would remind us, there are many more paradoxical spaces left to map. I look forward to more research which maps out these precarious experiences in places – where our stories hint at the extraordinary ways we employ our ordinary selves.

Notes

1. See M. Keith and S. Pile (eds), *Place and the Politics of Identity* (London: Routledge, 1993); N. Smith and C. Katz, 'Grounding metaphor: towards a spatialized politics', in M. Keith and S. Pile (eds), *Place and the Politics of Identity* (London: Routledge, 1993), pp.67–84.
2. J. Scales-Trent, *Notes of a White Black Woman: Race, Color, Community* (University Park, PA: The Pennsylvania State University, 1995), p.130.
3. J.O. Ifekwunigwe, *Scattered Belongings: Cultural Paradoxes of Race, Culture and Nation* (London: Routledge, 1998).
4. S. Hall, 'Cultural identity and diaspora', in J. Rutherford (ed.), *Identity: Community, Culture, Difference* (London: Lawrence and Wishart, 1990), p.222.
5. See, for example, P. Jackson, *Maps of Meaning* (London: Unwin Hyman, 1989); A. Kobayashi and L. Peake, 'Un-natural discourse: 'race' and gender in geography', *Gender, Place and Culture* 1, 3 (1994), pp.225–43.
6. L. Bondi, 'Locating identity politics', in M. Keith and S. Pile (eds), *Place and the Politics of Identity* (London: Routledge, 1993), pp.84–102.
7. M.P.P. Root (ed.), *Racially Mixed People in America* (London: Sage, 1992); M.P.P. Root, 'The multiracial experience: racial borders as a significant frontier in race relations', in M.P.P. Root (ed.), *The Multiracial Experience: Racial Borders as the New Frontier* (London: Sage, 1996), pp.xiii–15.
8. E.H. Erikson. 'Identity and the life cycle', *Psychological Issues* 1 (1959), pp.18–164; R.T. Carter, *The Influence of Race and Racial Identity in*

Psychotherapy: Towards a Racially Inclusive Model (New York: John Wiley & Sons, 1995).

9. R.T. Carter *The Influence of Race and Racial Identity in Psychotherapy: Towards a Racially Inclusive Model*, p.119.
10. B. Tizard and A. Phoenix, *Black, White or Mixed Race?* (London: Routledge, 1993); M.P.P. Root (ed.), *Racially Mixed People in America* (London: Sage, 1992).
11. T. Creswell, *In Place/Out of Place* (Minneapolis: University of Minnesota Press, 1996).
12. See J.O. Ifekwunigwe, *Scattered Belongings: Cultural Paradoxes of Race, Culture and Nation* (London: Routledge, 1998); K. Allman, '(Un)natural Boundaries: Mixed Race, Gender and Sexuality', in M.P.P. Root (ed.), *The Multiracial Experience: Racial Borders as the New Frontier* (London: Sage, 1996); C. Streeter, 'Ambiguous Bodies: Locating Black/White Women in Cultural Representations', in Root, *The Multiracial Experience*; F.W. Twine, 'Brown Skinned White Girls: Class, Culture and the Construction of White Identity in Suburban Communities', *Gender, Place and Culture* 3, 2 (1996), pp.205–24.
13. M.P.P. Root, *Women of Colour: Integrating Ethnic and Gender Identities in Psychotherapy* (New York: Guilford Press, 1994).
14. C. Ijima-Hall, 'Coloring outside the lines', in M.P.P. Root (ed.), *Racially Mixed People in America* (London: Sage, 1992); C.W. Stephan, 'Mixed-heritage individuals: ethnic identity and trait characteristics' in Root (ed.), *Racially Mixed People*; J. Gibbs and G. Hines, 'Negotiating ethnic identity: issues for black-white biracial adolescents' in Root (ed.), *Racially Mixed People*; M.P.P. Root. 'Resolving other status', in M.P.P. Root and S. Brown (eds), *Diversity and Complexity in Feminist Therapy* (New York: Haworth Press, 1990).
15. M. Mahtani, 'Mapping the Paradoxes of Multiethnicity: Stories of Multiethnic Women in Toronto, Canada', (unpublished Ph.D. thesis, Department of Geography, University College, London, 1999).
16. M.P.P. Root (ed.), *Racially Mixed People in America* (London: Sage, 1992).
17. L. Jones, *Bulletproof Diva: Tales of Race, Sex, and Hair* (New York: Doubleday, 1994), p.3.
18. See M. Song and D. Parker, 'Commonality, Difference, and the Dynamics of Disclosure in In-depth Interviewing', *Sociology*, 29, 2 (1995).
19. M. Keith, 'Knowing Your Place: The Imagined Geographies of Racial Subordination', in C. Philo (ed.), *New Words, New Worlds: Reconceptualizing Social and Cultural Geography* (Lampeter: Social and Cultural Geography Study Group of the Institute of British Geographers, 1991), pp.178–93.
20. G. Rose, *Feminism and Geography* (Minneapolis: University of Minnesota Press, 1993).
21. *Ibid*, p.143.
22. See bell hooks, *Yearning: Race, Gender and Cultural Politics*, (Boston: South End Press, 1990); Minnie Bruce Pratt, 'Identity: skin blood heart', in E.

Bulkin, M. Bruce Pratt (eds), *Yours in Struggle: Three Feminist Perspectives on Anti-Semitism and Racism* (New York: Long Hall Press, 1984).

23. Pratt, 'Identity: skin blood heart', p.17.
24. G. Rose, *Feminism and Geography* (Minneapolis: University of Minnesota Press, 1993), p.151.
25. *Ibid*, pp.152–53.
26. *Ibid*, p.160.
27. But see R.M. George, *The Politics of Home* (Cambridge: Cambridge University Press, 1996).
28. E. Probyn, *Outside Belongings* (London: Routledge, 1996).
29. *Ibid*, p.71.
30. *Ibid*, p.71.
31. *Ibid*, p.152.
32. *Ibid*, p.20.
33. *Ibid*, p.153.
34. *Ibid*.
35. J. Scales-Trent, *Notes of a White Black Woman: Race, Color, Community* (University Park, PA: The Pennsylvania State University, 1995), p.8.
36. M. Thornton, 'Hidden Agendas, Identity Theories and Multiracial People', in M.P.P. Root (ed.), *The Multiracial Experience: Racial Borders as the New Frontier* (London: Sage, 1996).
37. P. Williams, *Seeing a Colour-blind Future* (London: Virago Press, 1997), p.10.

Contributors

Frank Furedi teaches sociology at the University of Kent. His book *The Silent War* (1998) explored the transformation of race relations into a global issue during the twentieth century. He is also the author of *Paranoid Parenting* (2001), and is currently working on a book on the current crisis of identity, *The State of Emotion* (forthcoming).

Jayne O. Ifekwunigwe is Senior Lecturer in Anthropology and Sociology at the University of East London. Her most recent publication is *Scattered Belongings: Cultural Paradoxes of 'Race', Nation and Gender* (1999). Her current research projects include an ethnographic and photographic exploration of the political economy of cultural tourism in (post)apartheid Cape Town, South Africa, with a particular focus on township tours.

Barbara Ballis Lal is Associate Professor In Residence, Department of Sociology, University of California at Los Angeles. She teaches courses on sociological theory and political sociology, and convenes a seminar on The Chicago School of American Sociology, Symbolic Interaction and the Study of Race and Ethnicity in Cities. Her publications include, *The Romance of Culture in An Urban Civilization: Robert E. Park on Race and Ethnicity in Cities* (1990), 'Ethnic Identity Entrepreneurs: Their Role in Transracial and Intercountry Adoptions', *Asian and Pacific Migration Journal*, Vol. 6, Nos. 3–4, 1997 and 'Why the Fuss? The Real and the Symbolic Significance of Trans-racial and Intercountry-Adoptions,' in P. Morgan, *Adoption: The Continuing Debate* (1999). She lives in Los Angeles and in London with her husband, Professor Deepak Lal and their children Deepika and Akshay.

Minelle Mahtani completed her PhD at University College London in geography, exploring issues of racialised and gendered identity among 'mixed race' women in Toronto. She was a national television news producer at the Canadian Broadcasting Corporation for five years, and is currently a Killam Postdoctoral Fellow in the departments of geography and journalism at the University of British Columbia in Vancouver.

Laurie M. Mengel earned her BA at the University of California at Berkeley's Department of Ethnic Studies. After a year at the University of Hawaii at Manoa, she entered Brown University's Department of American Civilization where she is currently a PhD candidate. She is the author of 'Issei Women and Divorce in Hawai'i 1885–1907', in *Social Process in Hawai'i* (1998) in a special edition devoted to women in Hawai'i edited by Joyce Chinen, as well as other articles on Japanese American history and racial mixture.

April Moreno is a graduate of Anthropology and Cultural Process from Goldsmiths College, London. Her academic areas of interest are race, mixed race, national identity and visual studies. She is currently a teacher in Los Angeles, California.

Charlie Owen is a Senior Research Officer in the Thomas Coram Research Unit at the Institute of Education, University of London. His main research interest is the secondary analysis of official statistics. He also teaches research methods and the use of computers for both quantitative and qualitative analysis. He is a member of the Radical Statistics Group.

David Parker is a lecturer in the Department of Cultural Studies and Sociology, University of Birmingham. His publications include *Through Different Eyes: the Cultural Identities of Young Chinese People in Britain* (1995), and he is currently working on the themes of space, time and social identities.

Stephen Small is an Associate Professor in the Department of African American Studies, University of California at Berkeley, where he has taught since 1995. He earned his PhD in Sociology from the University of California, Berkeley (1989); his MSc in Social Science from the University of Bristol, England (1983); and his BA (Hons) in Economics and Sociology from the University of Kent at Canterbury, England (1979). Stephen Small's latest book will be published by New York

University Press early in 2001, entitled *The Matrix of Miscegenation: Black People of Mixed Origins Under Slavery in Jamaica and Georgia*. His most recent book is *Racialised Barriers: The Black Experience in the USA and England in the 1980s* (1994).

Miri Song received her BA from Harvard University and her PhD from the London School of Economics. She has been a lecturer in Sociology at the University of Kent since 1995. She is the author of a book about the role that children play in immigrant adaptation called *Helping Out: Children's Labor in Ethnic Businesses* (1999), and is currently completing a book called *Choosing Ethnic Identity?* (forthcoming).

Paul Spickard is Professor of History at the University of California, Santa Barbara, with affiliate appointments in Asian American Studies and Religious Studies. He holds an honours AB from Harvard University and an MA and PhD from the University of California, Berkeley. He has taught at ten universities in the USA and abroad and is the author or editor of eight books and many articles on the comparative history and sociology of race and ethnicity and related topics, including *Mixed Blood: Intermarriage and Ethnic Identity in Twentieth-Century America* (1989); *Japanese Americans* (1996); *We Are a People: Narrative and Multiplicity in Constructing Ethnic Identity* (2000); and, with G. Reginald Daniel as co-editor, *Uncompleted Independence: The Creation and Revision of American Racial Thinking* (forthcoming). Paul is currently working on another book, *Work and Hope: Black Los Angeles, 1930–1955*.

Index

Compiled by Auriol Griffith-Jones